GREEN ARROW

Sounds

OF Violence

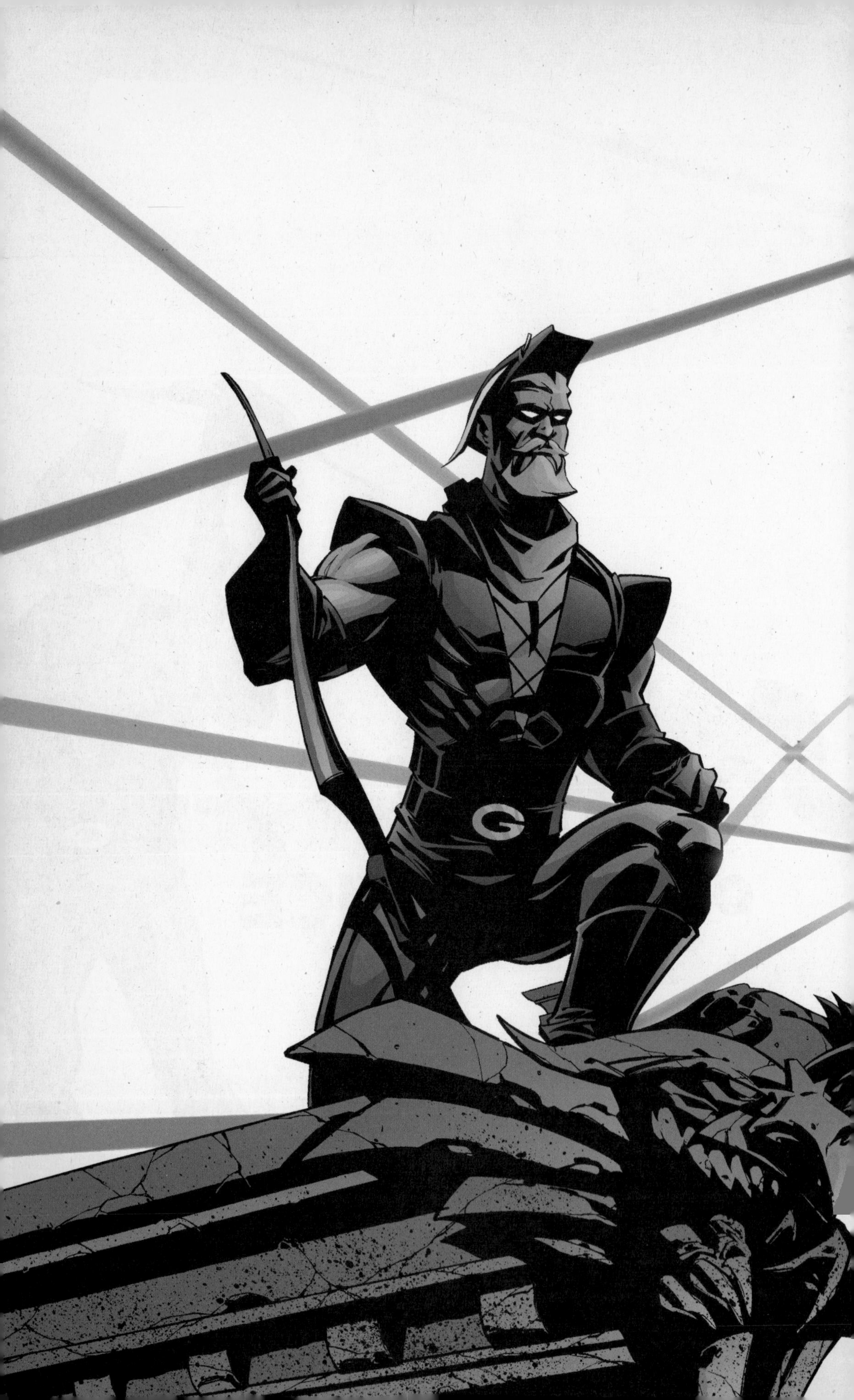

KEVIN SMITH
Writer

PHIL HESTER
Penciller

ANDE PARKS
Inker

JAMES SINCLAIR
Colorist

SEAN KONOT
Letterer

MATT WAGNER
Original Covers

GREEN ARROW

SOUNDS

OF VIOLENCE

DAN DIDIO
VP-Editorial

BOB SCHRECK
Editor-original series

BOB GREENBERGER
Senior Editor-collected edition

ROBBIN BROSTERMAN
Senior Art Director

PAUL LEVITZ
President & Publisher

GEORG BREWER
VP-Design & Retail Product Development

RICHARD BRUNING
VP-Creative Director

PATRICK CALDON
Senior VP-Finance & Operations

CHRIS CARAMALIS
VP-Finance

TERRI CUNNINGHAM
VP-Managing Editor

ALISON GILL
VP-Manufacturing

LILLIAN LASERSON
Senior VP & General Counsel

DAVID MCKILLIPS
VP-Advertising

JOHN NEE
VP-Business Development

CHERYL RUBIN
VP-Licensing & Merchandising

BOB WAYNE
VP-Sales & Marketing

3117206526ZZZZ

INTRODUCTION by PHIL HESTER

Comic-book creators are a delusional lot. At least I know I am.

I've been laboring under the pretense that the comic-buying public — that's you — wouldn't start forming an opinion of my work until it became halfway presentable. I believed that I could fire some sort of imaginary starting gun on my career, letting all of you know that I was finally ready to be seen and judged.

And of course, as my work grew and improved over the last 15 years that point crept closer and closer in time. When I was 21 I was not yet embarrassed by my work for some of the smallest publishers and fanzines. In my 20s I expected those works to be forgotten and only my fledgling efforts with major publishers to be official. As I entered my 30s, by the time a job left my drawing table and made it into print, it was old enough to disavow. I've fired that starting gun so many times now that I'm out of ammo, hoping against hope that you kind people would forget my most awkward, amateurish efforts, and only latch on to work no more than 18 months old.

Kevin Smith shattered that delusion. When Bob Schreck asked me to collaborate with Kevin, first on *Clerks* and then on GREEN ARROW, my first response was, "Of course!" — then, a few seconds later, "Why me?"

Because, in case you folks haven't noticed, I'm no Neal Adams, or Mike Grell, or Rodolfo Damaggio, or Don Newton, or Trevor Von... you get the picture. I'm not exactly a normal Green Arrow artist. That didn't seem to matter to Kevin or Bob. You see, Kevin turned out to be a fan of my run on SWAMP THING, a book I worked on with the lovely and talented

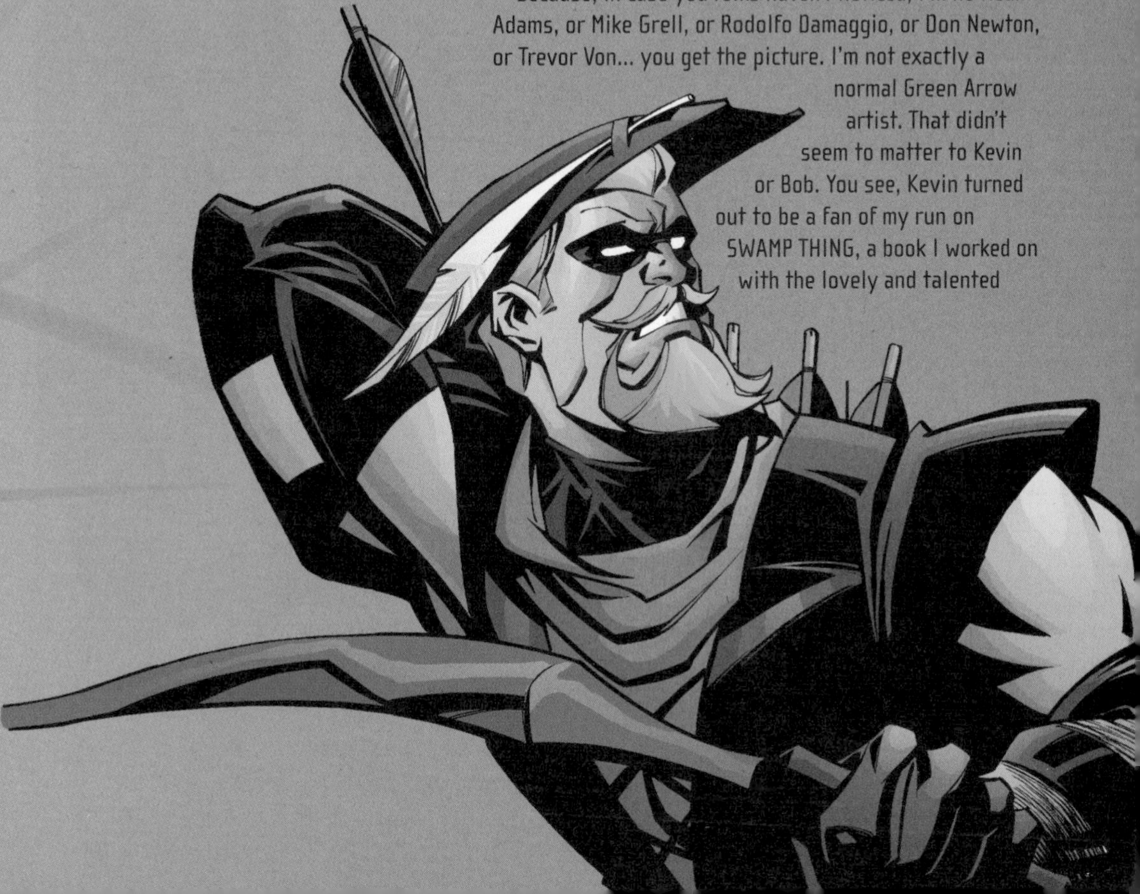

Mark Millar for about 30 issues when we were both in our early-to-mid-20s. Way, way behind my imaginary 18-month window. A brilliant run, to be sure, but not because of me — rather, in spite of me. In my opinion, the strength of Mark's writing pulled the book above the artwork it was mired in.

But that work stuck in Kevin's mind enough for him to want to work with me years later. I was shocked to learn that he even owned a piece of original art from that run.

That's when something I heard over 15 years ago, at my very first comic-book convention, finally made sense to me. It was the height of the black-and-white explosion of the mid-'80s, and if you could hold a pencil pointy side down you could get work. I was attending a panel consisting of the reigning comic-book intelligentsia deriding the quality of the writers and artists emerging at the time, myself among them. The great Will Eisner offered a word of caution. Of course I'm paraphrasing, and maybe the glare of Mr. Eisner's aura clouded my perception, but he pointed out that my generation of artists would be one of the first in history to have our work scrutinized from day one, ready or not. He informed the would-be arbiters of funny book aesthetics that the ugly ducklings of today would be their collaborators and partners in the near future.

It took me 15 years to realize it, but he was right. So you got to see me and Brian Bendis and Guy Davis and countless other artists of my generation grow up on the page in front of you. Some of that work is painful to us now, but we can't take it back, and hey, it looks like some of you even enjoyed it. And for me, at least some of it led to the most rewarding gig of my career to date, GREEN ARROW.

And since I'm unlikely to have a forum like this again, please indulge me as I express my gratitude toward the people I've worked with for the last couple of years.

Besides being my Dad's favorite comedic director, a genius screenwriter, and all around swell guy, Kevin Smith is a miracle worker. The evidence is there, people. He made GREEN ARROW a top ten book. GREEN ARROW. Not BATMAN, not SUPERMAN, not even AQUAMAN. *GREEN ARROW*. Imagine what he could do with something like JLA. But rest assured, I intend to test his powers. I'm pushing for our next collaboration to be a revival of Brother Power, The Geek. We'll see just how much juice the man has then!

His scripts have been a joy. I've been allowed to run rampant on the DC playground, playing with toys previously reserved for greater talents. I've read some of the funniest and most poignant scripts before anyone but my editors, and believe me, the funniest stuff was in the panel descriptions and margins, never seen by the reading public. Thanks for bringing me along on this ride, Kevin.

Nothing makes me happier than to hear the phrase "Hester and Parks." Although we shouldn't be mentioned in the same breath, ballpark, or universe as such great penciller/inker tandems as Kirby and Sinnott, Colan and Palmer, Miller and Janson, just to be known by that same nomenclature is the proudest achievement of my career. Thanks for saving my hide on every page, Anj.

Sean Konot remains the single most enthusiastic and stylistically satisfying letterer I've been privileged to work with. Guy Major and James Sinclair have transformed the messes we've laid in their laps into work of the highest quality with virtually no turnaround time at all. Thanks to all you guys for making us look like pros.

What can I say about the long-suffering Nachie Castro and his successor Morgan Dontanville? They did the heavy lifting every day on this book. It's impossible to imagine GREEN ARROW without them. The same goes to DC's unparalleled Production Department, and Bob Greenberger for putting this volume together.

Thanks also to Scott McCullar and those frequenting the various Green Arrow message boards for invaluable research and support. Hope we did you proud!

Finally, Bob Schreck. He's been manning the great

machine that is the comics industry for years, trying with more success than all but a few to steer this behemoth in the right direction. Look at some of the finest work of the last few decades and you'll see him behind the scenes. Talk with the most respected creators and you'll hear him counted as friend and advisor. Look for a group of laughing pros and fans alike at any convention and you'll find him at the head of the table.

Like many artists in this business, I've felt his presence before even meeting the man. He's been lurking at the edges of my career since the beginning, always looking for the right project to send my way. I'll always be in his debt, not just for GREEN ARROW but for the earlier jobs, the safe havens he carved out for me in which to develop my unique voice and earn a living. So, a dedication of sorts — this book, like so many others, could not exist without you.

One last thanks to the people reading this book. Thanks for hanging around long enough to make Green Arrow an important character again. I hope you enjoy this collection half as much as we enjoyed putting it together. If, for some reason, this book is your first exposure to Green Arrow, please drop by the monthly title some time. We're still having just as much fun.

Remember that starting gun? Well, it's gone for good now. I fired it for the last time when GREEN ARROW #1 hit the stands.

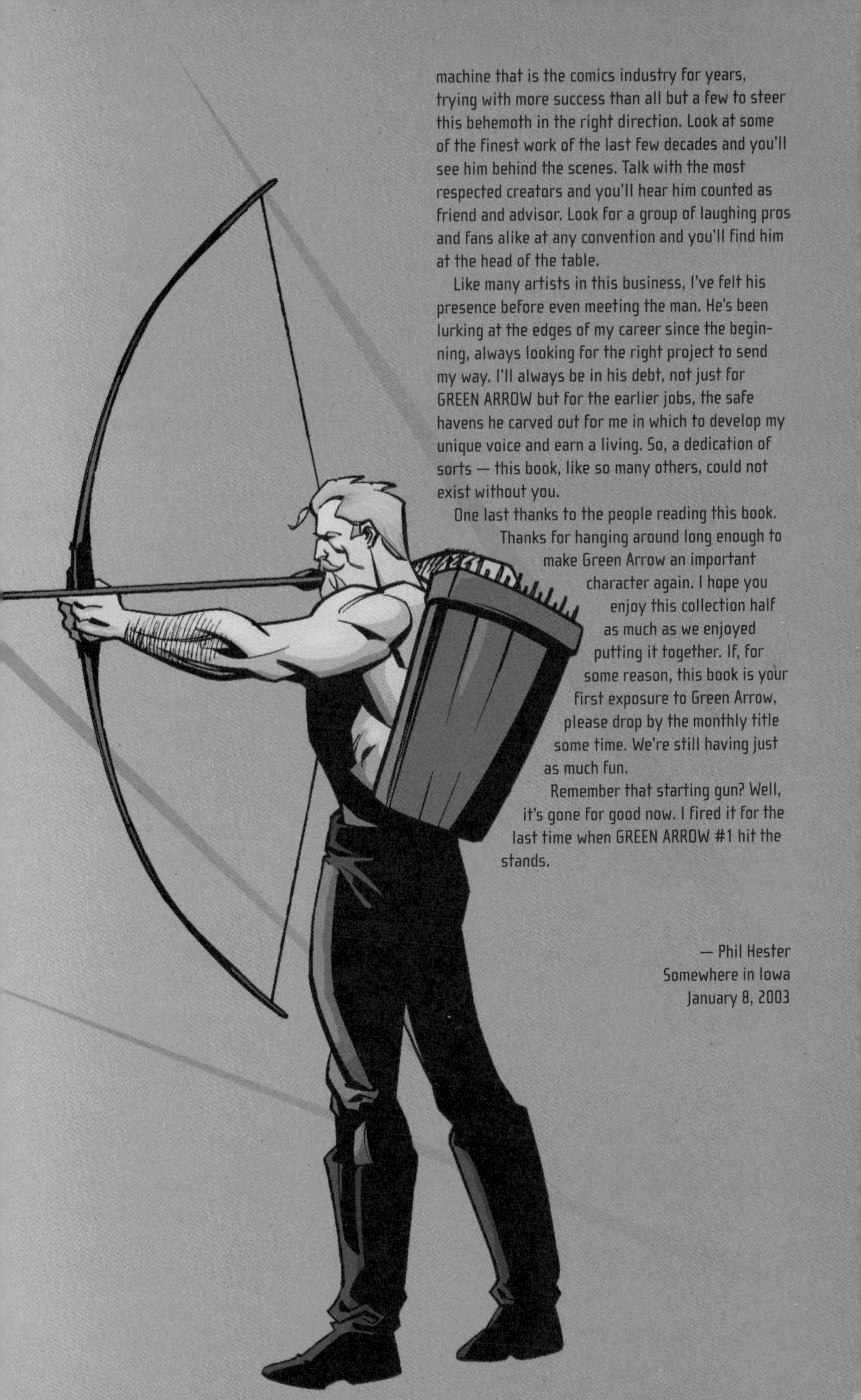

— Phil Hester
Somewhere in Iowa
January 8, 2003

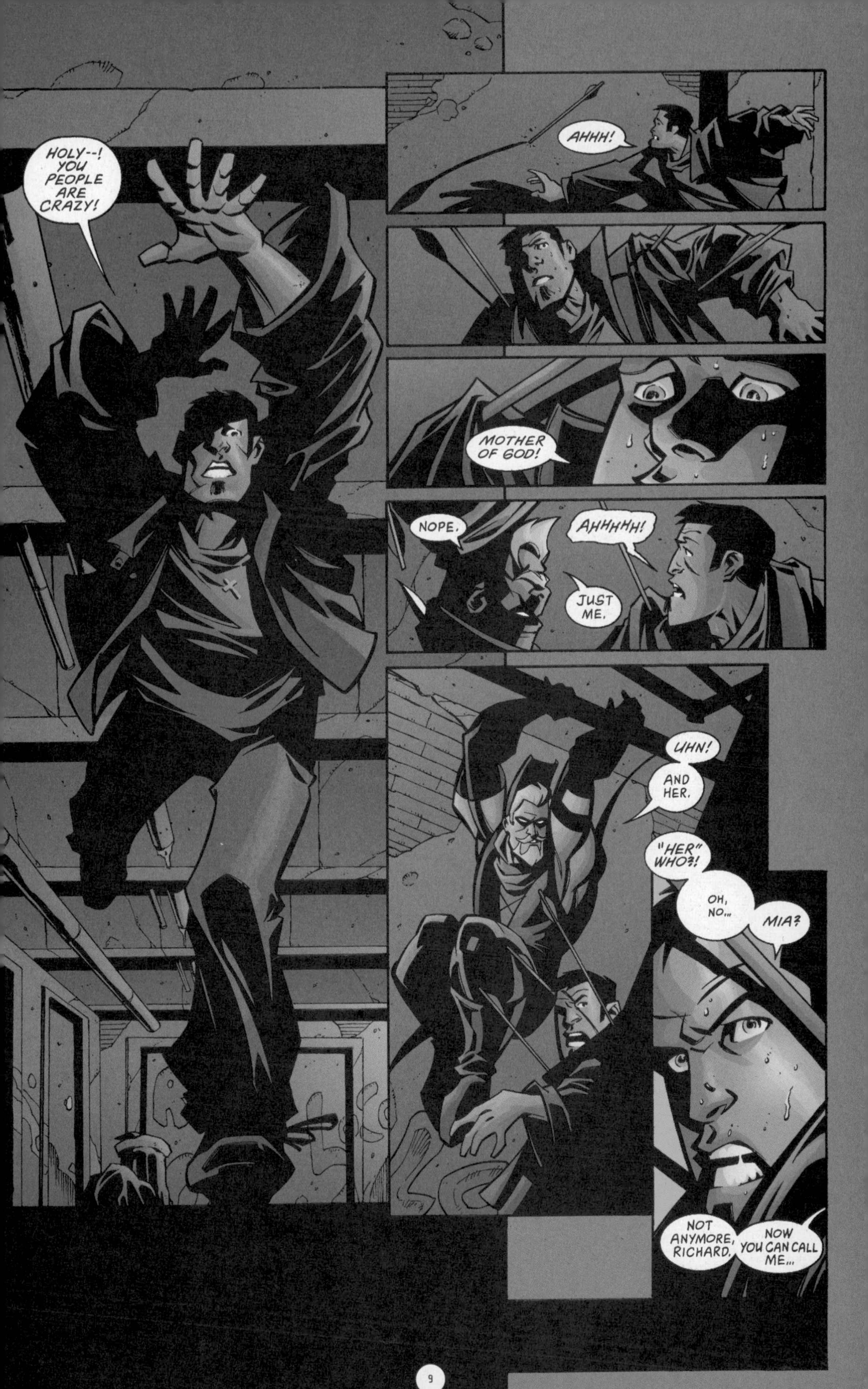
HOLY--! YOU PEOPLE ARE CRAZY!
AHHH!
MOTHER OF GOD!
NOPE.
AHHHHH!
JUST ME.
UHN!
AND HER.
"HER" WHO?!
OH, NO...
MIA?
NOT ANYMORE, RICHARD.
NOW YOU CAN CALL ME...

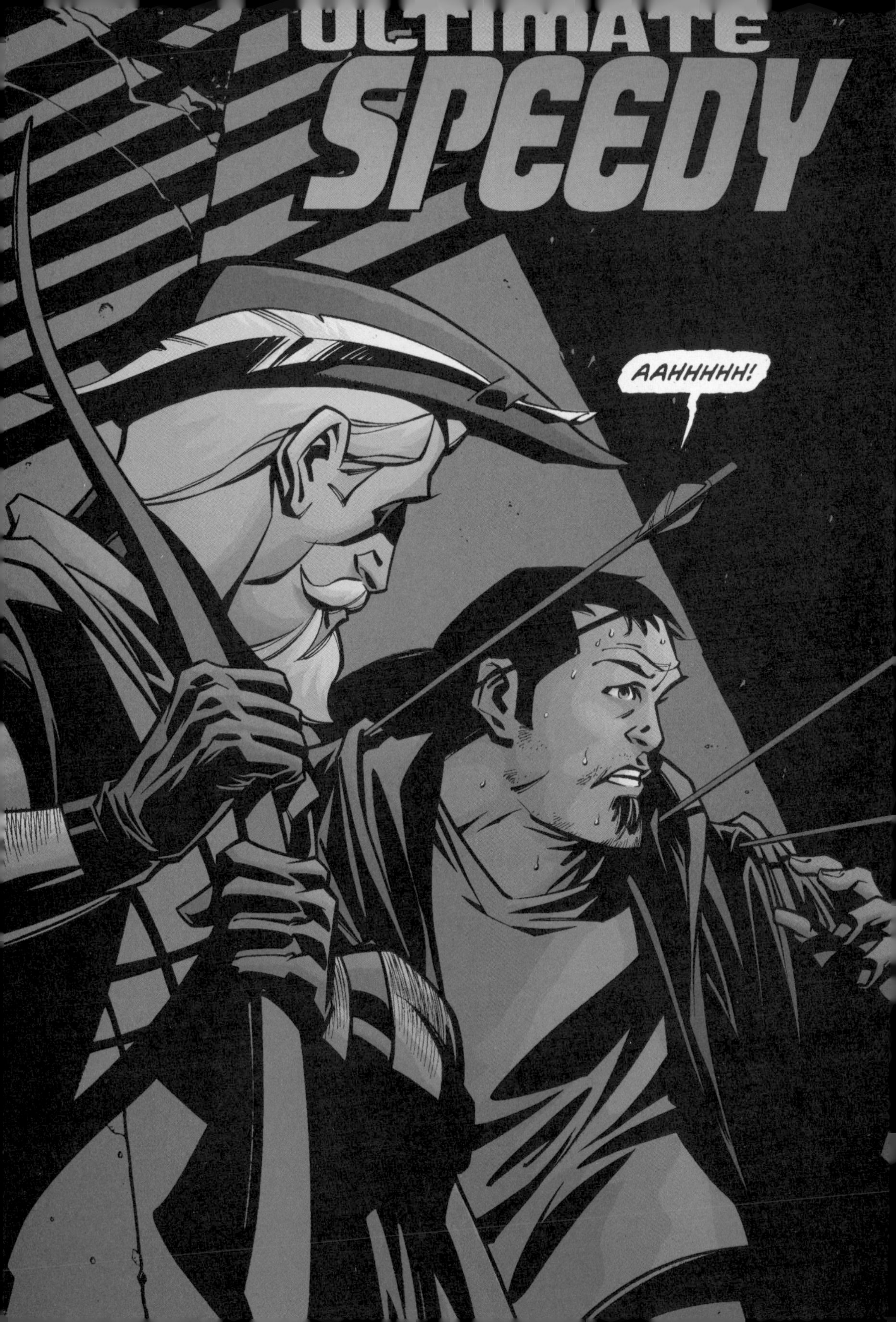
ULTIMATE
SPEEDY
AAHHHHH!

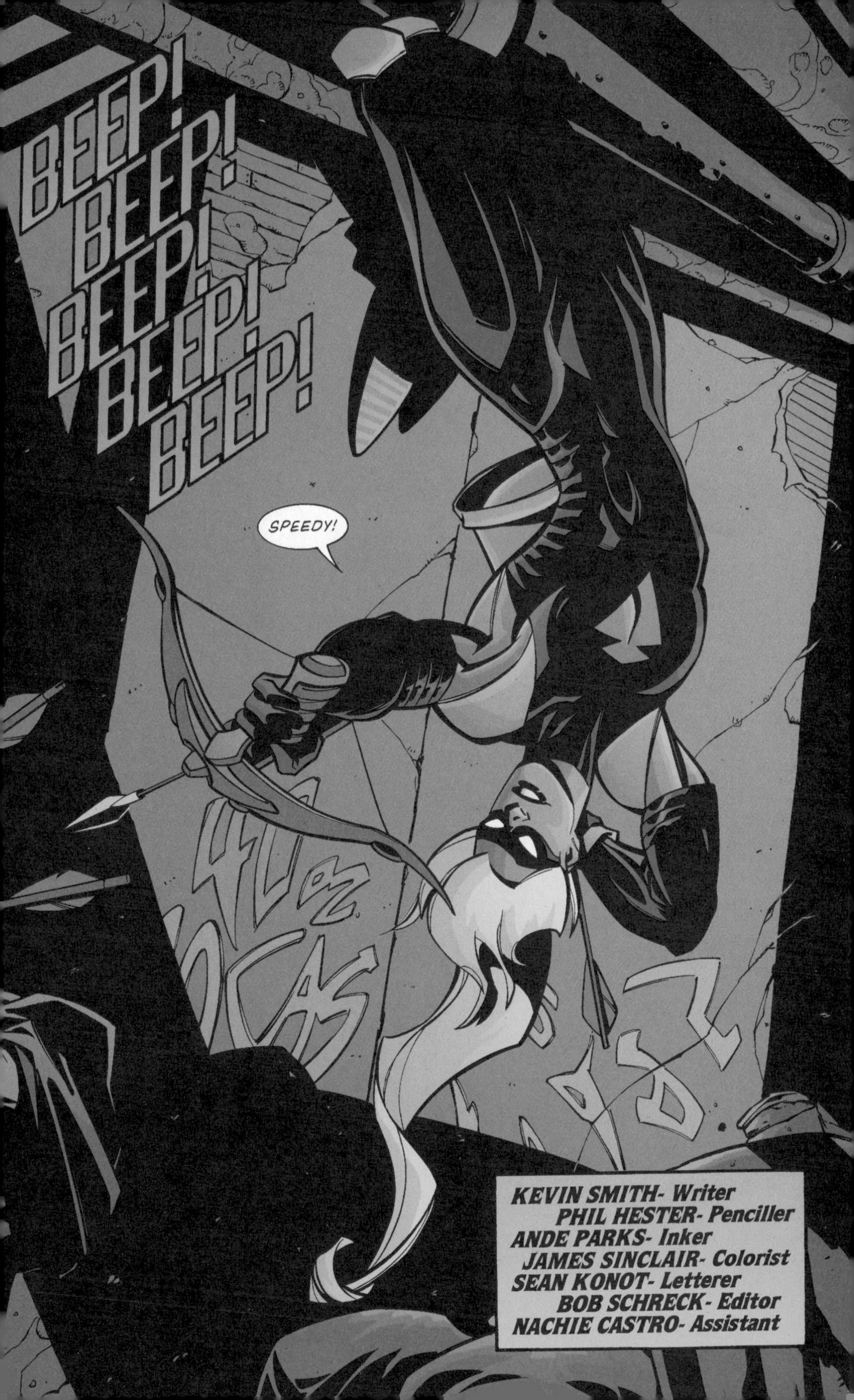
BEEP! BEEP! BEEP! BEEP! BEEP!
SPEEDY!
KEVIN SMITH- Writer
PHIL HESTER- Penciller
ANDE PARKS- Inker
JAMES SINCLAIR- Colorist
SEAN KONOT- Letterer
BOB SCHRECK- Editor
NACHIE CASTRO- Assistant

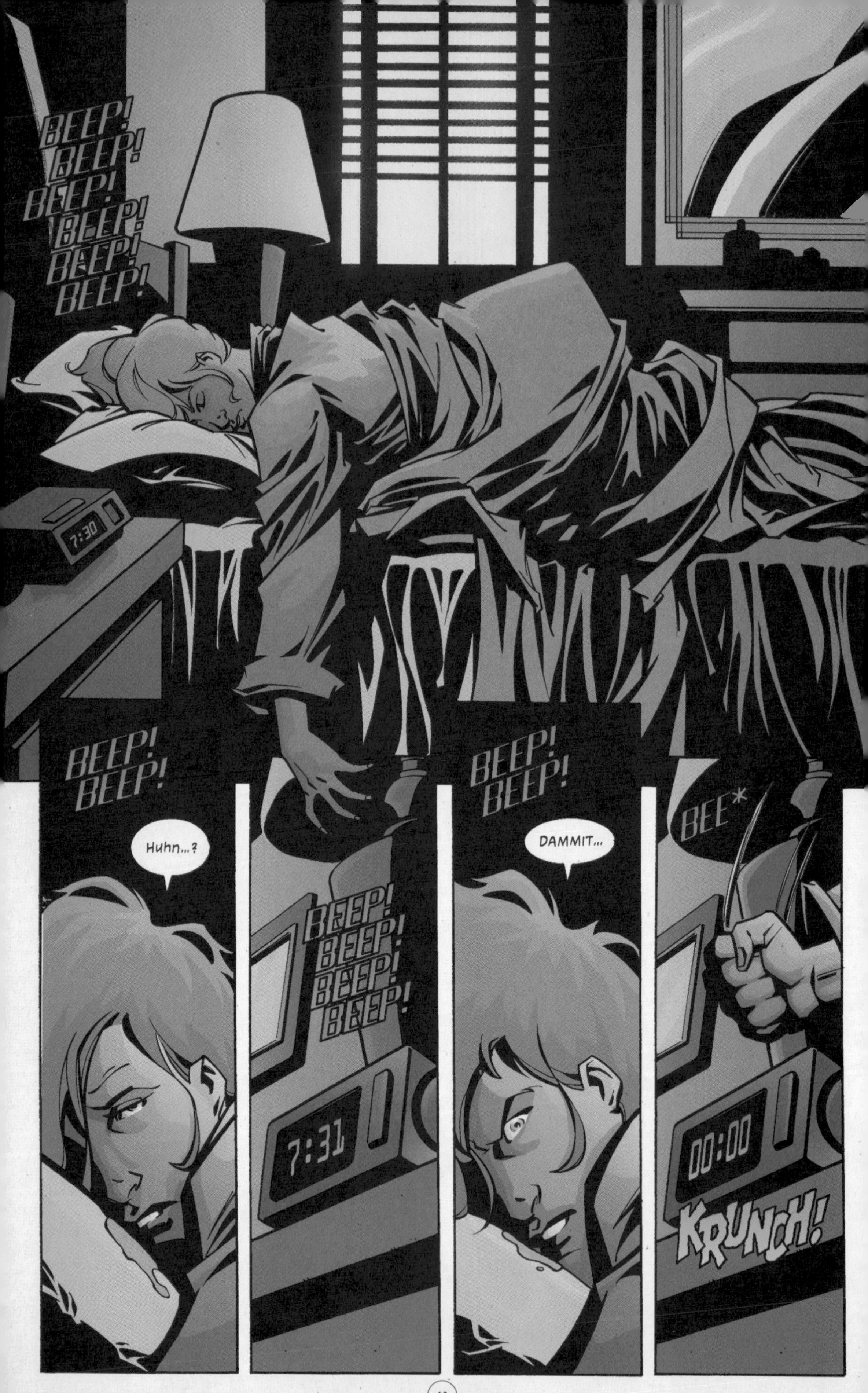
BEEP! BEEP! BEEP! BEEP! BEEP! BEEP!
7:30
BEEP! BEEP!
Huhn...?
BEEP! BEEP! BEEP! BEEP!
7:31
BEEP! BEEP!
DAMMIT...
BEE*
00:00
KRUNCH!

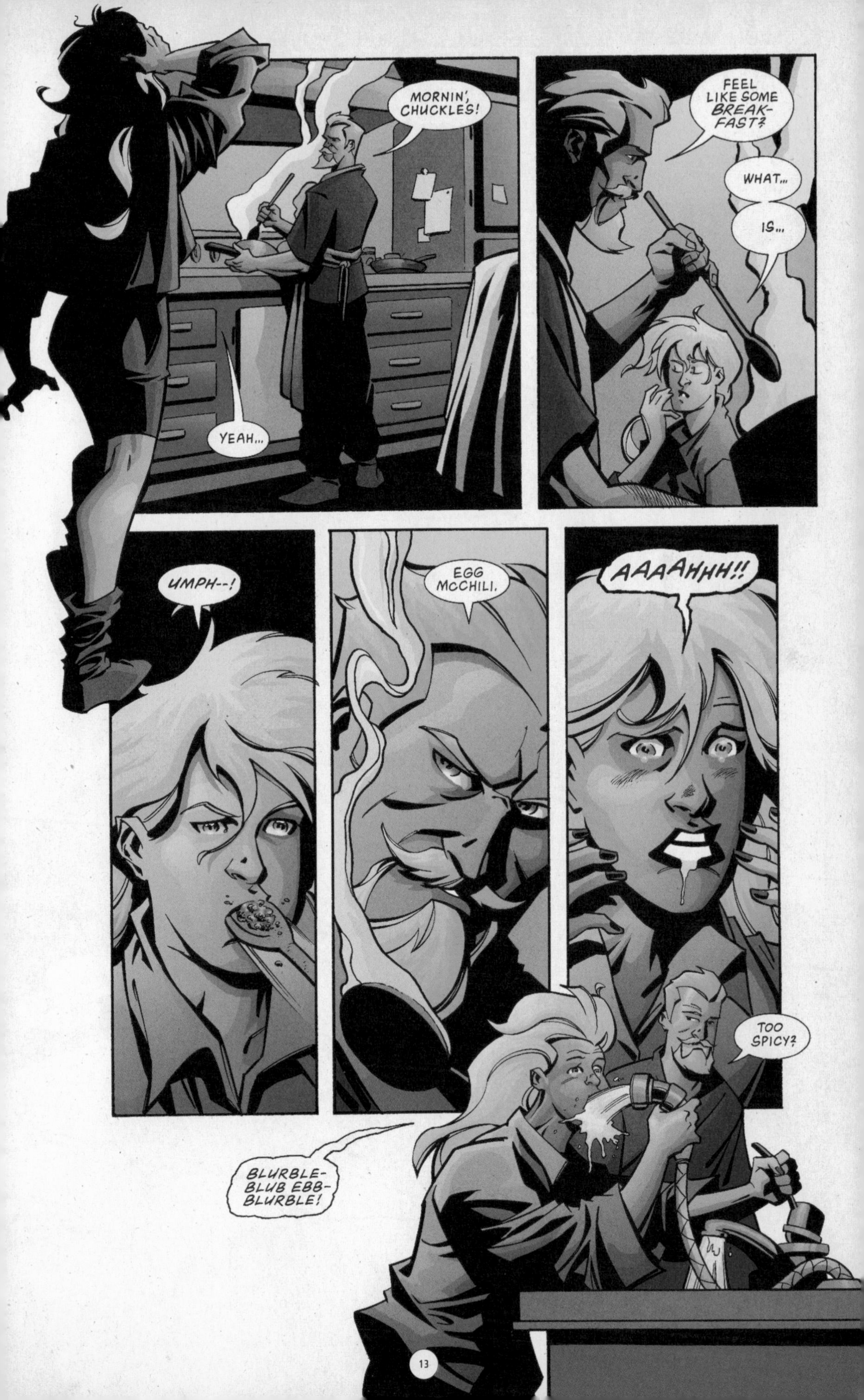
MORNIN', CHUCKLES!
YEAH...
FEEL LIKE SOME BREAK-FAST?
WHAT...
IS...
UMPH--!
EGG MCCHILI.
AAAAHHH!!
TOO SPICY?
BLURBLE-BLUB EBB-BLURBLE!

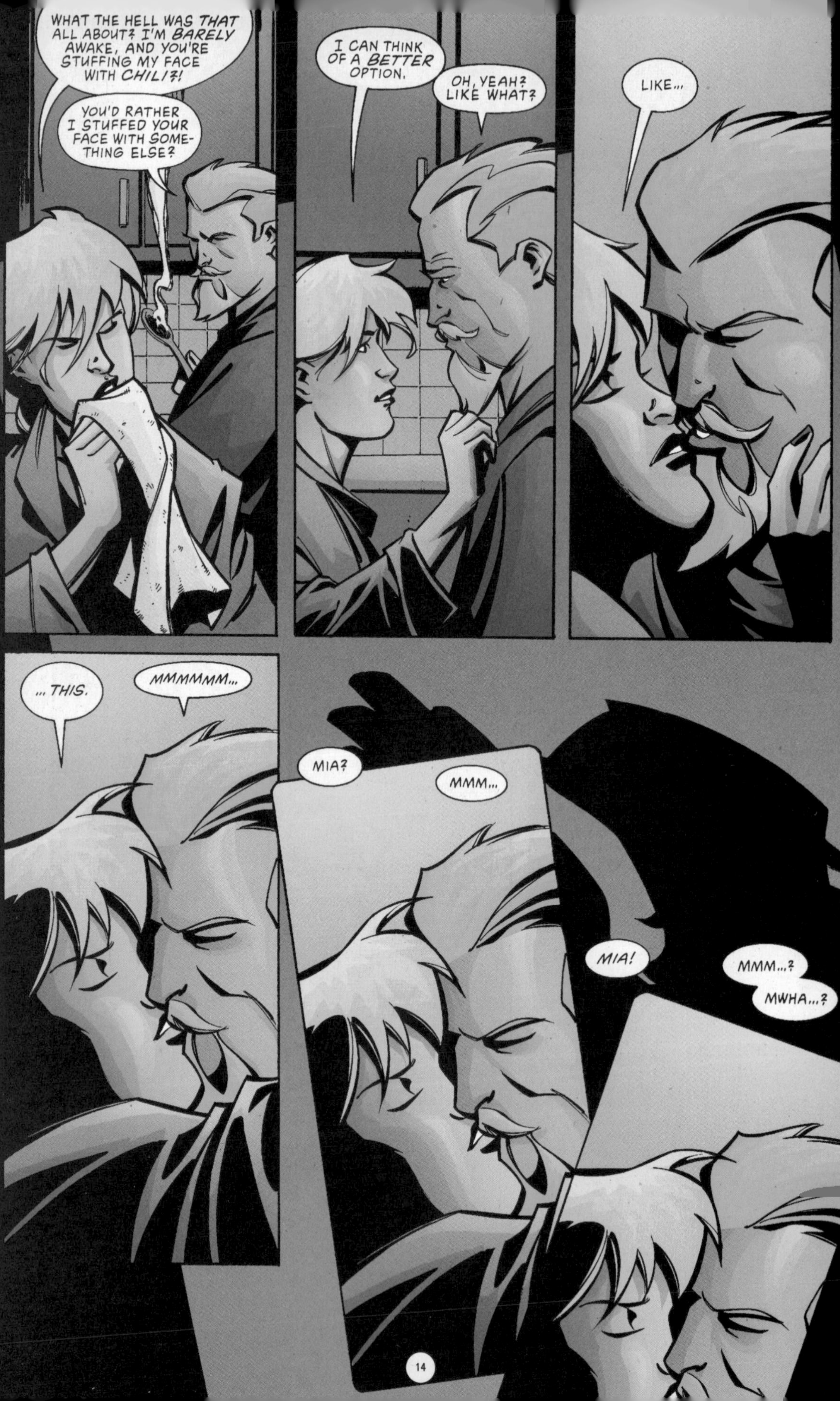
WHAT THE HELL WAS THAT ALL ABOUT? I'M BARELY AWAKE, AND YOU'RE STUFFING MY FACE WITH CHILI?!
YOU'D RATHER I STUFFED YOUR FACE WITH SOME-THING ELSE?
I CAN THINK OF A BETTER OPTION.
OH, YEAH? LIKE WHAT?
LIKE...
...THIS.
MMMMMM...
MIA?
MMM...
MIA!
MMM...?
MWHA...?

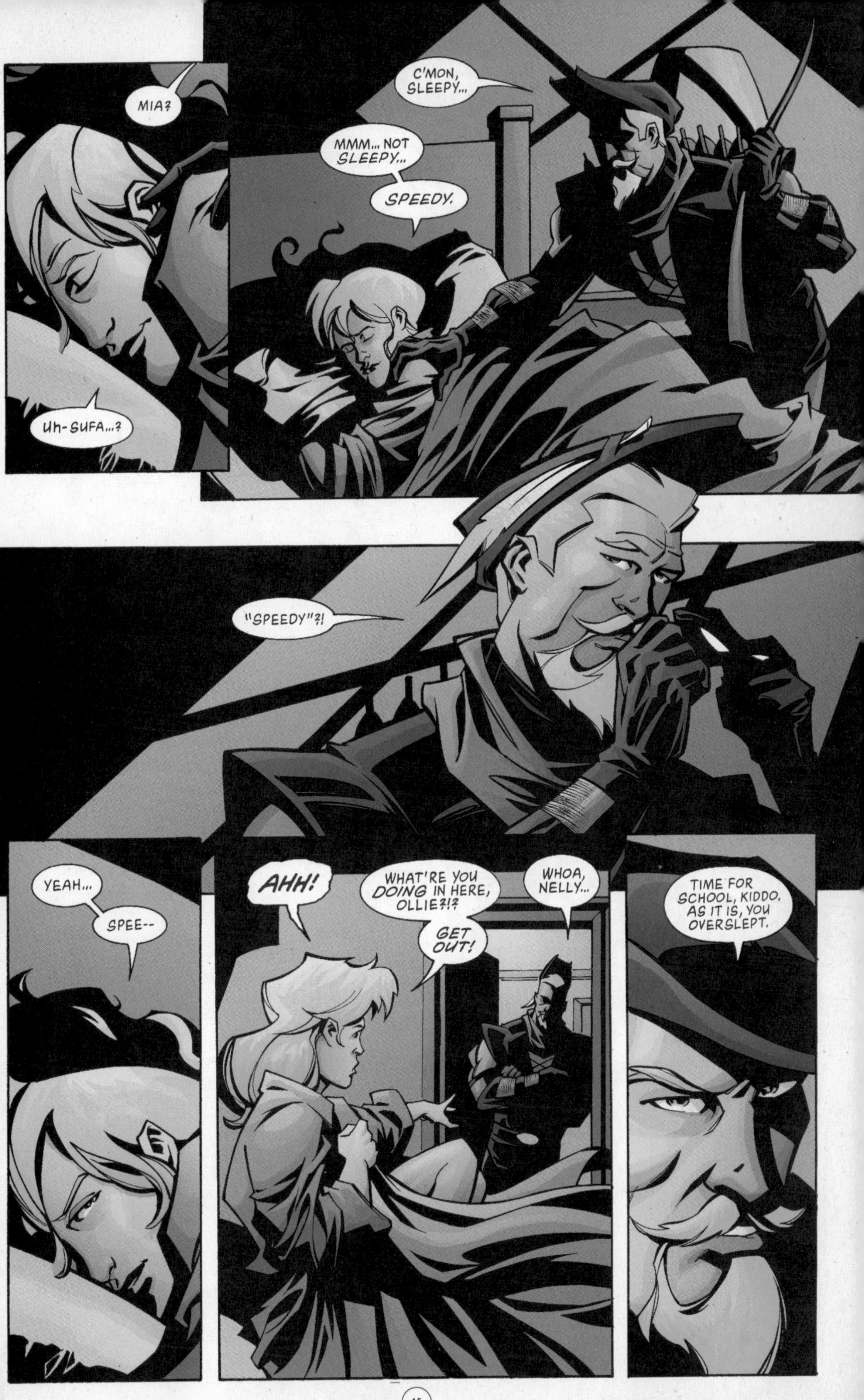
MIA?
Uh-SUFA...?
C'MON, SLEEPY...
MMM... NOT SLEEPY...
SPEEDY.
"SPEEDY"?!
YEAH...
SPEE--
AHH!
WHAT'RE YOU DOING IN HERE, OLLIE?!?
GET OUT!
WHOA, NELLY...
TIME FOR SCHOOL, KIDDO. AS IT IS, YOU OVERSLEPT.

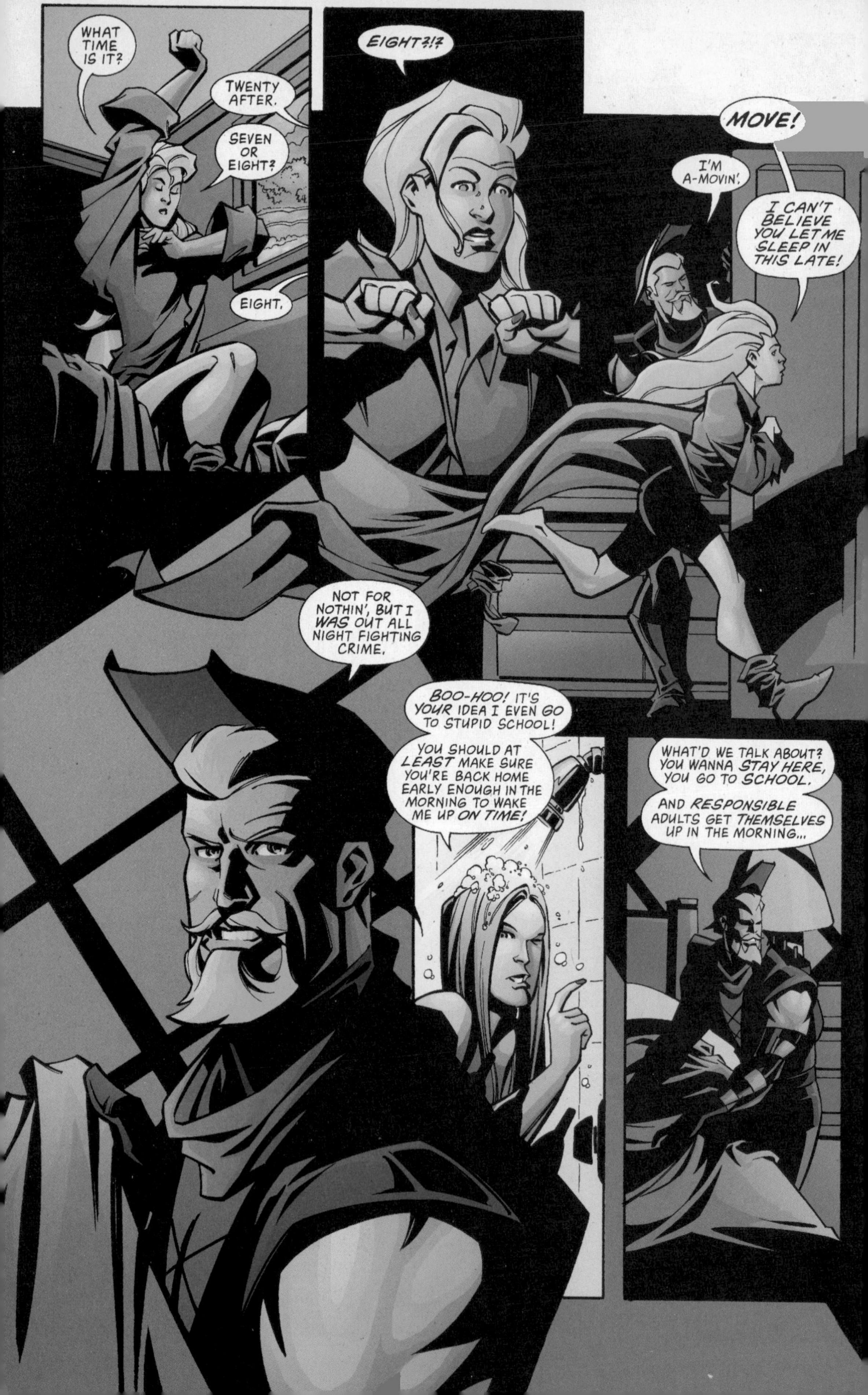
WHAT TIME IS IT?
TWENTY AFTER.
SEVEN OR EIGHT?
EIGHT.
EIGHT?!?
MOVE!
I'M A-MOVIN'.
I CAN'T BELIEVE YOU LET ME SLEEP IN THIS LATE!
NOT FOR NOTHIN', BUT I WAS OUT ALL NIGHT FIGHTING CRIME.
BOO-HOO! IT'S YOUR IDEA I EVEN GO TO STUPID SCHOOL!
YOU SHOULD AT LEAST MAKE SURE YOU'RE BACK HOME EARLY ENOUGH IN THE MORNING TO WAKE ME UP ON TIME!
WHAT'D WE TALK ABOUT? YOU WANNA STAY HERE, YOU GO TO SCHOOL.
AND RESPONSIBLE ADULTS GET THEMSELVES UP IN THE MORNING...

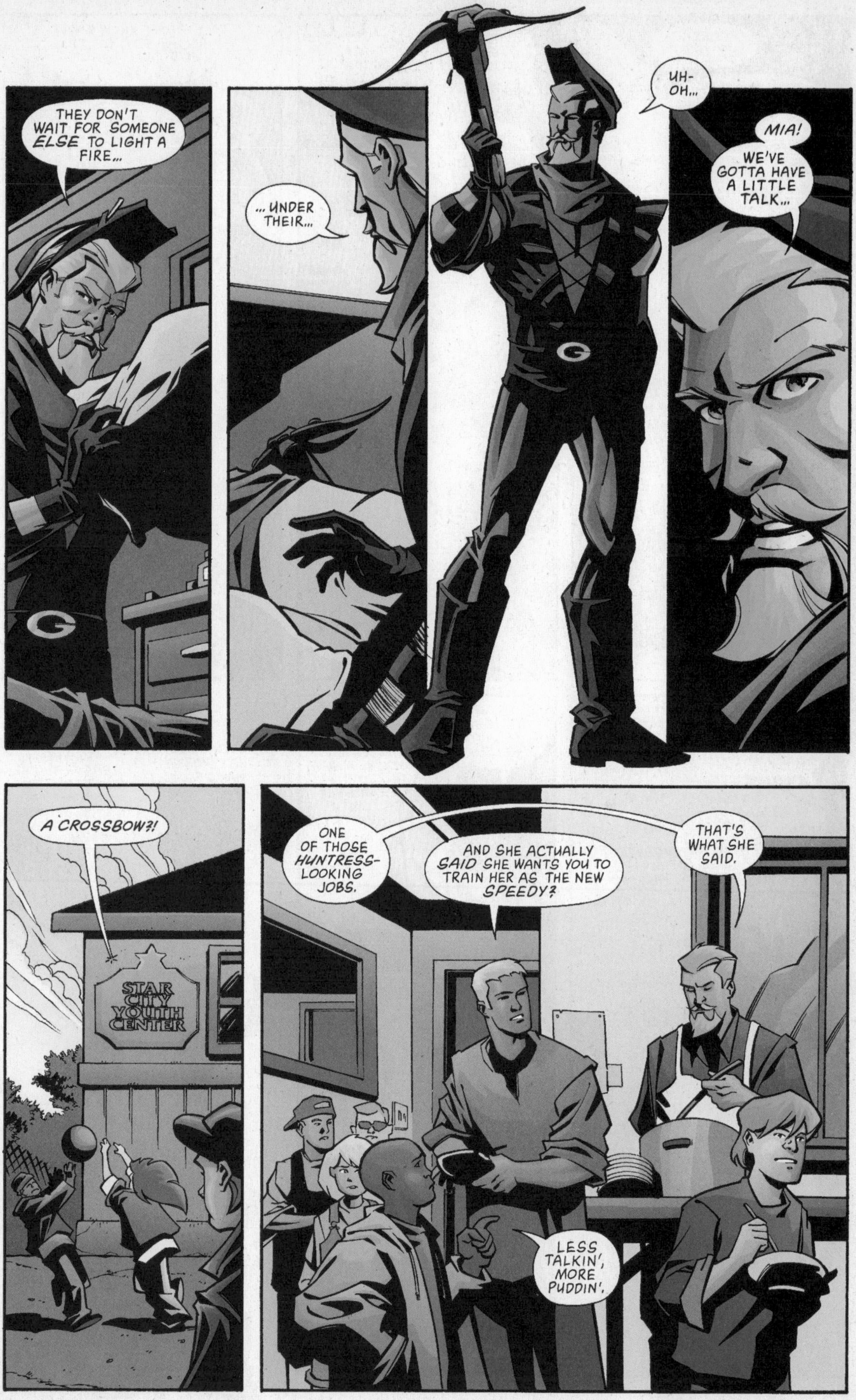
THEY DON'T WAIT FOR SOMEONE ELSE TO LIGHT A FIRE...
...UNDER THEIR...
UH-OH...
MIA!
WE'VE GOTTA HAVE A LITTLE TALK...
A CROSSBOW?!
STAR CITY YOUTH CENTER
ONE OF THOSE HUNTRESS-LOOKING JOBS.
AND SHE ACTUALLY SAID SHE WANTS YOU TO TRAIN HER AS THE NEW SPEEDY?
THAT'S WHAT SHE SAID.
LESS TALKIN', MORE PUDDIN'.

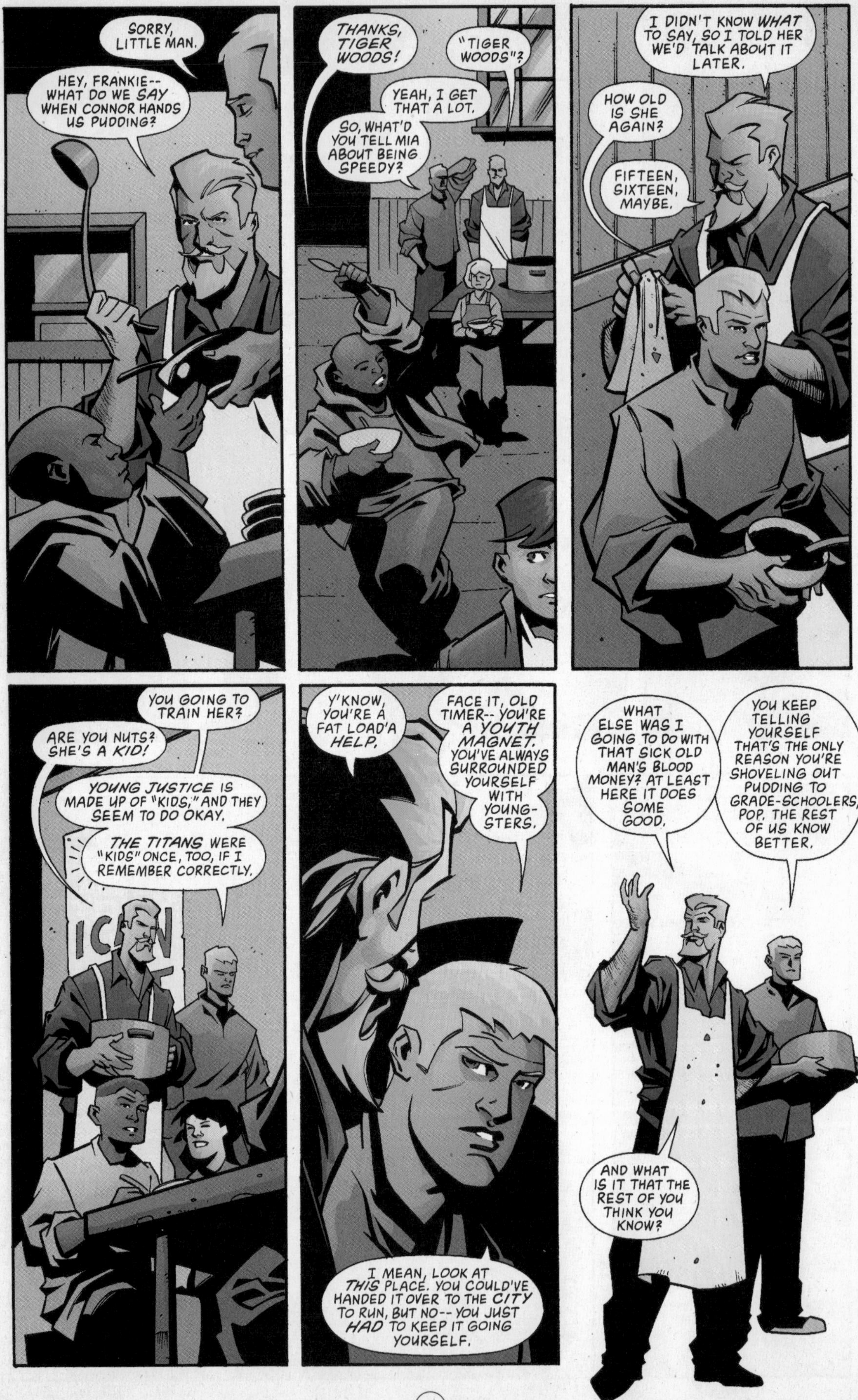
SORRY, LITTLE MAN.
HEY, FRANKIE-- WHAT DO WE SAY WHEN CONNOR HANDS US PUDDING?
THANKS, TIGER WOODS!
"TIGER WOODS"?
YEAH, I GET THAT A LOT.
SO, WHAT'D YOU TELL MIA ABOUT BEING SPEEDY?
I DIDN'T KNOW WHAT TO SAY, SO I TOLD HER WE'D TALK ABOUT IT LATER.
HOW OLD IS SHE AGAIN?
FIFTEEN, SIXTEEN, MAYBE.
YOU GOING TO TRAIN HER?
ARE YOU NUTS? SHE'S A KID!
YOUNG JUSTICE IS MADE UP OF "KIDS," AND THEY SEEM TO DO OKAY.
THE TITANS WERE "KIDS" ONCE, TOO, IF I REMEMBER CORRECTLY.
Y'KNOW, YOU'RE A FAT LOAD'A HELP.
FACE IT, OLD TIMER-- YOU'RE A YOUTH MAGNET. YOU'VE ALWAYS SURROUNDED YOURSELF WITH YOUNG-STERS.
I MEAN, LOOK AT THIS PLACE. YOU COULD'VE HANDED IT OVER TO THE CITY TO RUN, BUT NO-- YOU JUST HAD TO KEEP IT GOING YOURSELF.
WHAT ELSE WAS I GOING TO DO WITH THAT SICK OLD MAN'S BLOOD MONEY? AT LEAST HERE IT DOES SOME GOOD.
YOU KEEP TELLING YOURSELF THAT'S THE ONLY REASON YOU'RE SHOVELING OUT PUDDING TO GRADE-SCHOOLERS, POP. THE REST OF US KNOW BETTER.
AND WHAT IS IT THAT THE REST OF YOU THINK YOU KNOW?

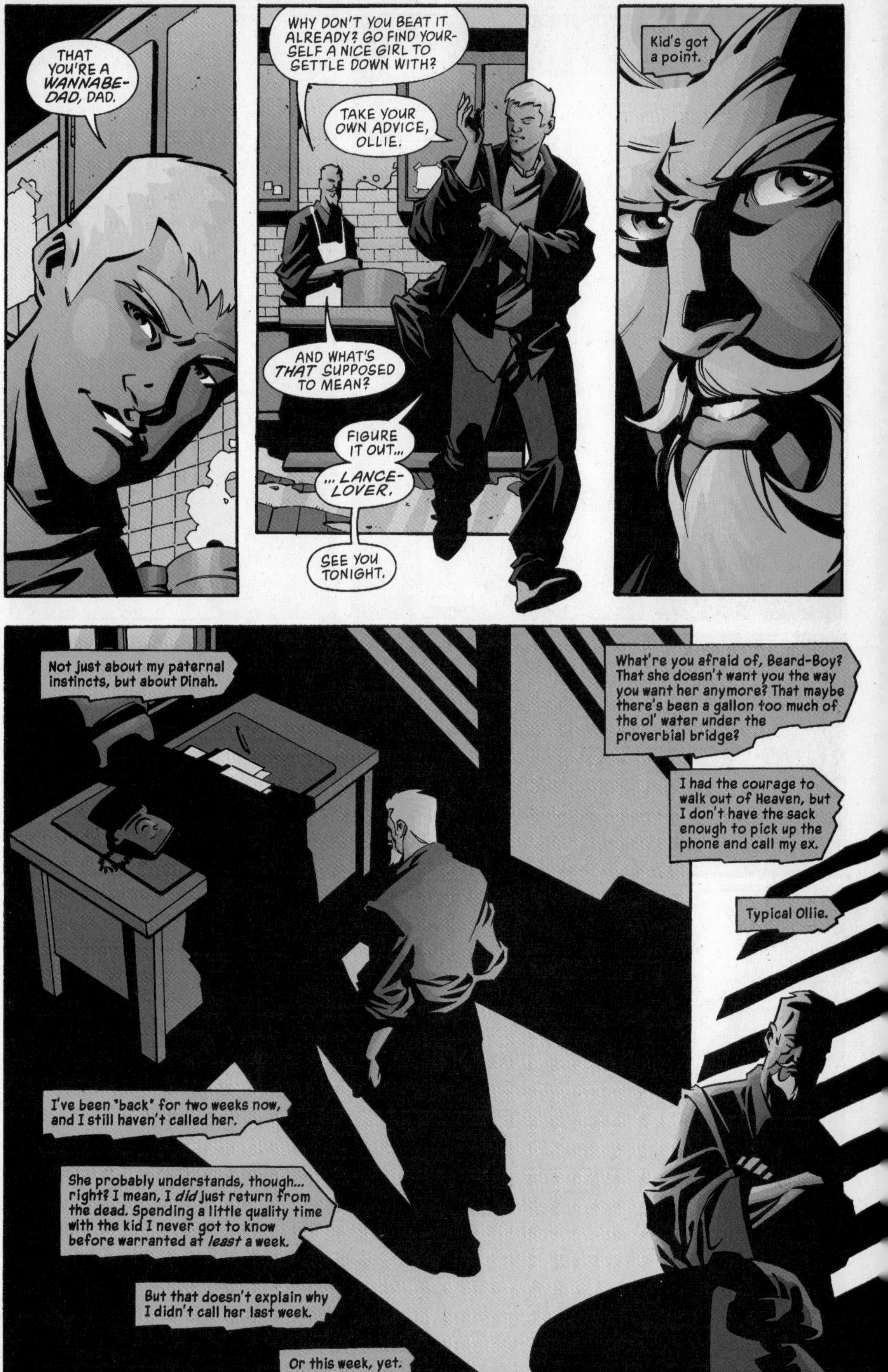

THAT YOU'RE A WANNABE-DAD, DAD.
WHY DON'T YOU BEAT IT ALREADY? GO FIND YOURSELF A NICE GIRL TO SETTLE DOWN WITH?
TAKE YOUR OWN ADVICE, OLLIE.
AND WHAT'S THAT SUPPOSED TO MEAN?
FIGURE IT OUT...
...LANCE-LOVER.
SEE YOU TONIGHT.
Kid's got a point.
Not just about my paternal instincts, but about Dinah.
I've been 'back' for two weeks now, and I still haven't called her.
She probably understands, though... right? I mean, I did just return from the dead. Spending a little quality time with the kid I never got to know before warranted at least a week.
But that doesn't explain why I didn't call her last week.
Or this week, yet.
What're you afraid of, Beard-Boy? That she doesn't want you the way you want her anymore? That maybe there's been a gallon too much of the ol' water under the proverbial bridge?
I had the courage to walk out of Heaven, but I don't have the sack enough to pick up the phone and call my ex.
Typical Ollie.

C'mon-- You've braved far worse than this.

YEAH...

OH, HELLO, MISTER "DO-AS-I-SAY-NOT-AS-I-DO."

YOU'RE LATE.

NOBODY.

YOU READY TO TAKE OVER? I'VE GOTTA GO HOME AND GRAB A SHOWER BEFORE I GO OUT TONIGHT.

DOCK ME.

SO, WHO'RE YOU TALKING TO?

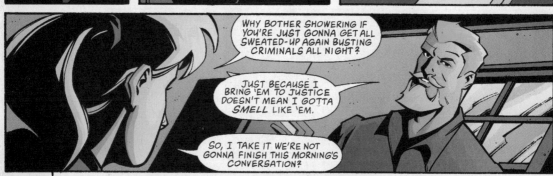

WHY BOTHER SHOWERING IF YOU'RE JUST GONNA GET ALL SWEATED-UP AGAIN BUSTING CRIMINALS ALL NIGHT?

JUST BECAUSE I BRING 'EM TO JUSTICE DOESN'T MEAN I GOTTA SMELL LIKE 'EM.

SO, I TAKE IT WE'RE NOT GONNA FINISH THIS MORNING'S CONVERSATION?

WE'LL DO IT TOMORROW MORNING.

MEANTIME, MAKE SURE YOU DO YOUR DISHES TONIGHT.

I GET HOME AGAIN TOMORROW MORNING AND I FIND ANY DISHES IN THAT SINK, YOU'RE WAKING UP TO A BED FULL'A ICE WATER.

YOU ALWAYS GONNA BE THIS EVASIVE?

DISHES, MIA.

YESSIR, YOUR ROYAL HIGHNESS.

JERK.

I HEARD THAT.

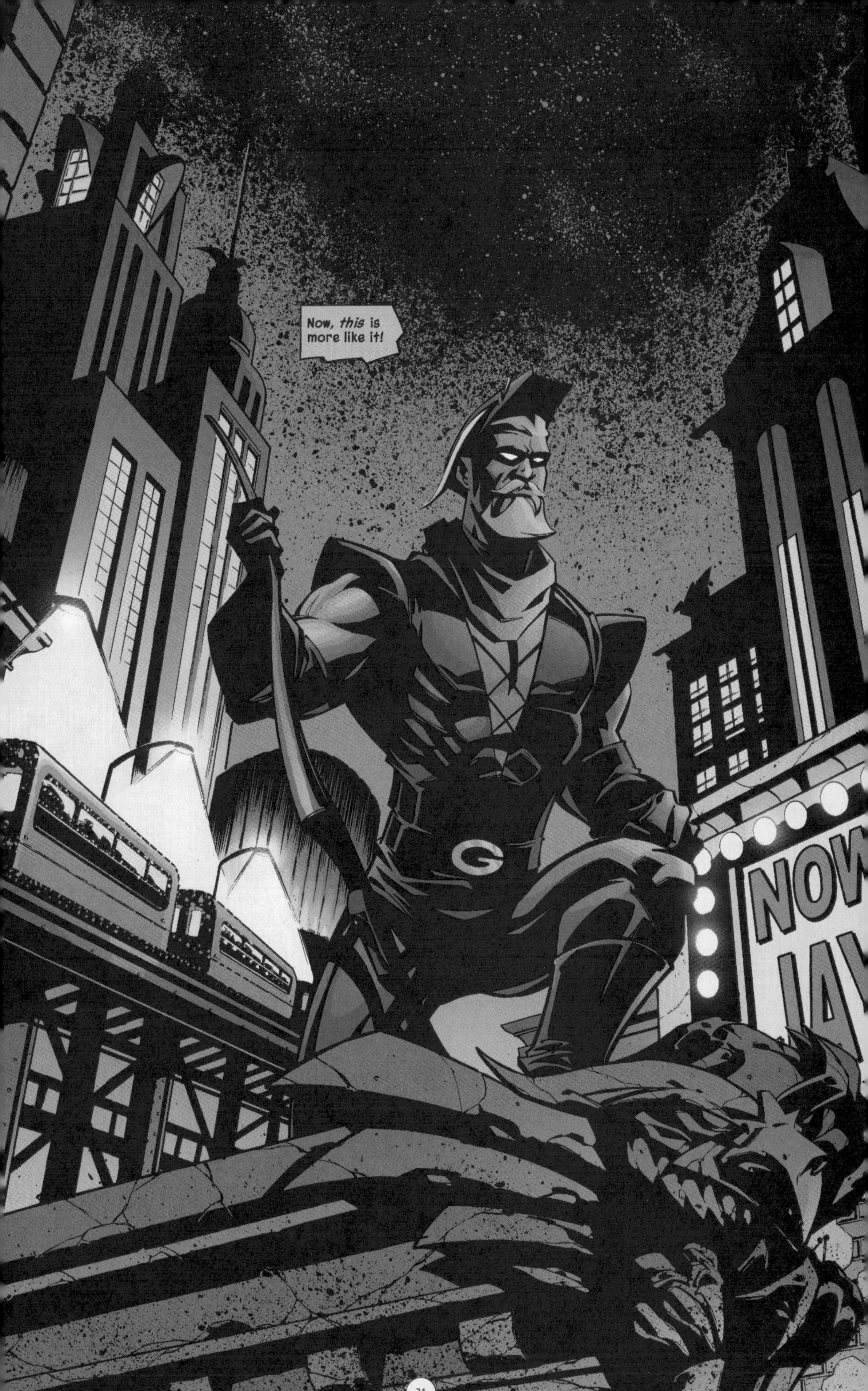
Now, *this* is more like it!
NOW

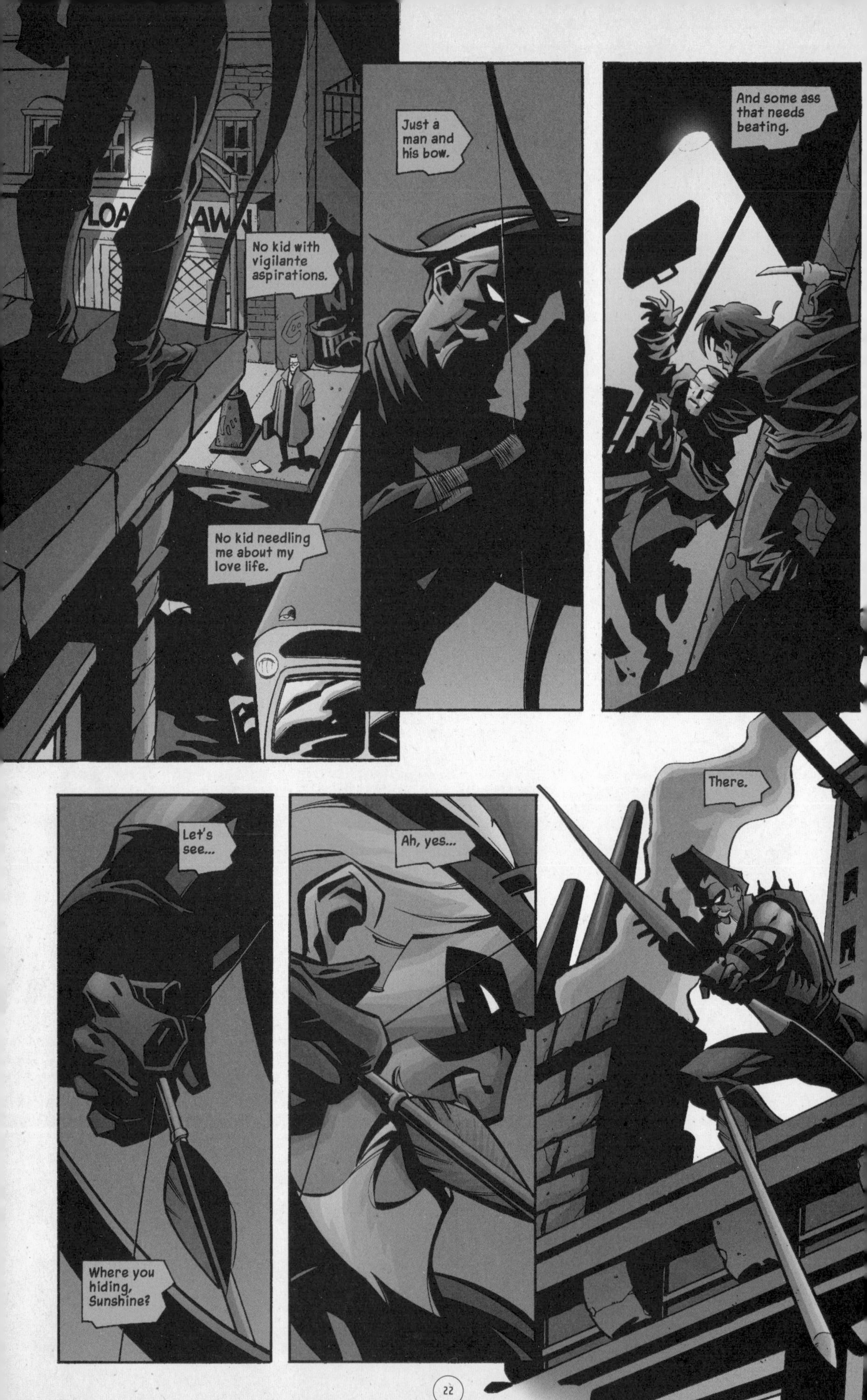
LOA AWN
No kid with vigilante aspirations.
No kid needling me about my love life.
Just a man and his bow.
And some ass that needs beating.
Let's see...
Where you hiding, Sunshine?
Ah, yes...
There.

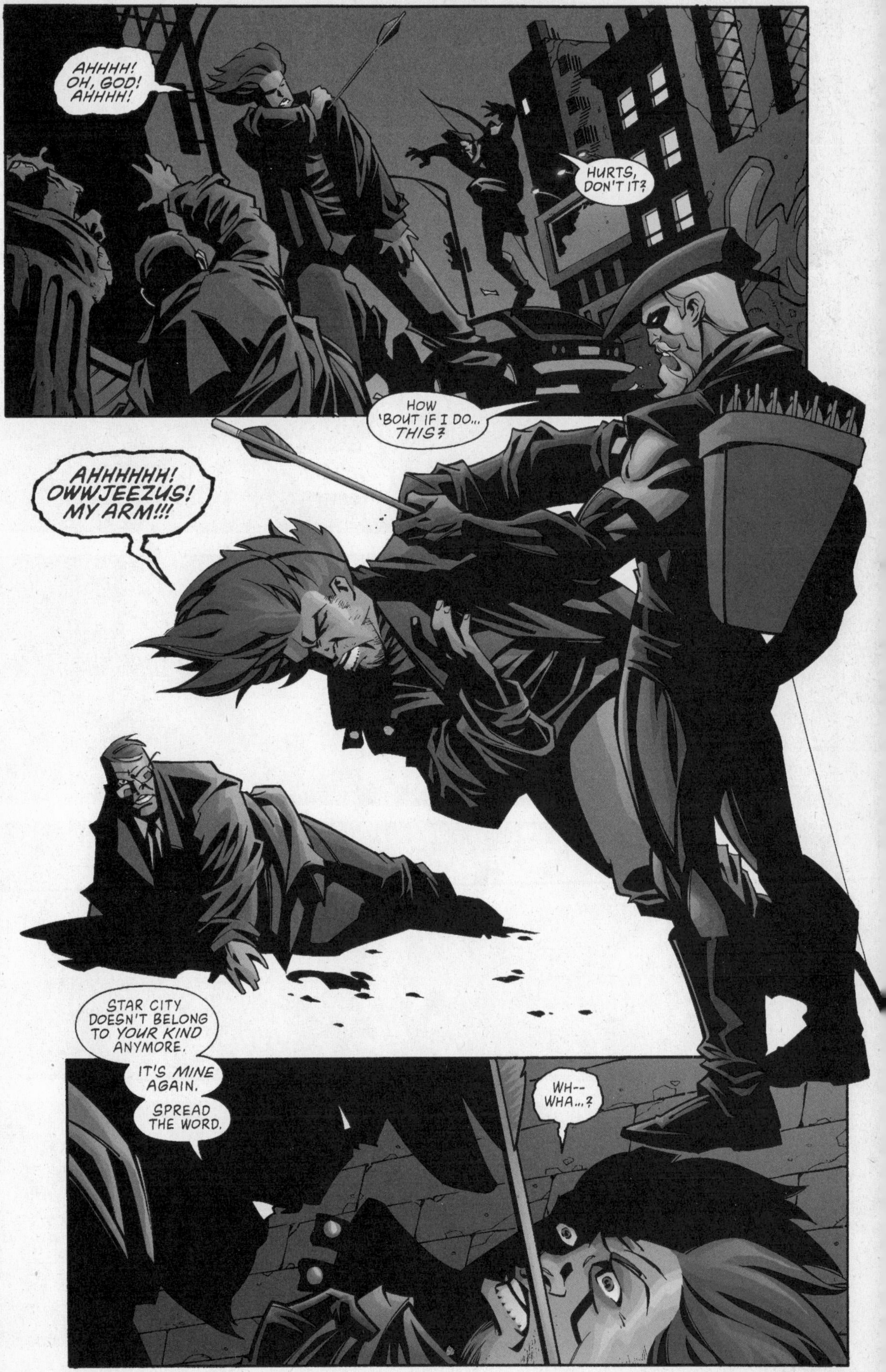
AHHHH! OH, GOD! AHHHH!
HURTS, DON'T IT?
HOW 'BOUT IF I DO... THIS?
AHHHHHH! OWWJEEZUS! MY ARM!!!
STAR CITY DOESN'T BELONG TO YOUR KIND ANYMORE.
IT'S MINE AGAIN.
SPREAD THE WORD.
WH-- WHA...?

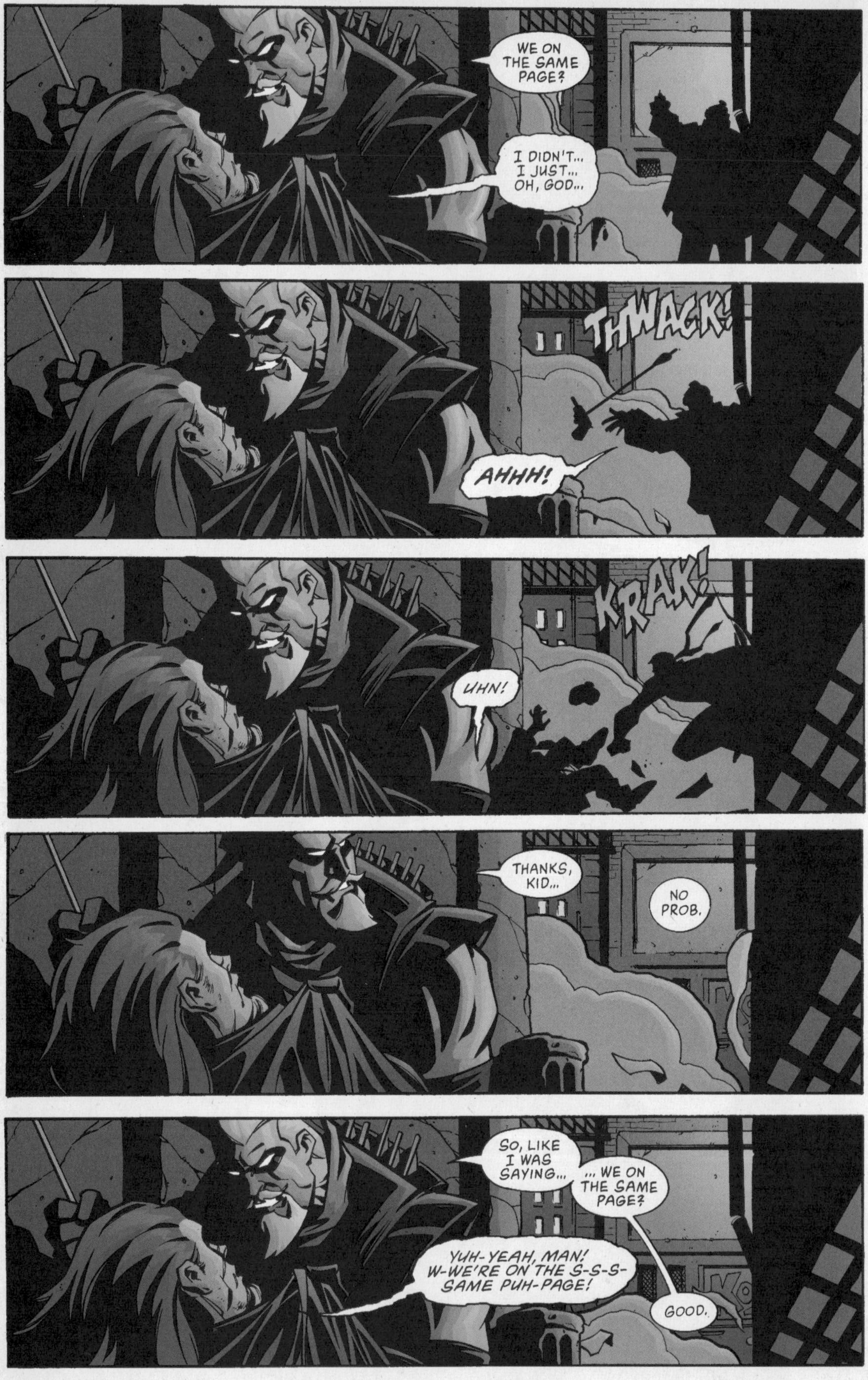
WE ON THE SAME PAGE?
I DIDN'T... I JUST... OH, GOD...
THWACK!
AHHH!
KRAK!
UHN!
THANKS, KID...
NO PROB.
SO, LIKE I WAS SAYING...
... WE ON THE SAME PAGE?
YUH-YEAH, MAN! W-WE'RE ON THE S-S-SAME PUH-PAGE!
GOOD.

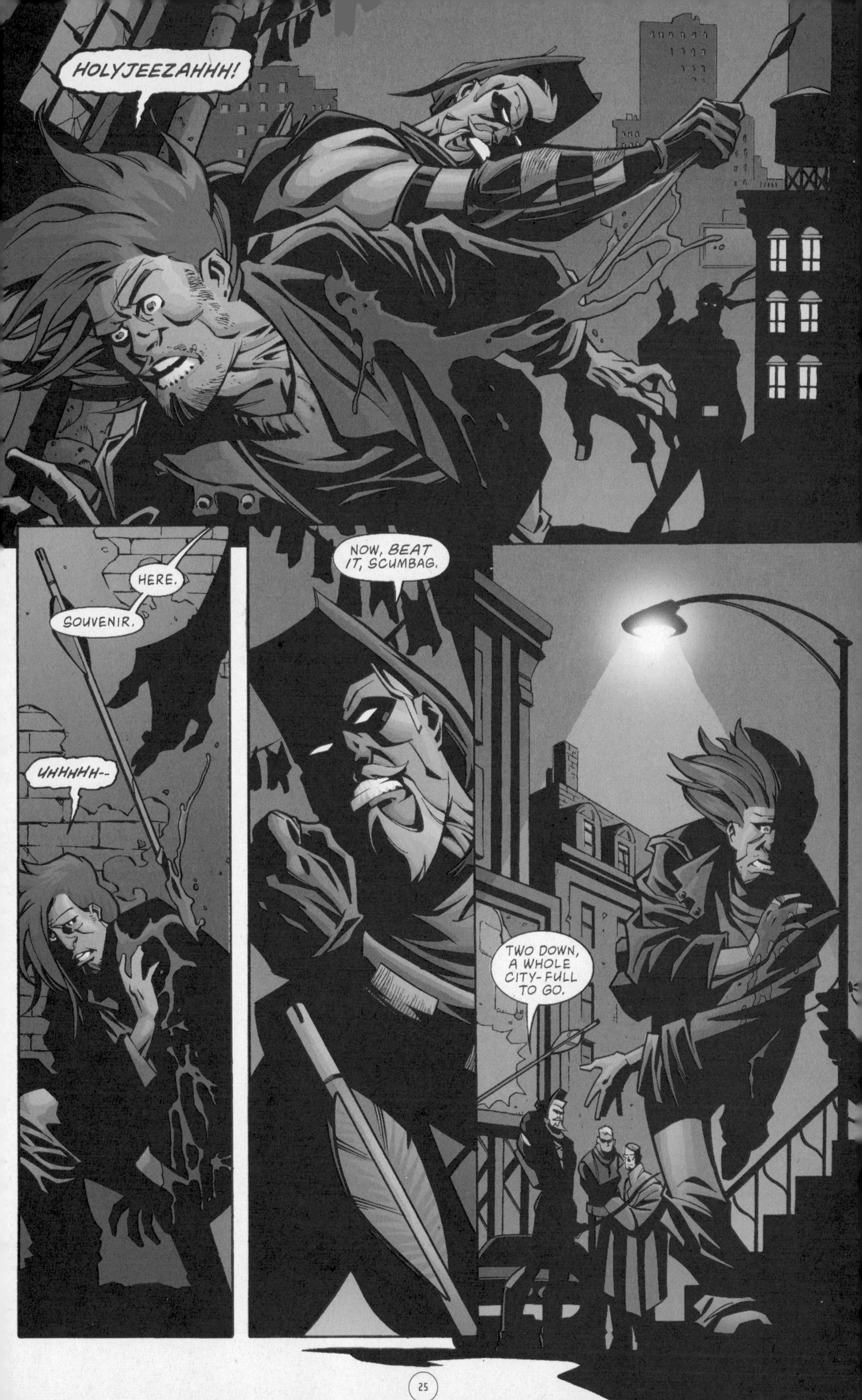
HOLYJEEZAHHH!
HERE.
SOUVENIR.
UHHHHH--
NOW, BEAT IT, SCUMBAG.
TWO DOWN, A WHOLE CITY-FULL TO GO.

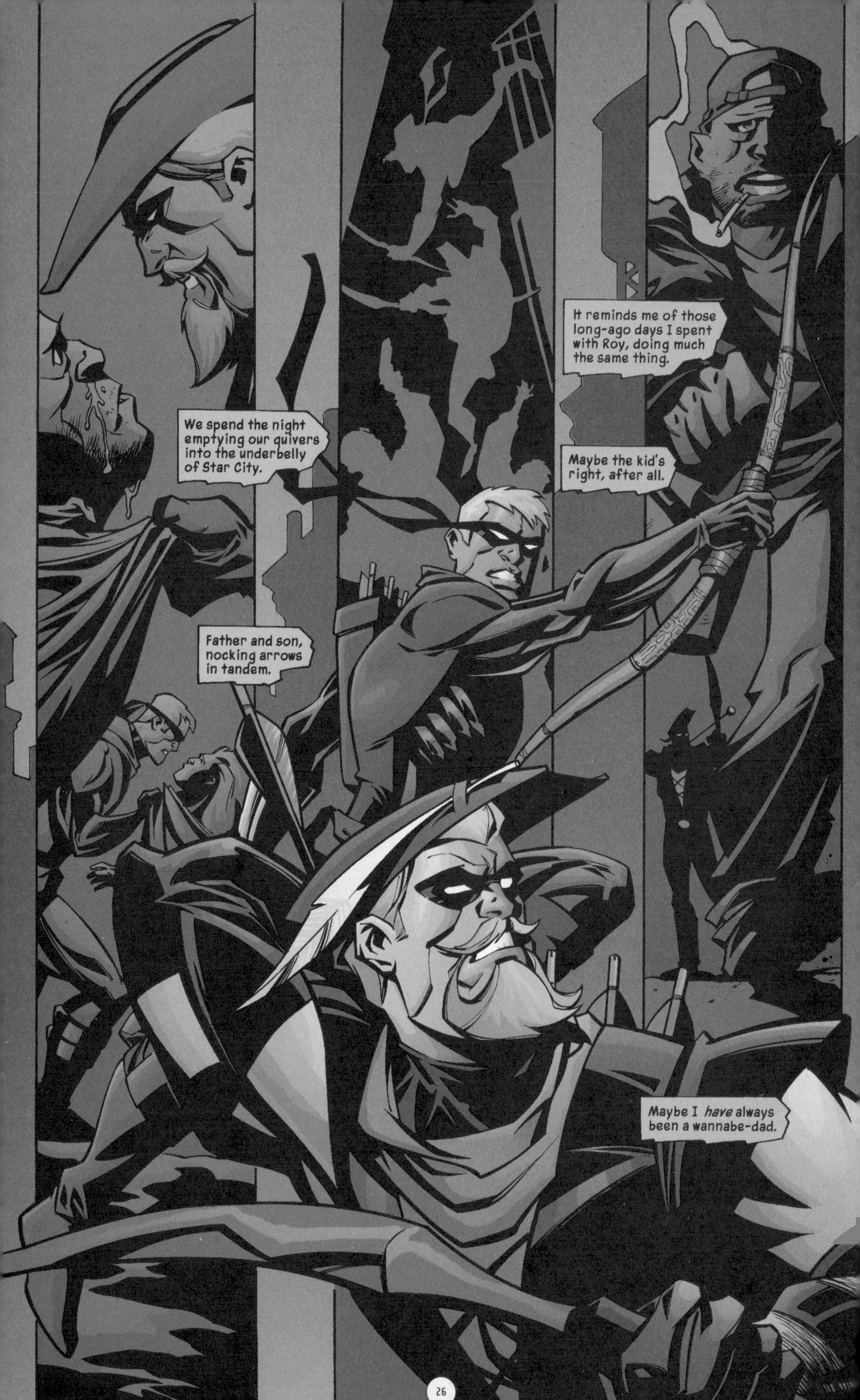
We spend the night emptying our quivers into the underbelly of Star City.
It reminds me of those long-ago days I spent with Roy, doing much the same thing.
Maybe the kid's right, after all.
Father and son, nocking arrows in tandem.
Maybe I *have* always been a wannabe-dad.

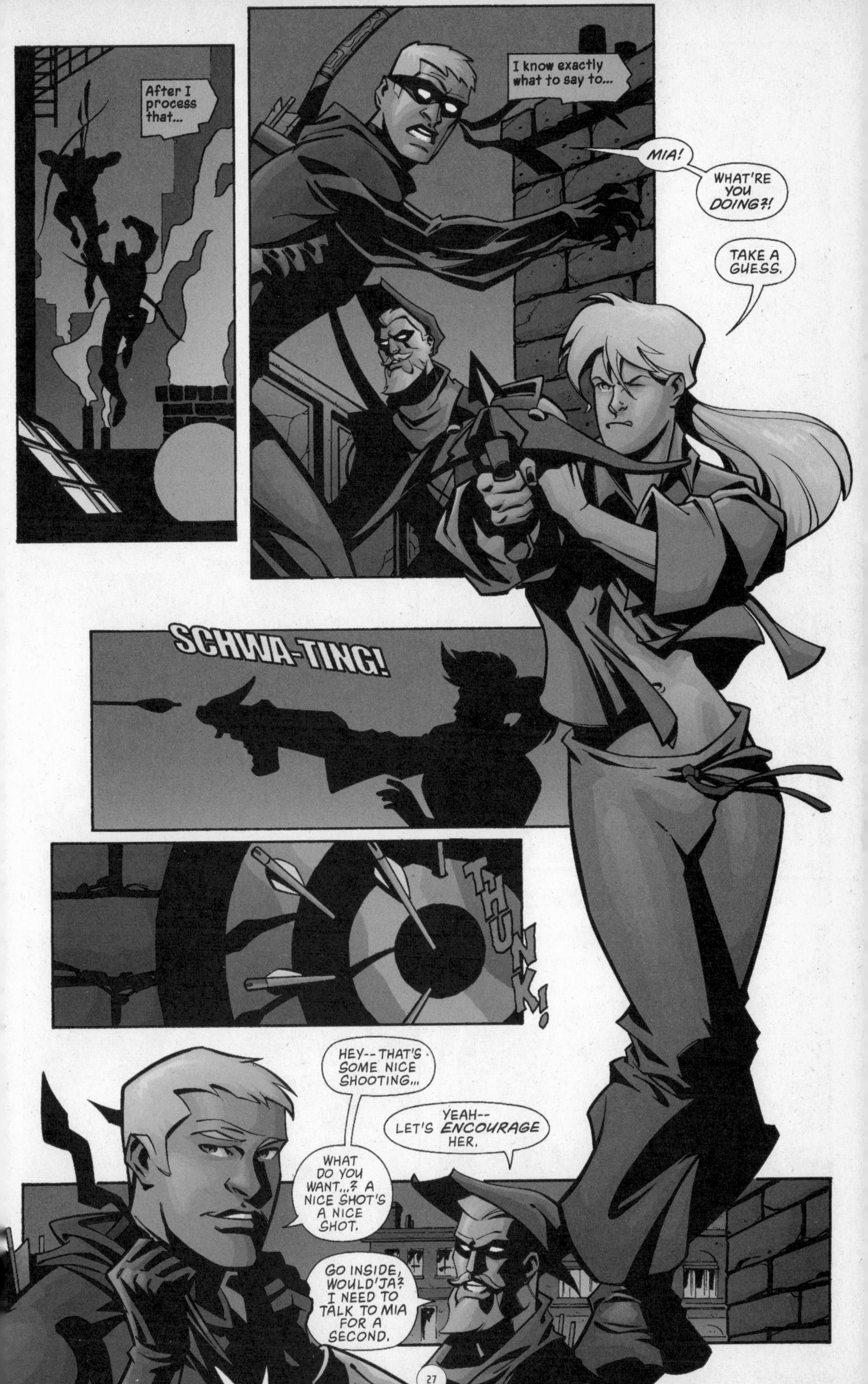
After I process that...
I know exactly what to say to...
MIA!
WHAT'RE YOU DOING?!
TAKE A GUESS.
SCHWA-TING!
THUNK!
HEY--THAT'S SOME NICE SHOOTING...
YEAH-- LET'S ENCOURAGE HER.
WHAT DO YOU WANT...? A NICE SHOT'S A NICE SHOT.
GO INSIDE, WOULD'JA? I NEED TO TALK TO MIA FOR A SECOND.

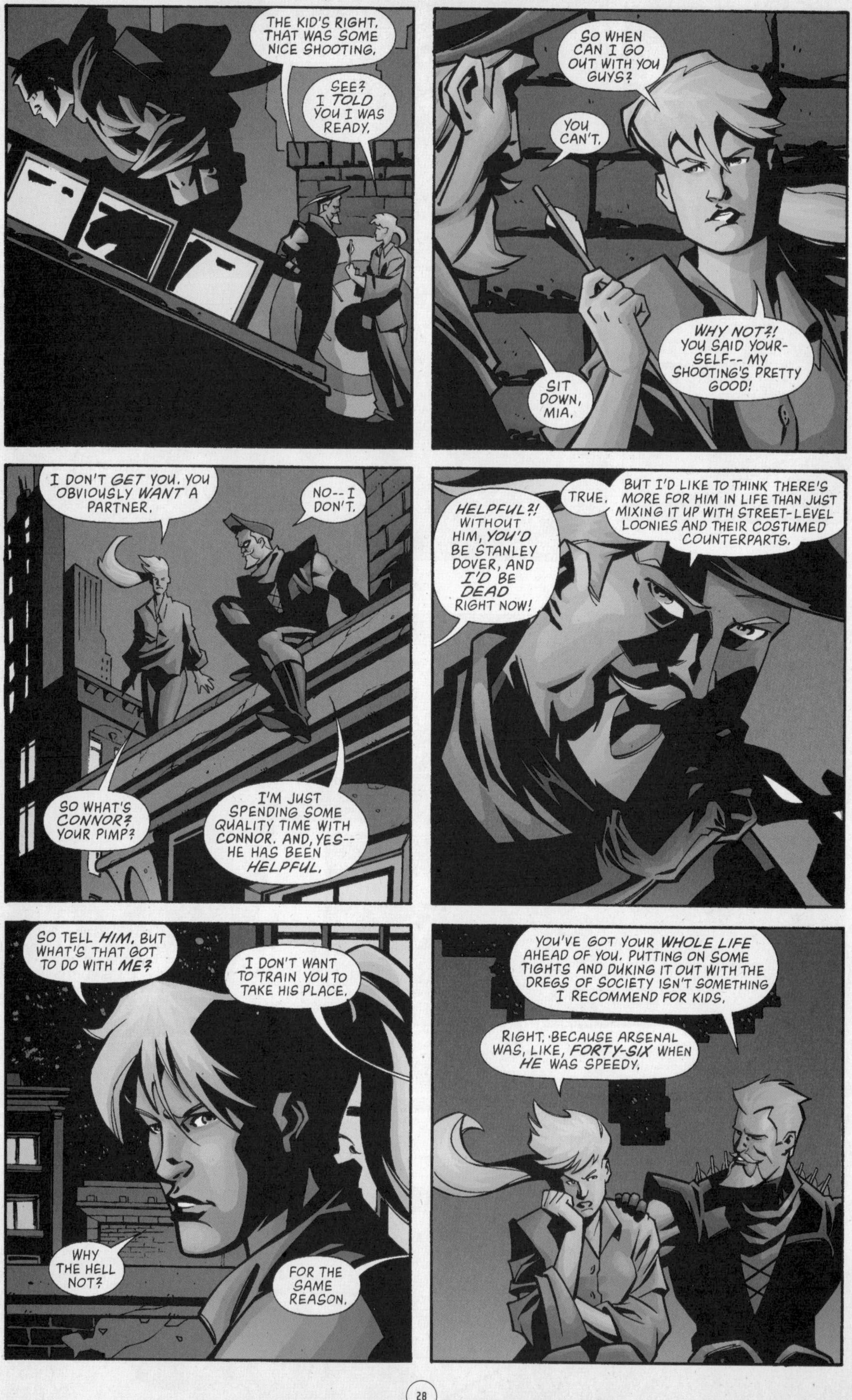
THE KID'S RIGHT. THAT WAS SOME NICE SHOOTING.
SEE? I TOLD YOU I WAS READY.
SO WHEN CAN I GO OUT WITH YOU GUYS?
YOU CAN'T.
WHY NOT?! YOU SAID YOURSELF-- MY SHOOTING'S PRETTY GOOD!
SIT DOWN, MIA.
I DON'T GET YOU. YOU OBVIOUSLY WANT A PARTNER.
NO-- I DON'T.
I'M JUST SPENDING SOME QUALITY TIME WITH CONNOR. AND, YES-- HE HAS BEEN HELPFUL.
SO WHAT'S CONNOR? YOUR PIMP?
HELPFUL?! WITHOUT HIM, YOU'D BE STANLEY DOVER, AND I'D BE DEAD RIGHT NOW!
TRUE.
BUT I'D LIKE TO THINK THERE'S MORE FOR HIM IN LIFE THAN JUST MIXING IT UP WITH STREET-LEVEL LOONIES AND THEIR COSTUMED COUNTERPARTS.
SO TELL HIM. BUT WHAT'S THAT GOT TO DO WITH ME?
I DON'T WANT TO TRAIN YOU TO TAKE HIS PLACE.
WHY THE HELL NOT?
FOR THE SAME REASON.
YOU'VE GOT YOUR WHOLE LIFE AHEAD OF YOU. PUTTING ON SOME TIGHTS AND DUKING IT OUT WITH THE DREGS OF SOCIETY ISN'T SOMETHING I RECOMMEND FOR KIDS.
RIGHT. BECAUSE ARSENAL WAS, LIKE, FORTY-SIX WHEN HE WAS SPEEDY.

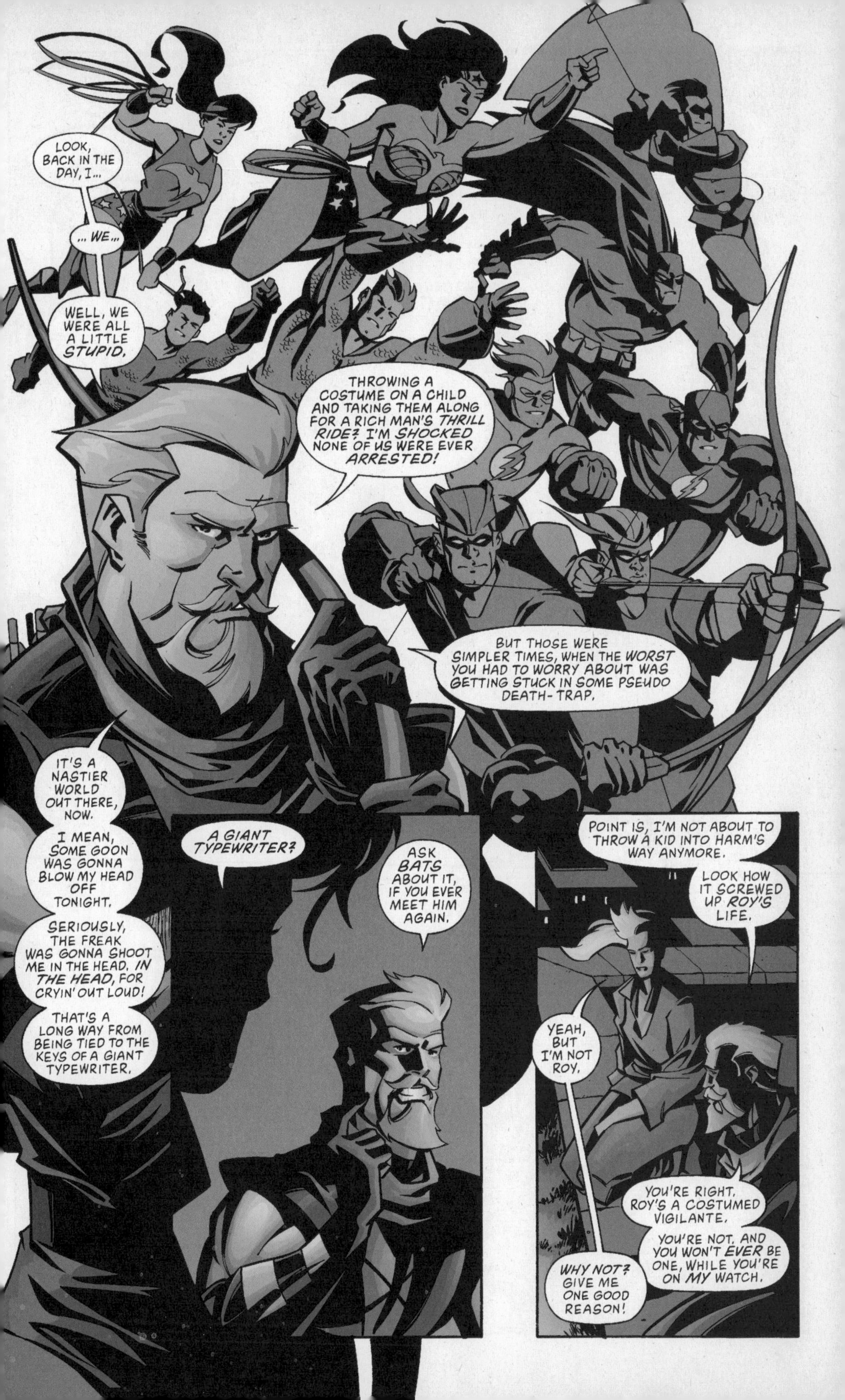

LOOK, BACK IN THE DAY, I...
...WE...
WELL, WE WERE ALL A LITTLE STUPID.
THROWING A COSTUME ON A CHILD AND TAKING THEM ALONG FOR A RICH MAN'S THRILL RIDE? I'M SHOCKED NONE OF US WERE EVER ARRESTED!
BUT THOSE WERE SIMPLER TIMES, WHEN THE WORST YOU HAD TO WORRY ABOUT WAS GETTING STUCK IN SOME PSEUDO DEATH-TRAP.
IT'S A NASTIER WORLD OUT THERE, NOW.
I MEAN, SOME GOON WAS GONNA BLOW MY HEAD OFF TONIGHT.
SERIOUSLY, THE FREAK WAS GONNA SHOOT ME IN THE HEAD. IN THE HEAD, FOR CRYIN' OUT LOUD!
THAT'S A LONG WAY FROM BEING TIED TO THE KEYS OF A GIANT TYPEWRITER.
A GIANT TYPEWRITER?
ASK BATS ABOUT IT, IF YOU EVER MEET HIM AGAIN.
POINT IS, I'M NOT ABOUT TO THROW A KID INTO HARM'S WAY ANYMORE.
LOOK HOW IT SCREWED UP ROY'S LIFE.
YEAH, BUT I'M NOT ROY.
YOU'RE RIGHT. ROY'S A COSTUMED VIGILANTE.
YOU'RE NOT. AND YOU WON'T EVER BE ONE, WHILE YOU'RE ON MY WATCH.
WHY NOT? GIVE ME ONE GOOD REASON!

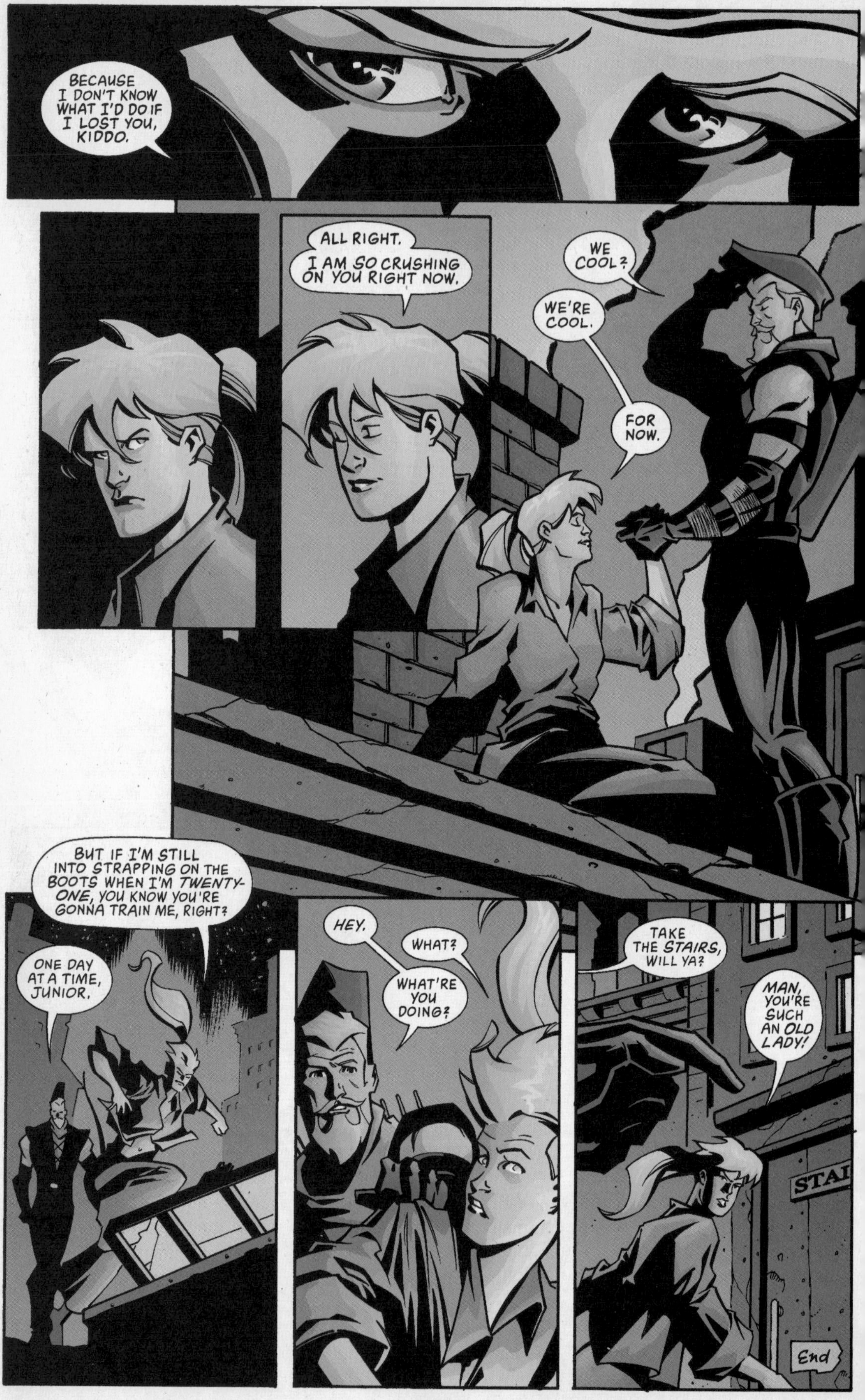

BECAUSE I DON'T KNOW WHAT I'D DO IF I LOST YOU, KIDDO.
ALL RIGHT. I AM SO CRUSHING ON YOU RIGHT NOW.
WE COOL?
WE'RE COOL.
FOR NOW.
BUT IF I'M STILL INTO STRAPPING ON THE BOOTS WHEN I'M TWENTY-ONE, YOU KNOW YOU'RE GONNA TRAIN ME, RIGHT?
ONE DAY AT A TIME, JUNIOR.
HEY.
WHAT?
WHAT'RE YOU DOING?
TAKE THE STAIRS, WILL YA?
MAN, YOU'RE SUCH AN OLD LADY!
STAI
End

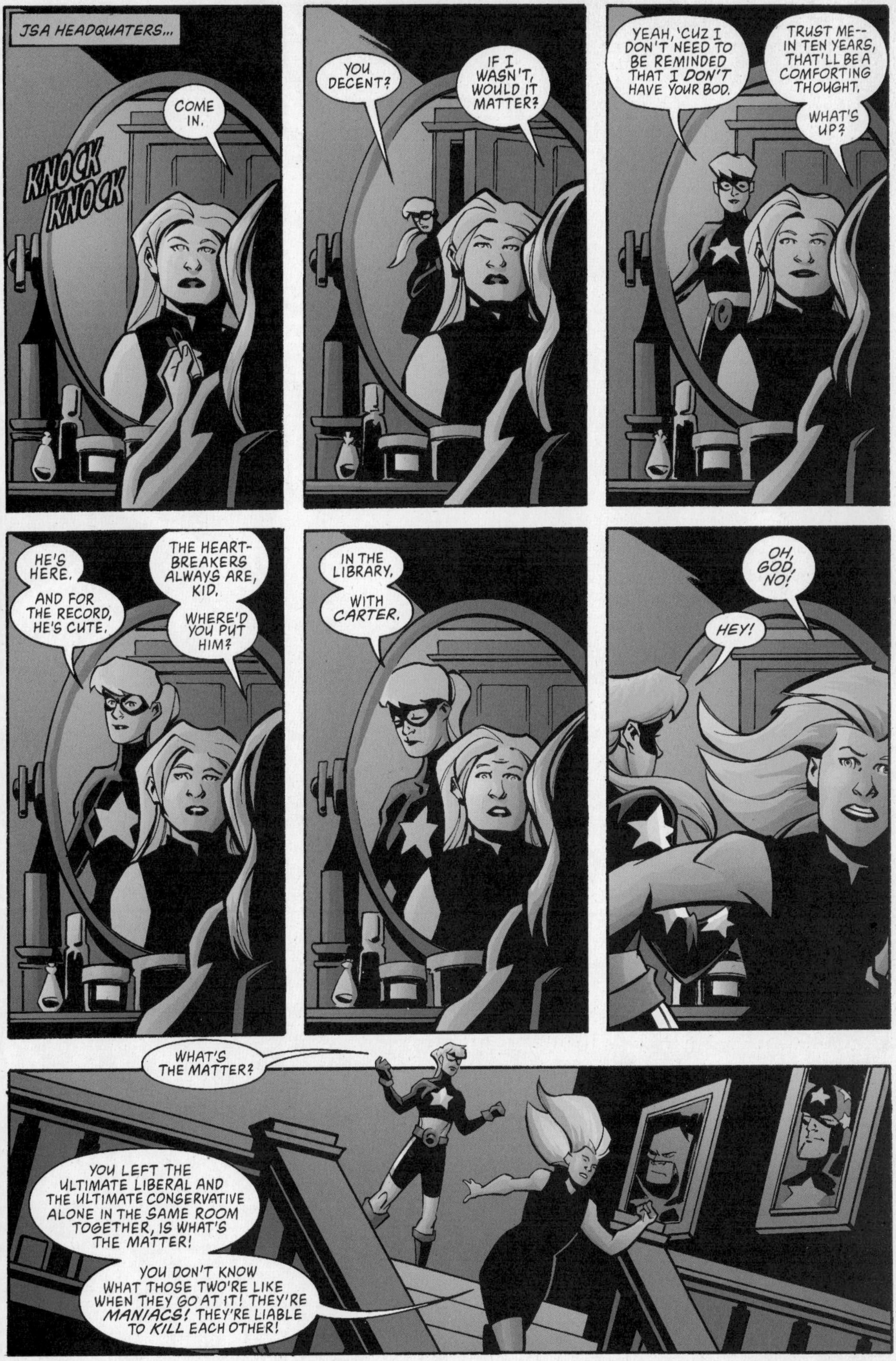
JSA HEADQUATERS...
KNOCK KNOCK
COME IN.
YOU DECENT?
IF I WASN'T, WOULD IT MATTER?
YEAH, 'CUZ I DON'T NEED TO BE REMINDED THAT I *DON'T* HAVE YOUR BOD.
TRUST ME-- IN TEN YEARS, THAT'LL BE A COMFORTING THOUGHT.
WHAT'S UP?
HE'S HERE.
AND FOR THE RECORD, HE'S CUTE.
THE HEART-BREAKERS ALWAYS ARE, KID.
WHERE'D YOU PUT HIM?
IN THE LIBRARY.
WITH *CARTER*.
OH, GOD, NO!
HEY!
WHAT'S THE MATTER?
YOU LEFT THE ULTIMATE LIBERAL AND THE ULTIMATE CONSERVATIVE ALONE IN THE SAME ROOM TOGETHER, IS WHAT'S THE MATTER!
YOU DON'T KNOW WHAT THOSE TWO'RE LIKE WHEN THEY GO AT IT! THEY'RE *MANIACS!* THEY'RE LIABLE TO *KILL* EACH OTHER!

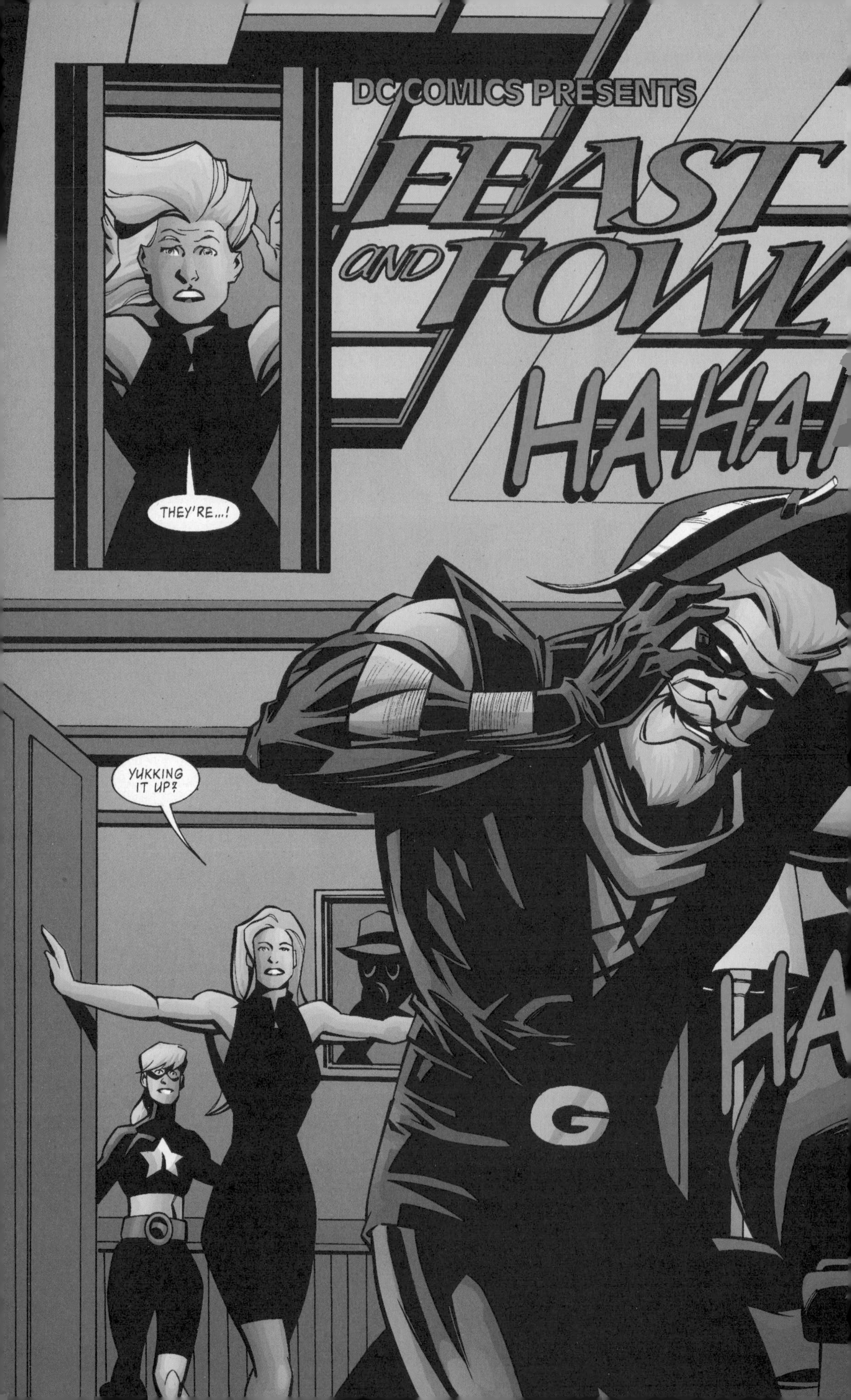
DC COMICS PRESENTS
FEAST AND FOWL
HA HA
THEY'RE...!
YUKKING IT UP?
HA

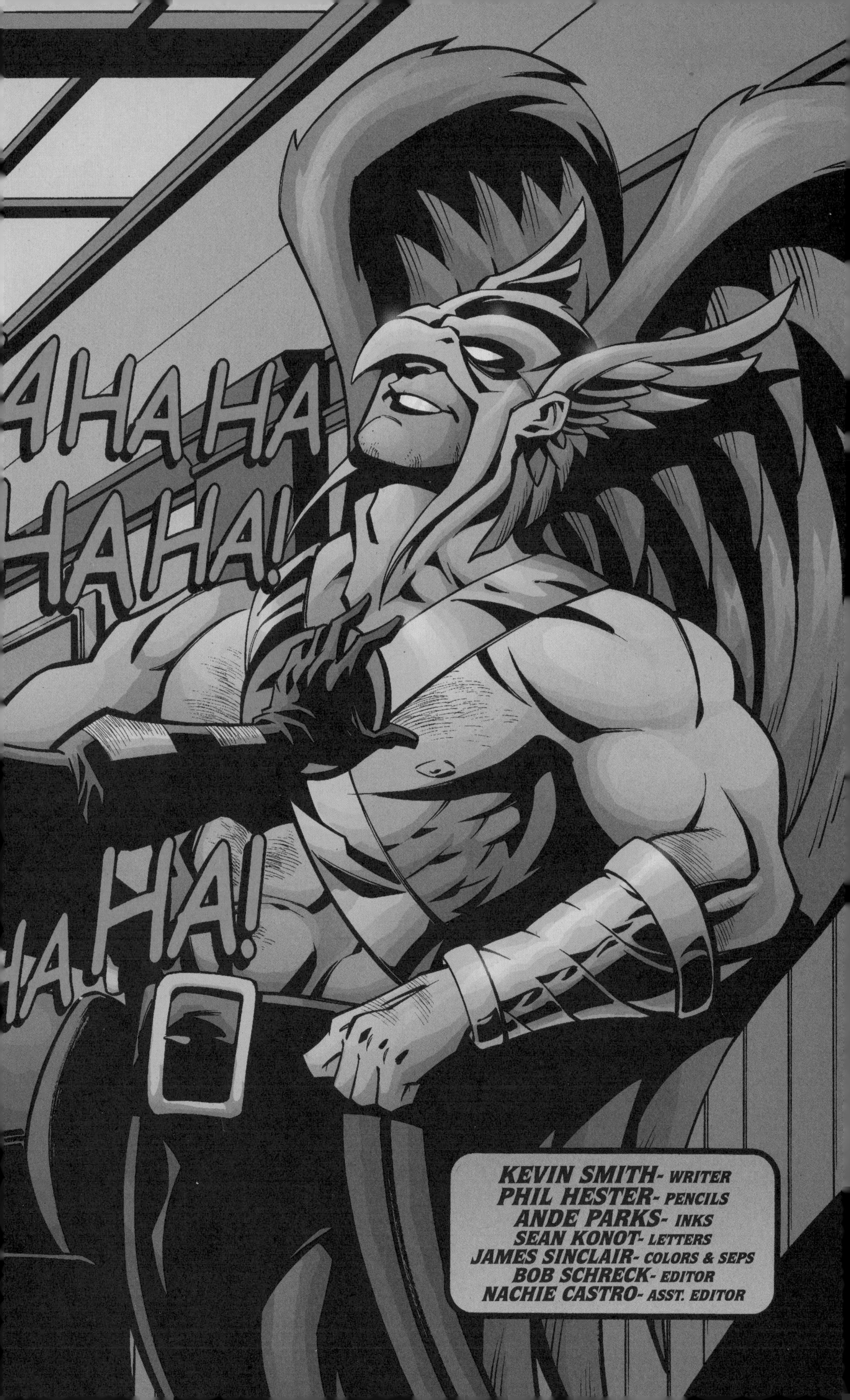

AHAHA HA
HAHA!
HA. HA!
KEVIN SMITH- WRITER
PHIL HESTER- PENCILS
ANDE PARKS- INKS
SEAN KONOT- LETTERS
JAMES SINCLAIR- COLORS & SEPS
BOB SCHRECK- EDITOR
NACHIE CASTRO- ASST. EDITOR

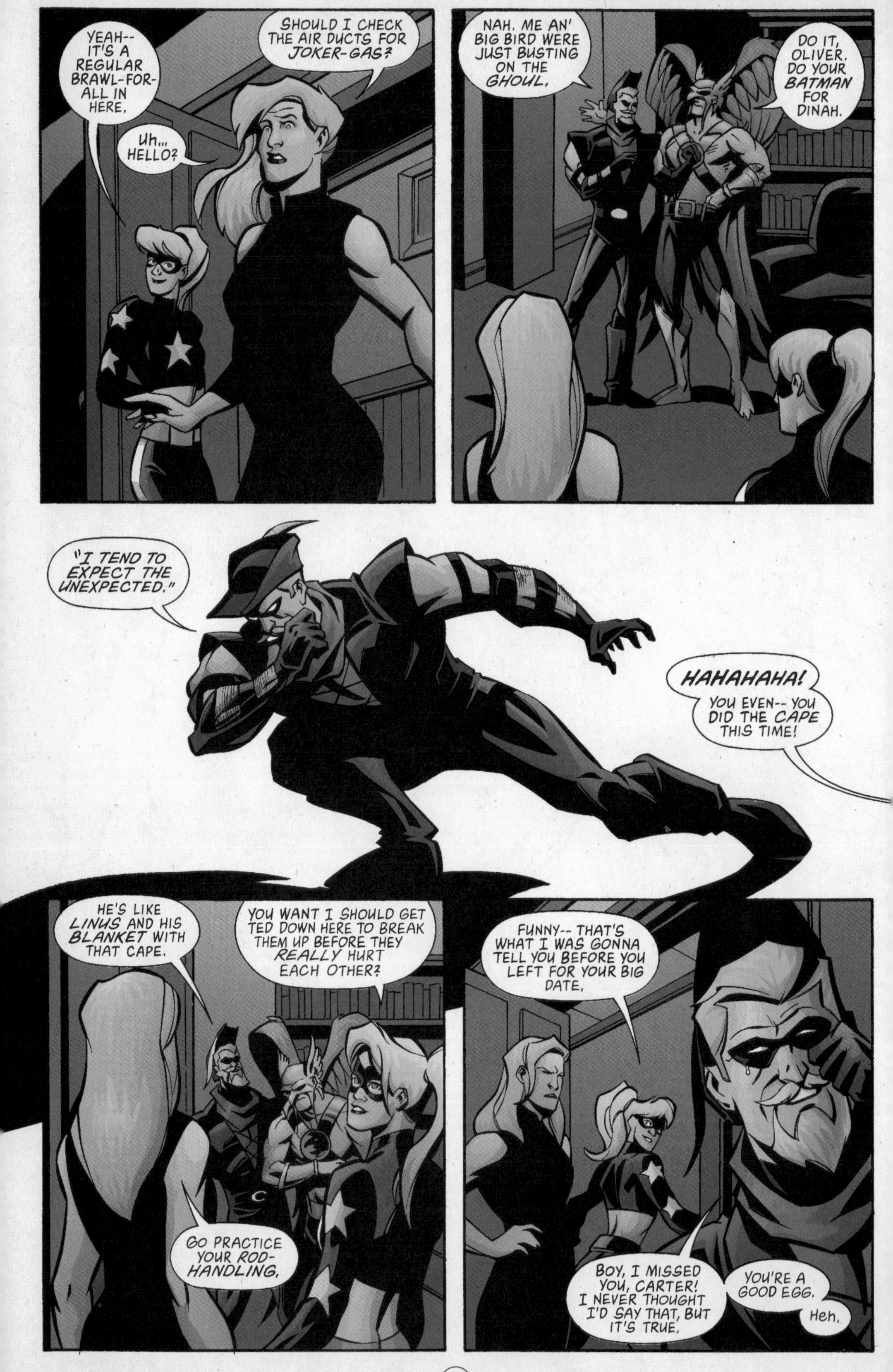
YEAH-- IT'S A REGULAR BRAWL-FOR-ALL IN HERE.
SHOULD I CHECK THE AIR DUCTS FOR JOKER-GAS?
UH... HELLO?
NAH. ME AN' BIG BIRD WERE JUST BUSTING ON THE GHOUL.
DO IT, OLIVER. DO YOUR BATMAN FOR DINAH.
"I TEND TO EXPECT THE UNEXPECTED."
HAHAHAHA!
YOU EVEN-- YOU DID THE CAPE THIS TIME!
HE'S LIKE LINUS AND HIS BLANKET WITH THAT CAPE.
YOU WANT I SHOULD GET TED DOWN HERE TO BREAK THEM UP BEFORE THEY REALLY HURT EACH OTHER?
GO PRACTICE YOUR ROD-HANDLING.
FUNNY-- THAT'S WHAT I WAS GONNA TELL YOU BEFORE YOU LEFT FOR YOUR BIG DATE.
BOY, I MISSED YOU, CARTER! I NEVER THOUGHT I'D SAY THAT, BUT IT'S TRUE.
YOU'RE A GOOD EGG.
Heh.

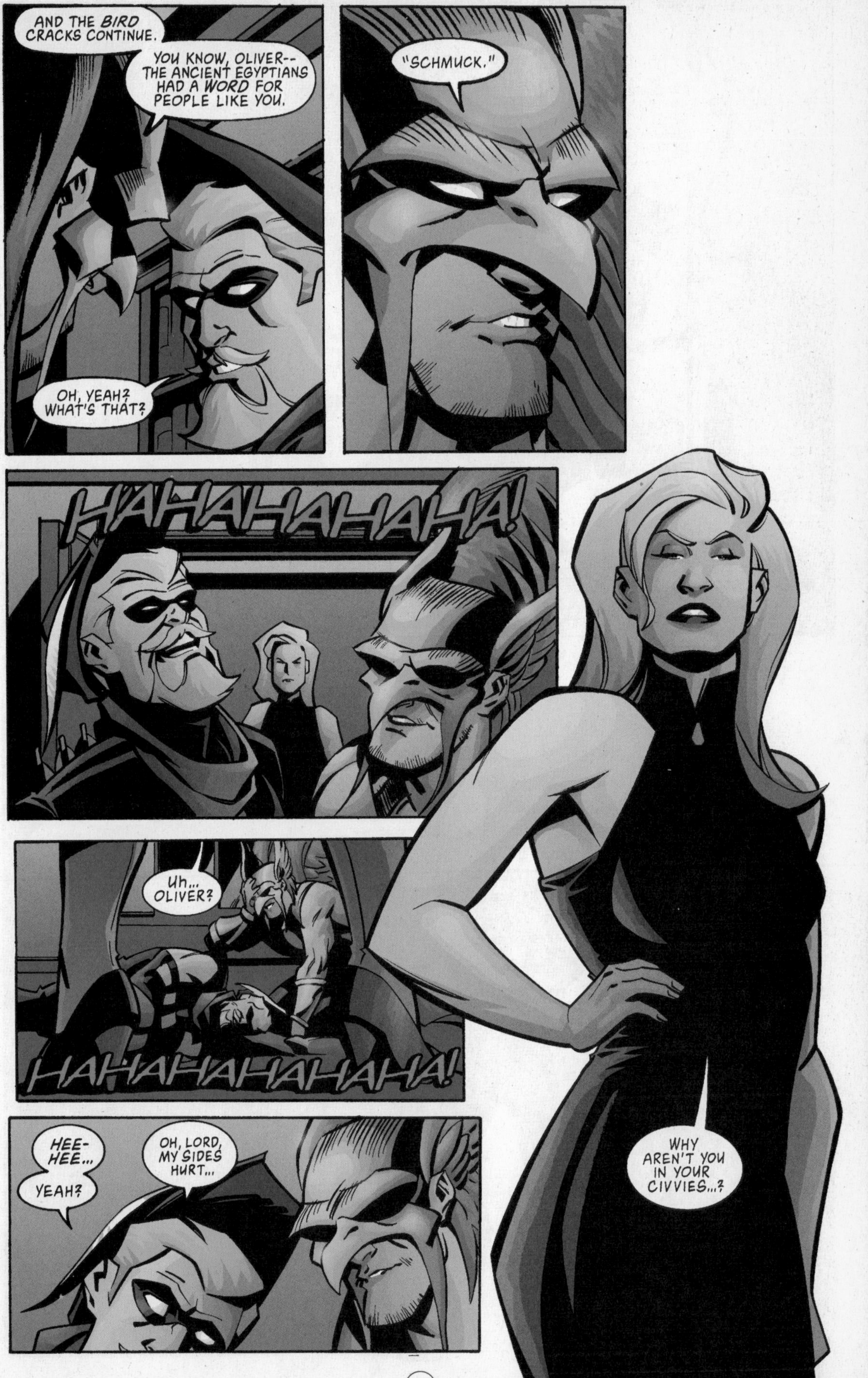
AND THE BIRD CRACKS CONTINUE.
YOU KNOW, OLIVER-- THE ANCIENT EGYPTIANS HAD A WORD FOR PEOPLE LIKE YOU.
OH, YEAH? WHAT'S THAT?
"SCHMUCK."
HAHAHAHAHAHA!
UH... OLIVER?
HAHAHAHAHAHAHA!
HEE-HEE...
OH, LORD, MY SIDES HURT...
YEAH?
WHY AREN'T YOU IN YOUR CIVVIES...?

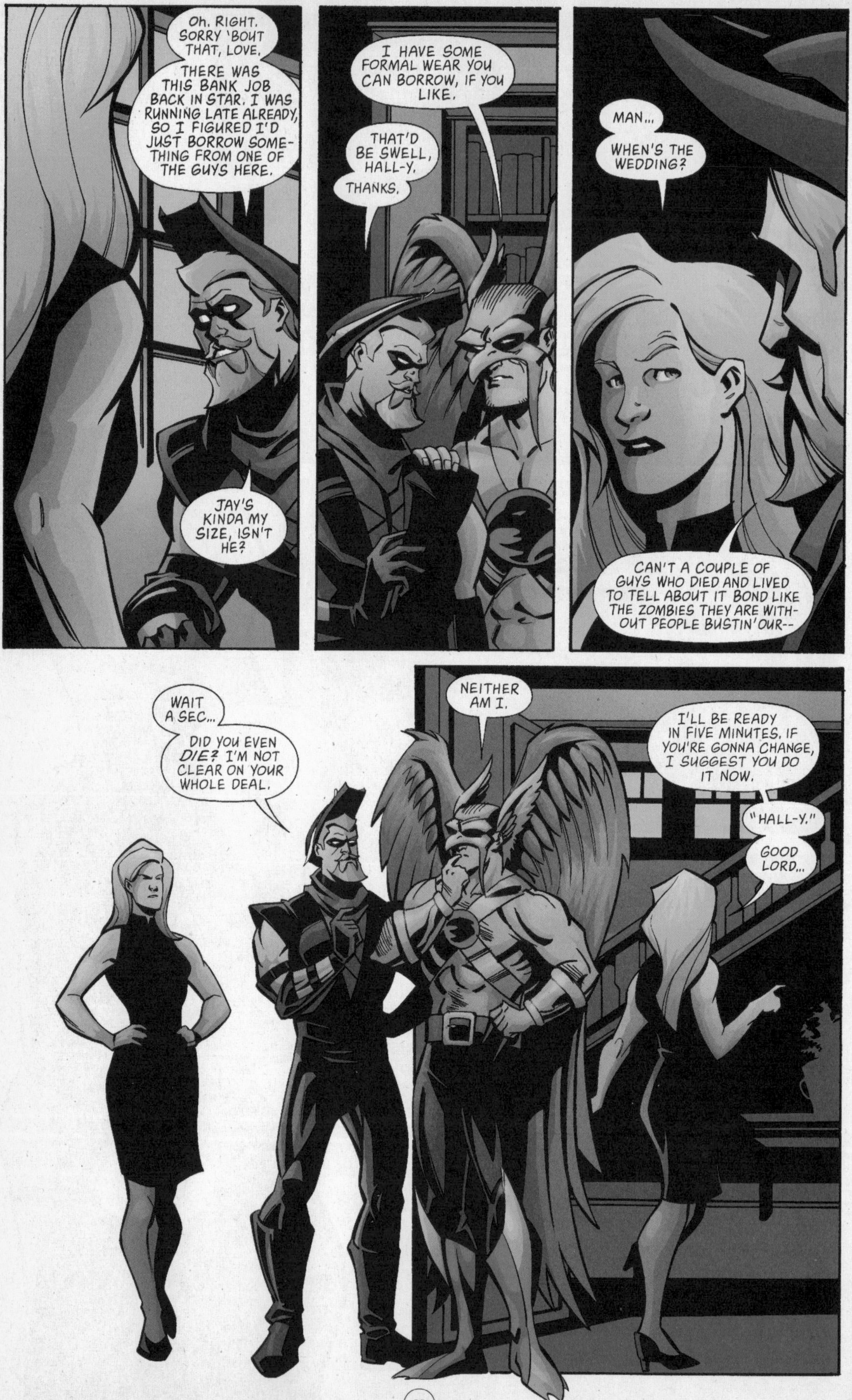
OH. RIGHT. SORRY 'BOUT THAT, LOVE.
THERE WAS THIS BANK JOB BACK IN STAR. I WAS RUNNING LATE ALREADY, SO I FIGURED I'D JUST BORROW SOME-THING FROM ONE OF THE GUYS HERE.
JAY'S KINDA MY SIZE, ISN'T HE?
I HAVE SOME FORMAL WEAR YOU CAN BORROW, IF YOU LIKE.
THAT'D BE SWELL, HALL-Y.
THANKS.
MAN...
WHEN'S THE WEDDING?
CAN'T A COUPLE OF GUYS WHO DIED AND LIVED TO TELL ABOUT IT BOND LIKE THE ZOMBIES THEY ARE WITH-OUT PEOPLE BUSTIN' OUR--
WAIT A SEC...
DID YOU EVEN *DIE*? I'M NOT CLEAR ON YOUR WHOLE DEAL.
NEITHER AM I.
I'LL BE READY IN FIVE MINUTES. IF YOU'RE GONNA CHANGE, I SUGGEST YOU DO IT NOW.
"HALL-Y."
GOOD LORD...

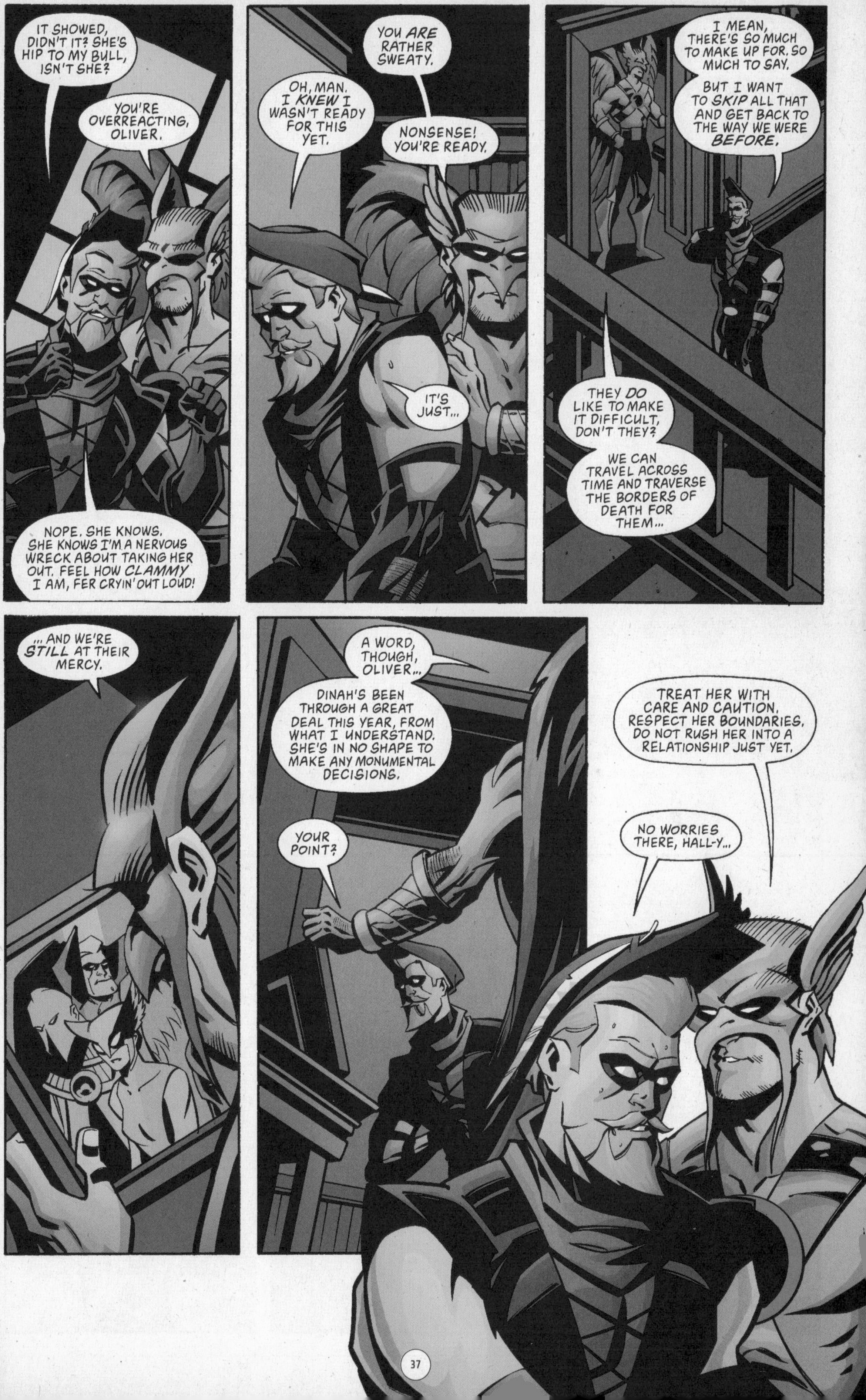
IT SHOWED, DIDN'T IT? SHE'S HIP TO MY BULL, ISN'T SHE?
YOU'RE OVERREACTING, OLIVER.
NOPE. SHE KNOWS. SHE KNOWS I'M A NERVOUS WRECK ABOUT TAKING HER OUT. FEEL HOW CLAMMY I AM, FER CRYIN' OUT LOUD!
YOU ARE RATHER SWEATY.
OH, MAN. I KNEW I WASN'T READY FOR THIS YET.
NONSENSE! YOU'RE READY.
IT'S JUST...
I MEAN, THERE'S SO MUCH TO MAKE UP FOR. SO MUCH TO SAY.
BUT I WANT TO SKIP ALL THAT AND GET BACK TO THE WAY WE WERE BEFORE.
THEY DO LIKE TO MAKE IT DIFFICULT, DON'T THEY?
WE CAN TRAVEL ACROSS TIME AND TRAVERSE THE BORDERS OF DEATH FOR THEM...
...AND WE'RE STILL AT THEIR MERCY.
A WORD, THOUGH, OLIVER...
DINAH'S BEEN THROUGH A GREAT DEAL THIS YEAR, FROM WHAT I UNDERSTAND. SHE'S IN NO SHAPE TO MAKE ANY MONUMENTAL DECISIONS.
YOUR POINT?
TREAT HER WITH CARE AND CAUTION. RESPECT HER BOUNDARIES. DO NOT RUSH HER INTO A RELATIONSHIP JUST YET.
NO WORRIES THERE, HALL-Y...

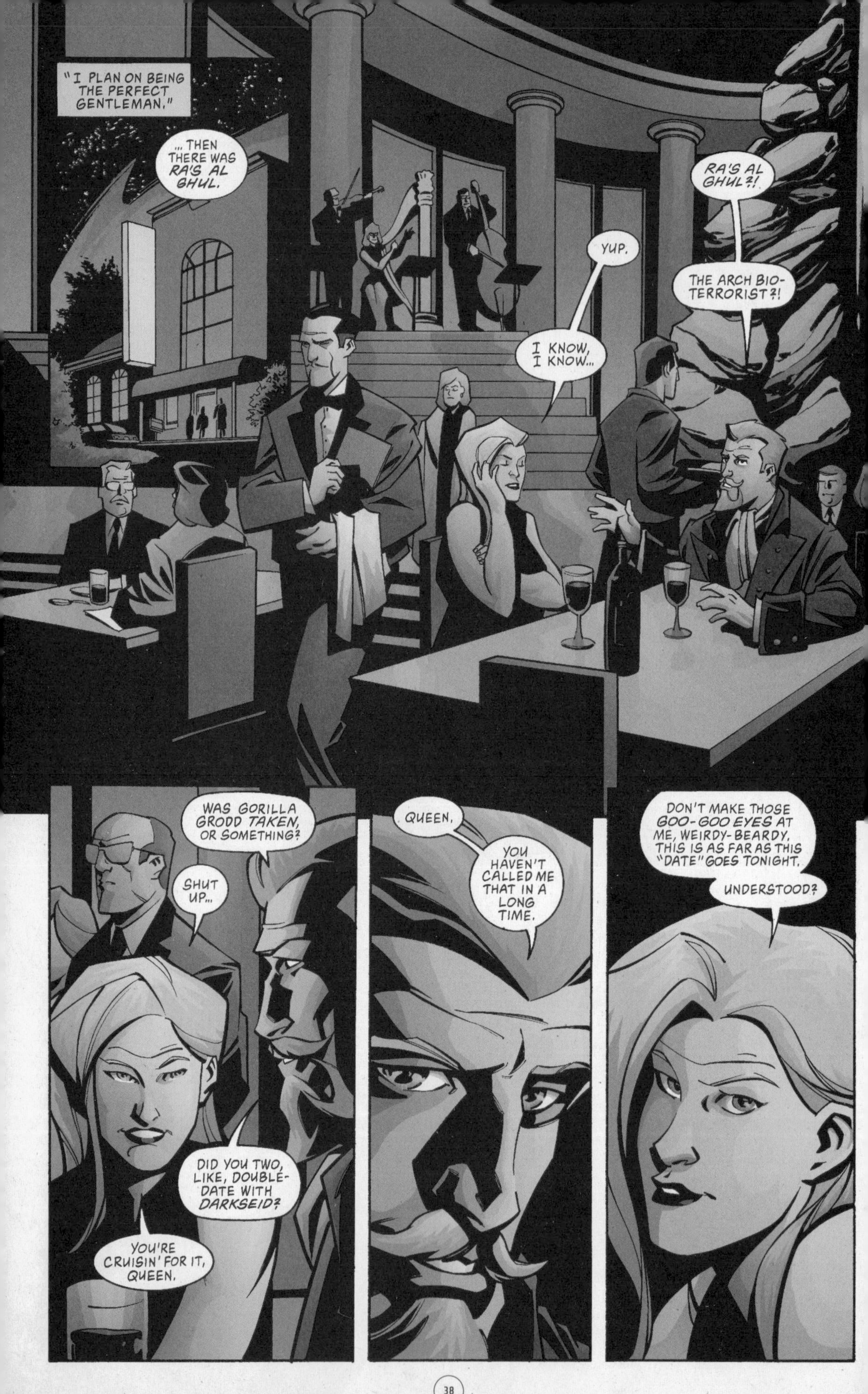
"I PLAN ON BEING THE PERFECT GENTLEMAN."
...THEN THERE WAS RA'S AL GHUL.
RA'S AL GHUL?!
THE ARCH BIO-TERRORIST?!
YUP.
I KNOW, I KNOW...
WAS GORILLA GRODD TAKEN, OR SOMETHING?
SHUT UP...
DID YOU TWO, LIKE, DOUBLE-DATE WITH DARKSEID?
YOU'RE CRUISIN' FOR IT, QUEEN.
QUEEN.
YOU HAVEN'T CALLED ME THAT IN A LONG TIME.
DON'T MAKE THOSE GOO-GOO EYES AT ME, WEIRDY-BEARDY. THIS IS AS FAR AS THIS "DATE" GOES TONIGHT.
UNDERSTOOD?

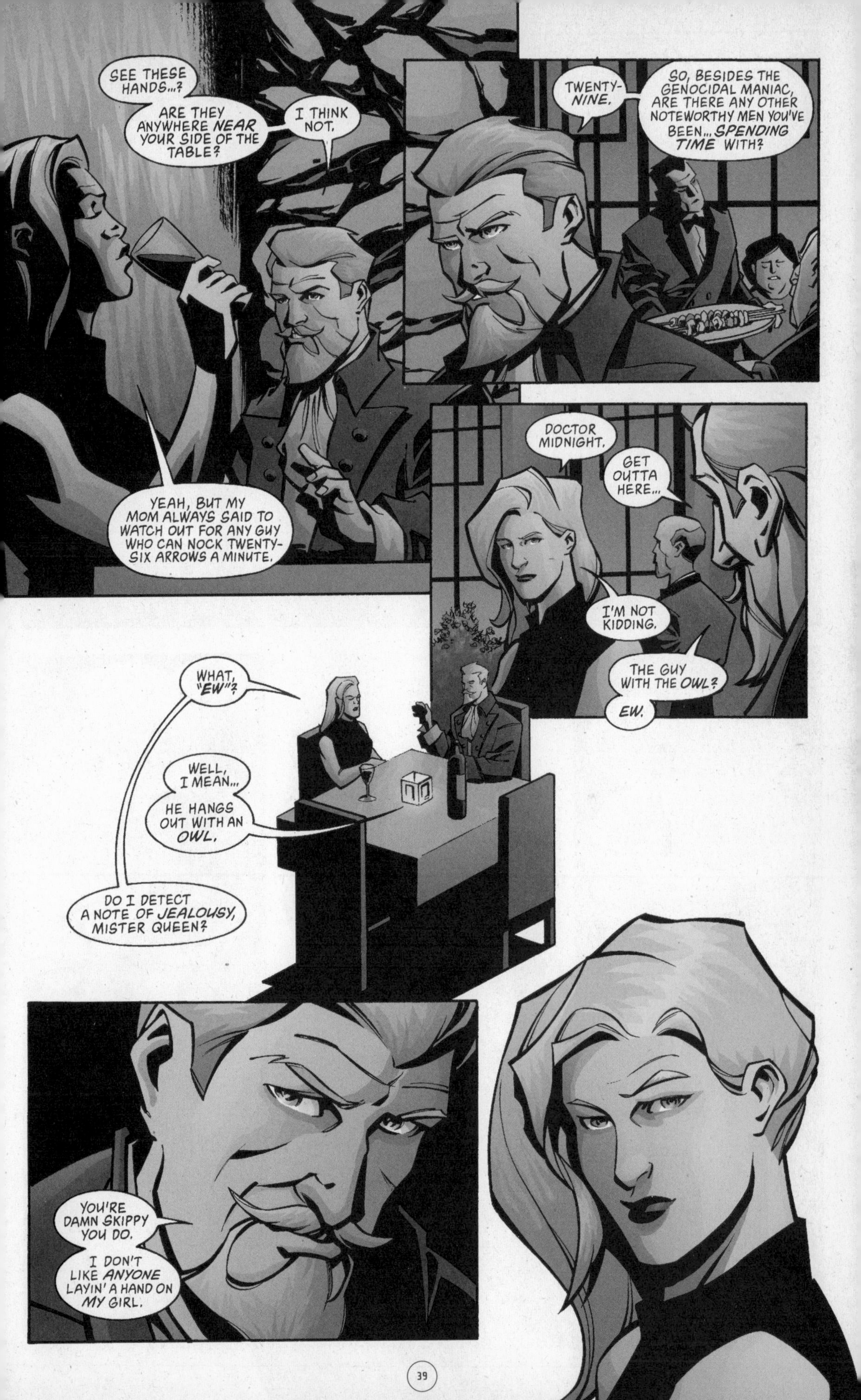
SEE THESE HANDS...?
ARE THEY ANYWHERE NEAR YOUR SIDE OF THE TABLE?
I THINK NOT.
YEAH, BUT MY MOM ALWAYS SAID TO WATCH OUT FOR ANY GUY WHO CAN NOCK TWENTY-SIX ARROWS A MINUTE.
TWENTY-NINE.
SO, BESIDES THE GENOCIDAL MANIAC, ARE THERE ANY OTHER NOTEWORTHY MEN YOU'VE BEEN... SPENDING TIME WITH?
DOCTOR MIDNIGHT.
GET OUTTA HERE...
I'M NOT KIDDING.
THE GUY WITH THE OWL?
EW.
WHAT, "EW"?
WELL, I MEAN...
HE HANGS OUT WITH AN OWL.
DO I DETECT A NOTE OF JEALOUSY, MISTER QUEEN?
YOU'RE DAMN SKIPPY YOU DO.
I DON'T LIKE ANYONE LAYIN' A HAND ON MY GIRL.

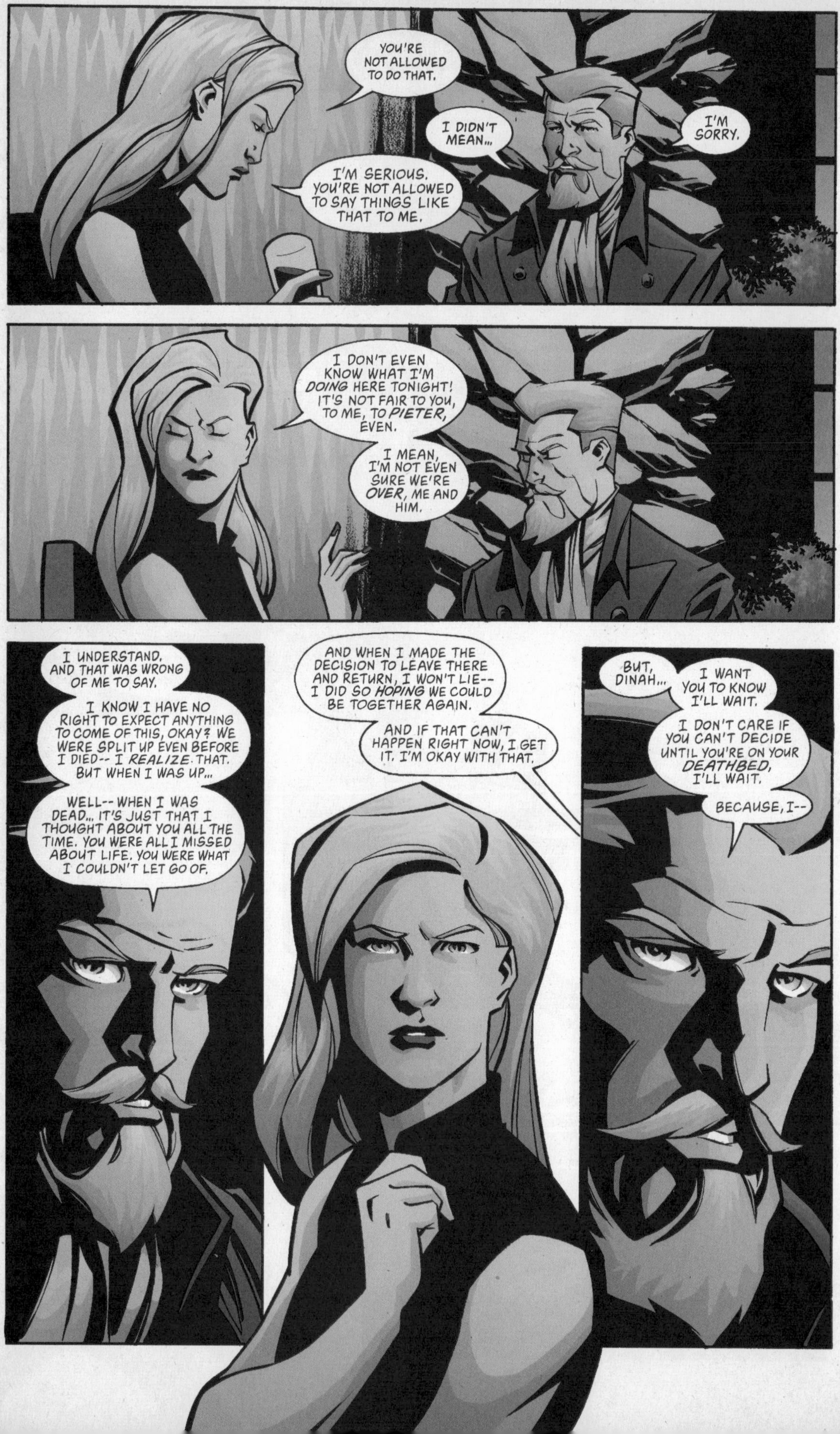
YOU'RE NOT ALLOWED TO DO THAT.
I DIDN'T MEAN...
I'M SORRY.
I'M SERIOUS. YOU'RE NOT ALLOWED TO SAY THINGS LIKE THAT TO ME.
I DON'T EVEN KNOW WHAT I'M DOING HERE TONIGHT! IT'S NOT FAIR TO YOU, TO ME, TO PIETER, EVEN.
I MEAN, I'M NOT EVEN SURE WE'RE OVER, ME AND HIM.
I UNDERSTAND, AND THAT WAS WRONG OF ME TO SAY.
I KNOW I HAVE NO RIGHT TO EXPECT ANYTHING TO COME OF THIS, OKAY? WE WERE SPLIT UP EVEN BEFORE I DIED-- I REALIZE THAT. BUT WHEN I WAS UP...
WELL-- WHEN I WAS DEAD... IT'S JUST THAT I THOUGHT ABOUT YOU ALL THE TIME. YOU WERE ALL I MISSED ABOUT LIFE. YOU WERE WHAT I COULDN'T LET GO OF.
AND WHEN I MADE THE DECISION TO LEAVE THERE AND RETURN, I WON'T LIE-- I DID SO HOPING WE COULD BE TOGETHER AGAIN.
AND IF THAT CAN'T HAPPEN RIGHT NOW, I GET IT. I'M OKAY WITH THAT.
BUT, DINAH...
I WANT YOU TO KNOW I'LL WAIT.
I DON'T CARE IF YOU CAN'T DECIDE UNTIL YOU'RE ON YOUR DEATHBED, I'LL WAIT.
BECAUSE, I--

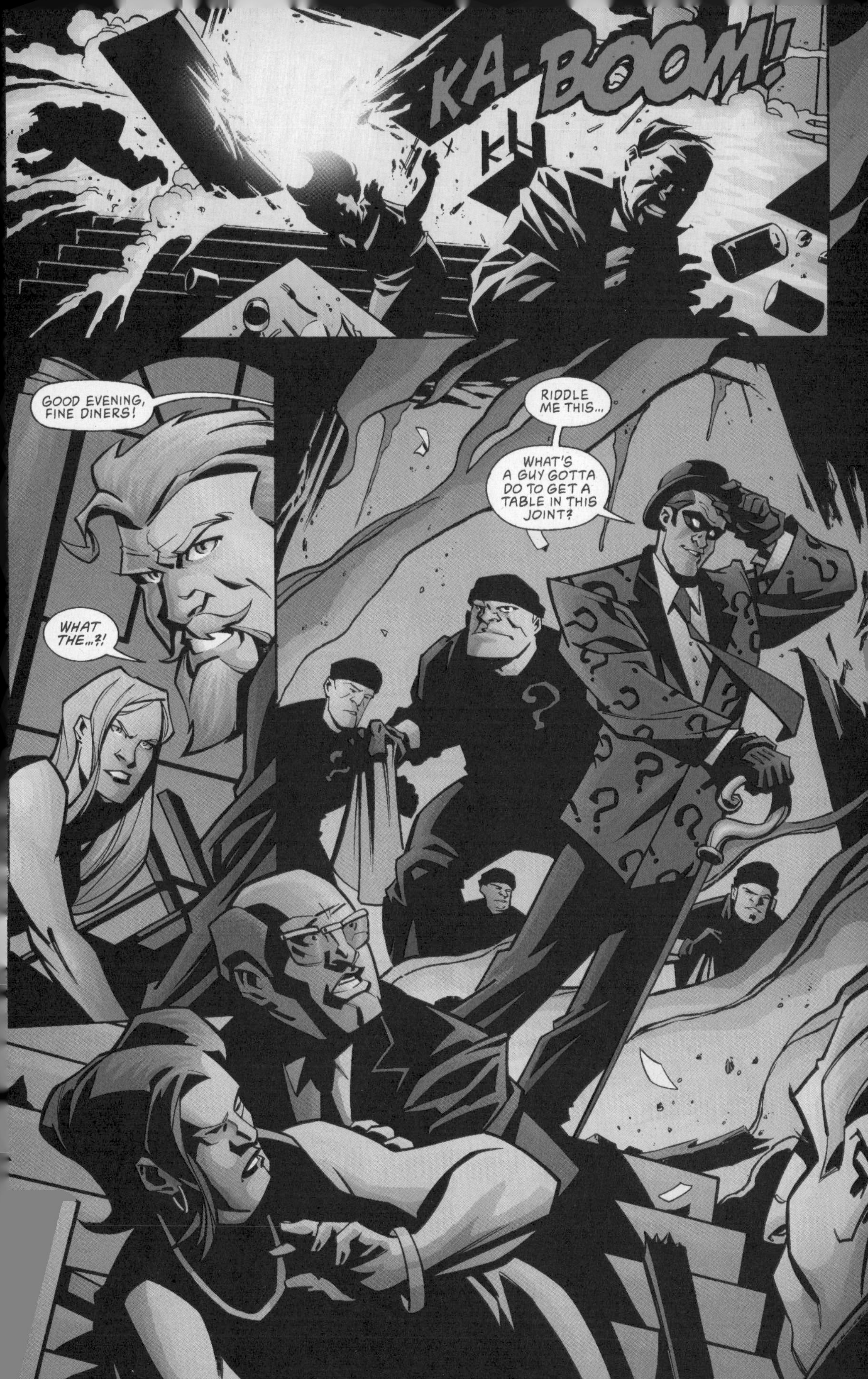
KA-BOOM!
GOOD EVENING, FINE DINERS!
WHAT THE...?!
RIDDLE ME THIS...
WHAT'S A GUY GOTTA DO TO GET A TABLE IN THIS JOINT?

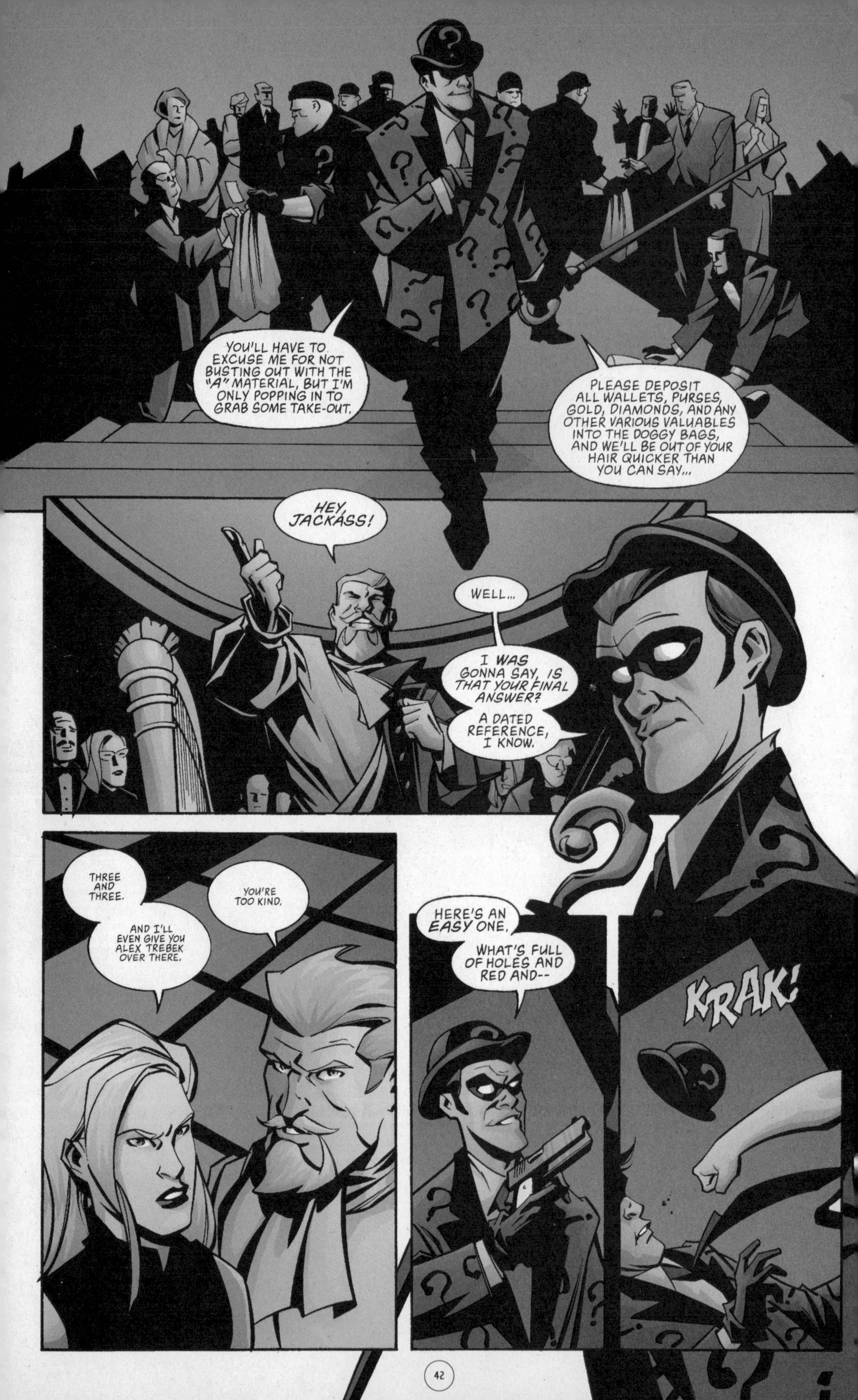
YOU'LL HAVE TO EXCUSE ME FOR NOT BUSTING OUT WITH THE "A" MATERIAL, BUT I'M ONLY POPPING IN TO GRAB SOME TAKE-OUT.
PLEASE DEPOSIT ALL WALLETS, PURSES, GOLD, DIAMONDS, AND ANY OTHER VARIOUS VALUABLES INTO THE DOGGY BAGS, AND WE'LL BE OUT OF YOUR HAIR QUICKER THAN YOU CAN SAY...
HEY, JACKASS!
WELL...
I WAS GONNA SAY, IS THAT YOUR FINAL ANSWER?
A DATED REFERENCE, I KNOW.
THREE AND THREE.
AND I'LL EVEN GIVE YOU ALEX TREBEK OVER THERE.
YOU'RE TOO KIND.
HERE'S AN EASY ONE.
WHAT'S FULL OF HOLES AND RED AND--
KRAK!

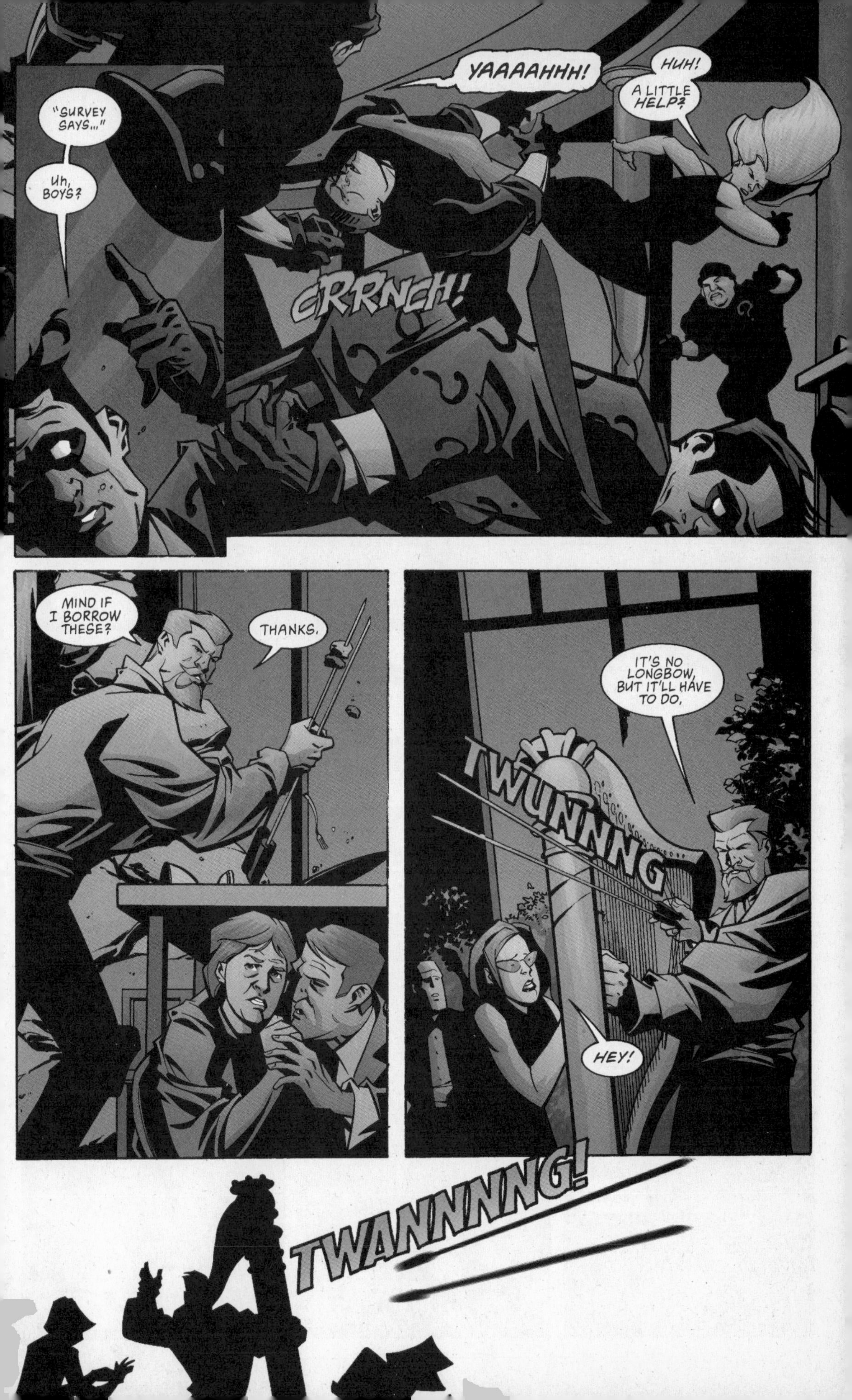
"SURVEY SAYS..."
Uh, BOYS?
YAAAAAHHH!
HUH!
A LITTLE HELP?
CRRNCH!
MIND IF I BORROW THESE?
THANKS.
IT'S NO LONGBOW, BUT IT'LL HAVE TO DO.
TWUNNNG
HEY!
TWANNNNG!

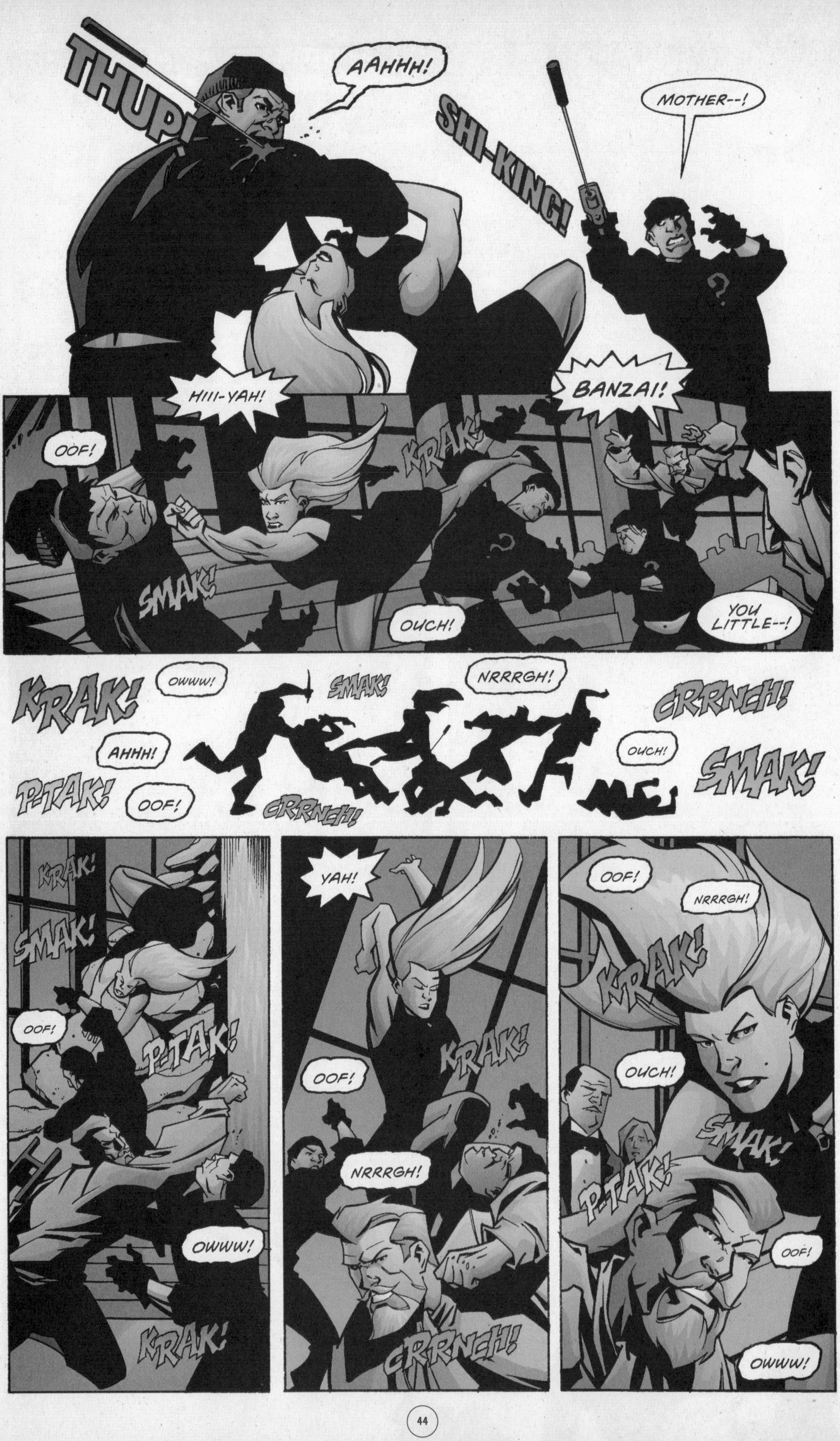
THUP!
AAHHH!
SHI-KING!
MOTHER--!
HIII-YAH!
BANZAI!
OOF!
KRAK!
SMAK!
OUCH!
YOU LITTLE--!
KRAK!
OWWW!
SMAK!
NRRRGH!
CRRNCH!
AHHH!
OUCH!
P-TAK!
OOF!
CRRNCH!
SMAK!
KRAK!
SMAK!
OOF!
P-TAK!
OWWW!
KRAK!
YAH!
OOF!
KRAK!
NRRRGH!
CRRNCH!
OOF!
NRRRGH!
KRAK!
OUCH!
SMAK!
P-TAK!
OOF!
OWWW!

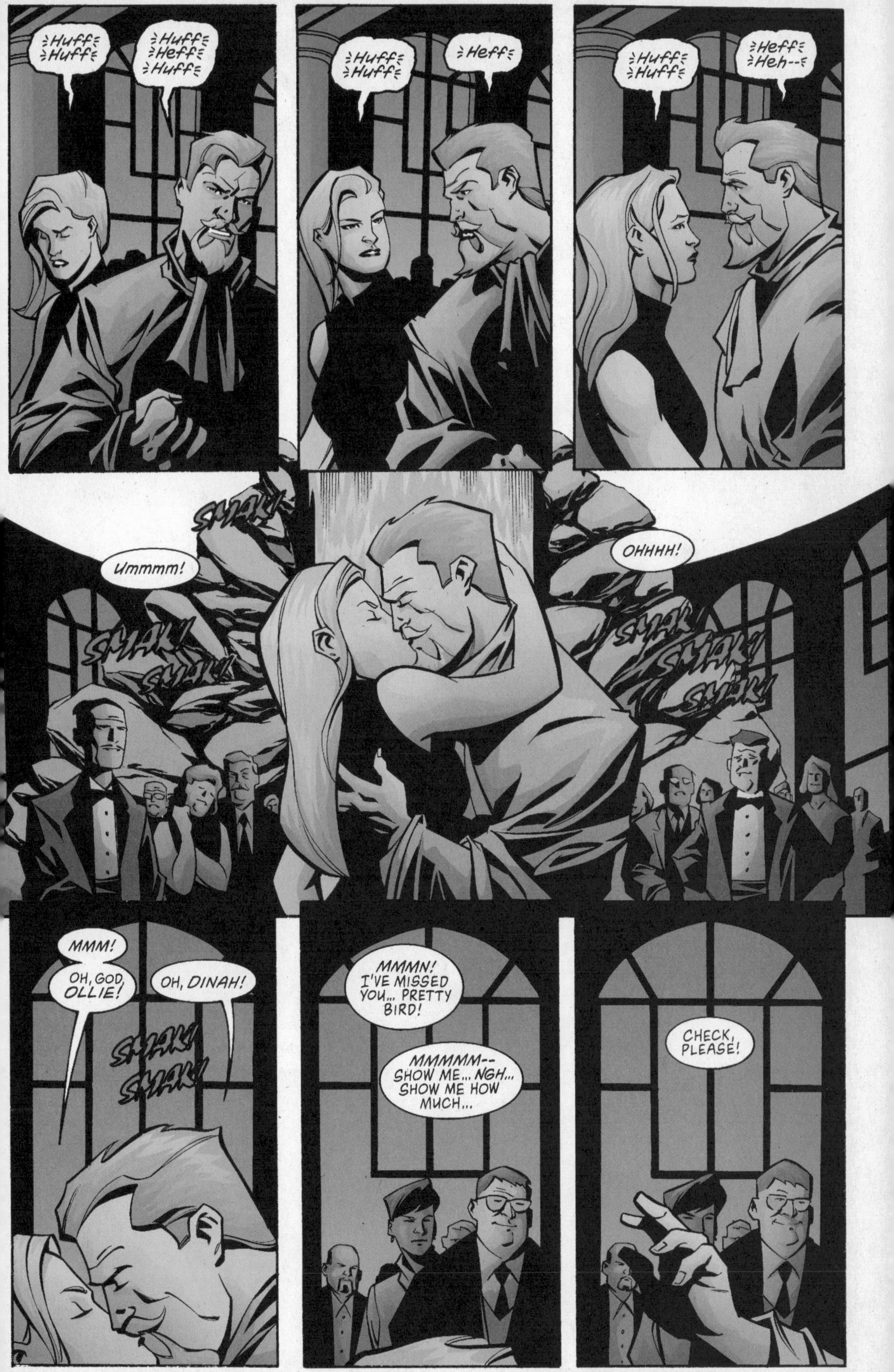
Huff Huff
Huff Heff Huff
Huff Huff
Heff
Huff Huff
Heff Heh--
SMAK!
Ummmm!
OHHHH!
SMAK! SMAK!
SMAK! SMAK! SMAK!
MMM!
OH, GOD, OLLIE!
OH, DINAH!
SMAK! SMAK!
MMMN! I'VE MISSED YOU... PRETTY BIRD!
MMMMM-- SHOW ME... NGH... SHOW ME HOW MUCH...
CHECK, PLEASE!

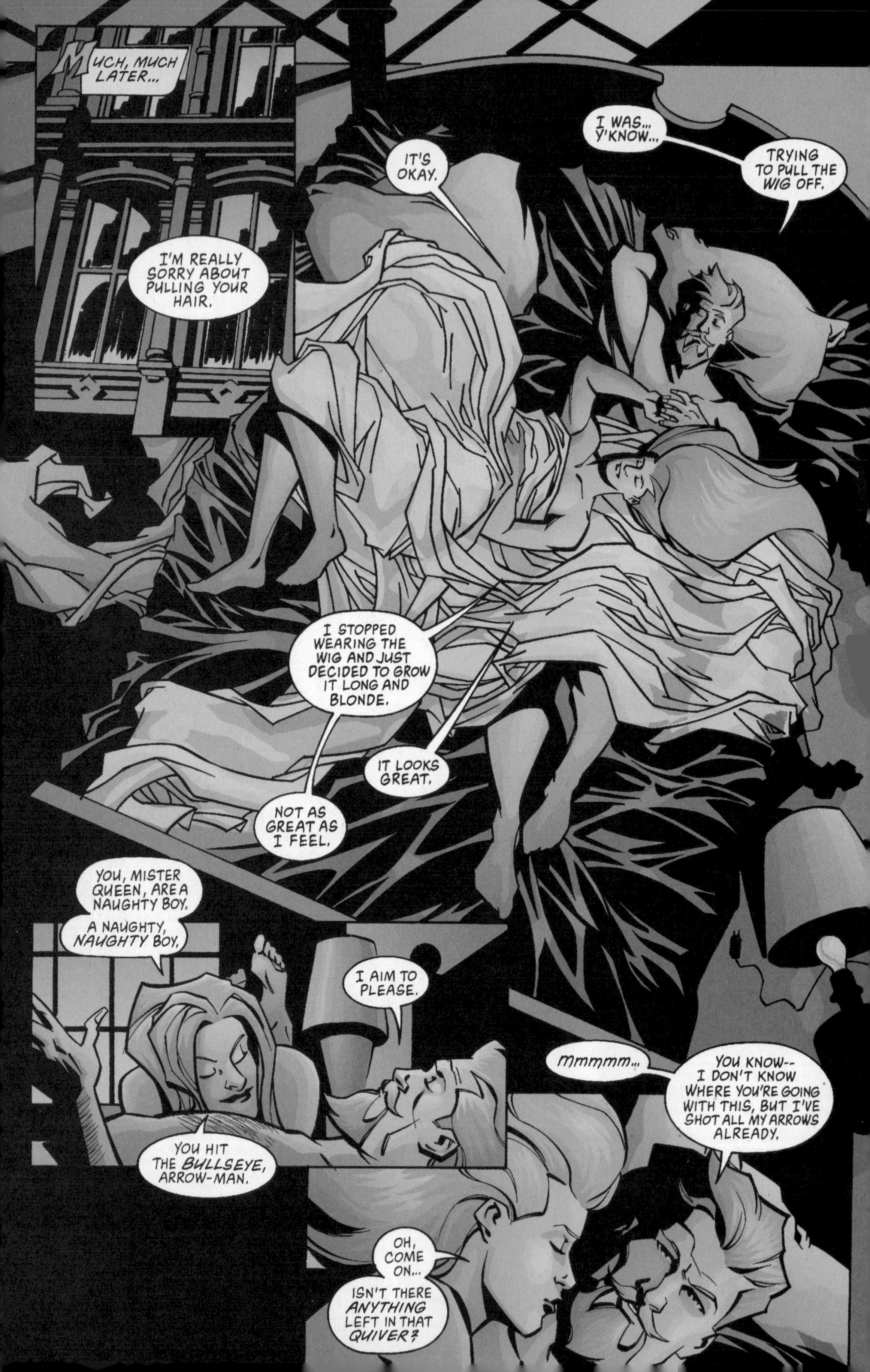
MUCH, MUCH LATER...
I'M REALLY SORRY ABOUT PULLING YOUR HAIR.
IT'S OKAY.
I WAS... Y'KNOW...
TRYING TO PULL THE WIG OFF.
I STOPPED WEARING THE WIG AND JUST DECIDED TO GROW IT LONG AND BLONDE.
IT LOOKS GREAT.
NOT AS GREAT AS I FEEL.
YOU, MISTER QUEEN, ARE A NAUGHTY BOY.
A NAUGHTY, NAUGHTY BOY.
I AIM TO PLEASE.
YOU HIT THE BULLSEYE, ARROW-MAN.
mmmmm...
YOU KNOW-- I DON'T KNOW WHERE YOU'RE GOING WITH THIS, BUT I'VE SHOT ALL MY ARROWS ALREADY.
OH, COME ON...
ISN'T THERE ANYTHING LEFT IN THAT QUIVER?

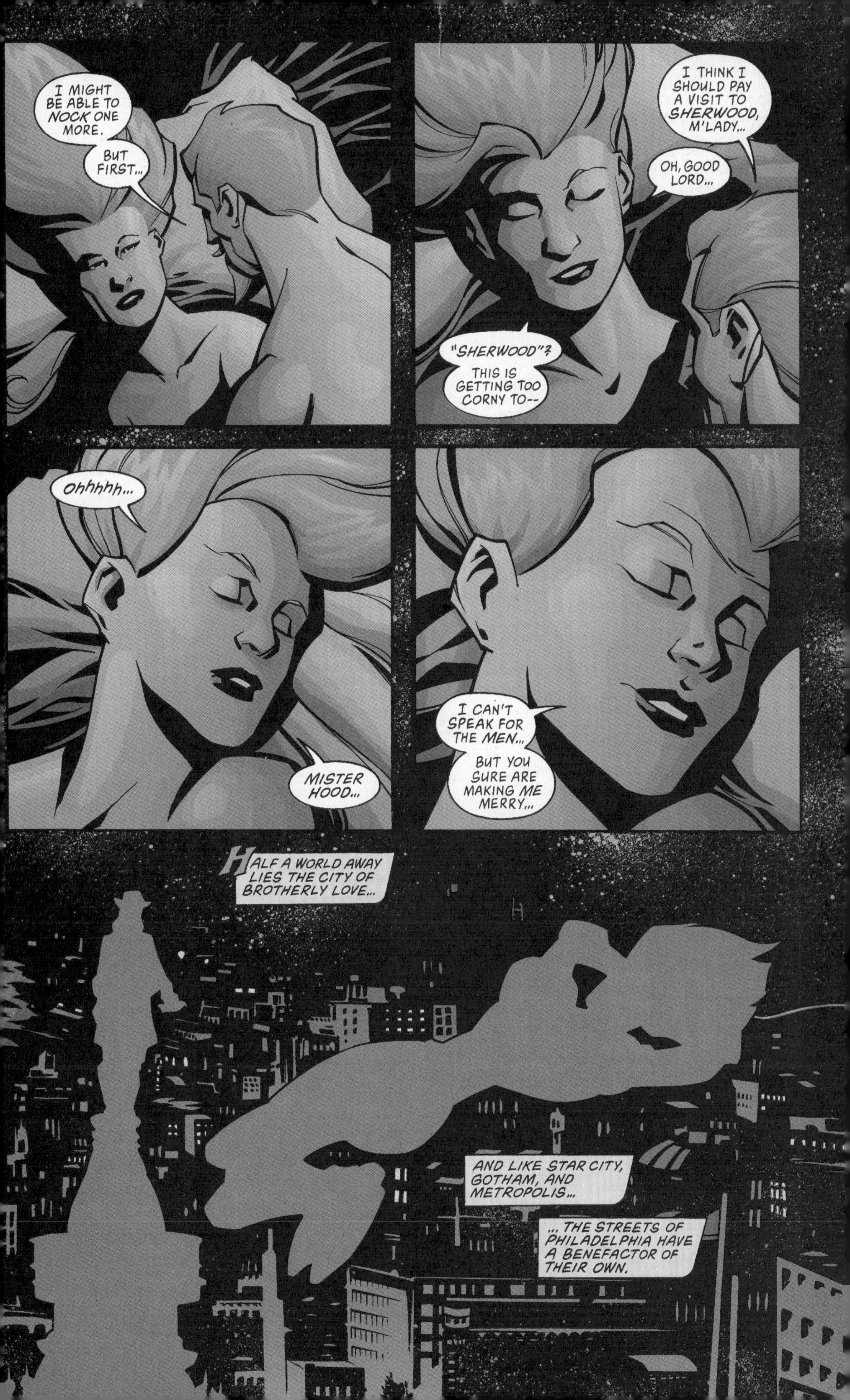
I MIGHT BE ABLE TO NOCK ONE MORE.
BUT FIRST...
I THINK I SHOULD PAY A VISIT TO SHERWOOD, M'LADY...
OH, GOOD LORD...
"SHERWOOD"? THIS IS GETTING TOO CORNY TO--
Ohhhhh...
MISTER HOOD...
I CAN'T SPEAK FOR THE MEN...
BUT YOU SURE ARE MAKING ME MERRY...
HALF A WORLD AWAY LIES THE CITY OF BROTHERLY LOVE...
AND LIKE STAR CITY, GOTHAM, AND METROPOLIS...
... THE STREETS OF PHILADELPHIA HAVE A BENEFACTOR OF THEIR OWN.

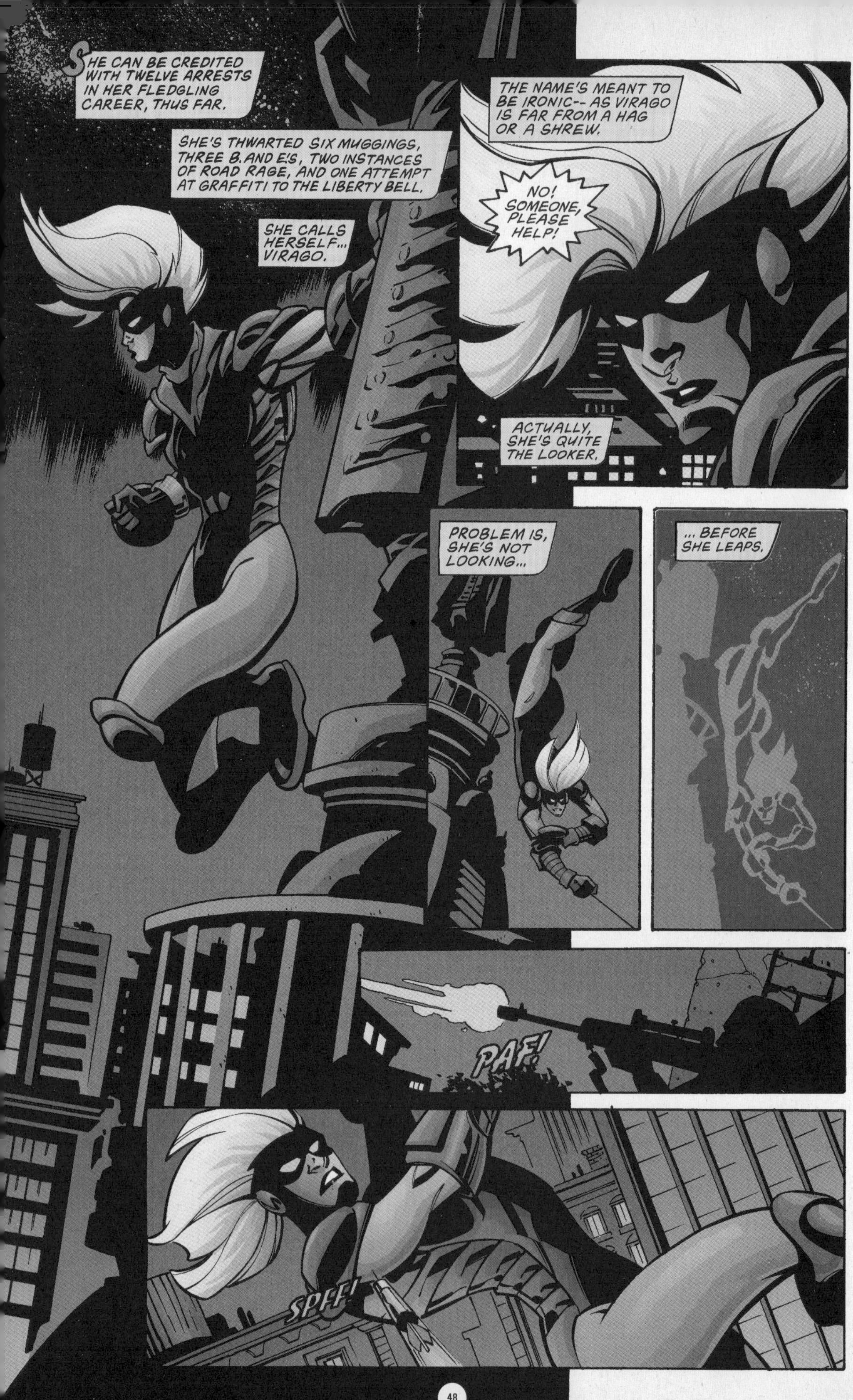
SHE CAN BE CREDITED WITH TWELVE ARRESTS IN HER FLEDGLING CAREER, THUS FAR.
SHE'S THWARTED SIX MUGGINGS, THREE B. AND E.'S, TWO INSTANCES OF ROAD RAGE, AND ONE ATTEMPT AT GRAFFITI TO THE LIBERTY BELL.
SHE CALLS HERSELF... VIRAGO.
THE NAME'S MEANT TO BE IRONIC-- AS VIRAGO IS FAR FROM A HAG OR A SHREW.
NO! SOMEONE, PLEASE HELP!
ACTUALLY, SHE'S QUITE THE LOOKER.
PROBLEM IS, SHE'S NOT LOOKING...
...BEFORE SHE LEAPS.
PAF!
SPFF!

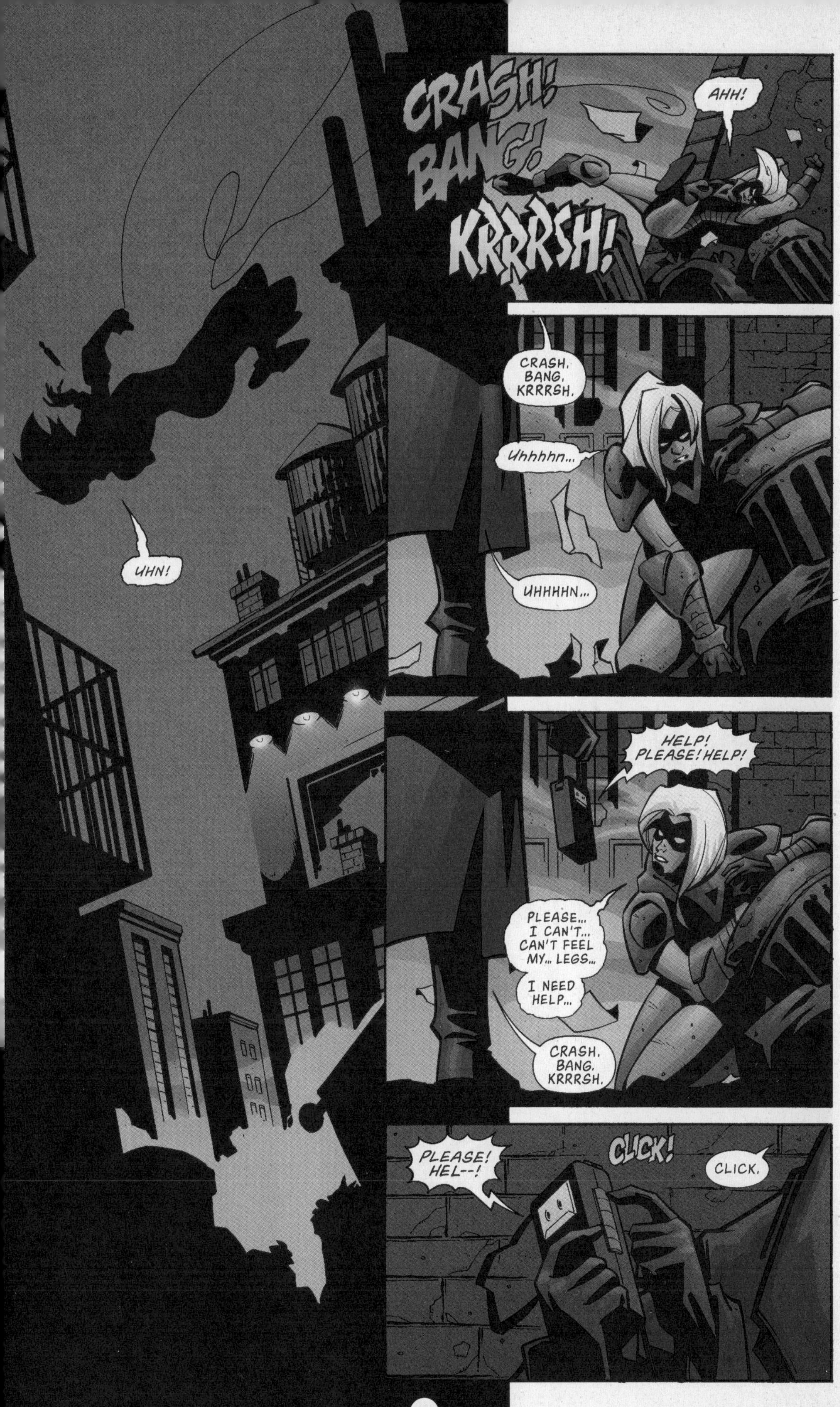
UHN!
CRASH! BANG! KRRRSH!
AHH!
CRASH, BANG, KRRRSH.
Uhhhhn...
UHHHHN...
HELP! PLEASE! HELP!
PLEASE... I CAN'T... CAN'T FEEL MY... LEGS...
I NEED HELP...
CRASH. BANG. KRRRSH.
PLEASE! HEL--!
CLICK!
CLICK.

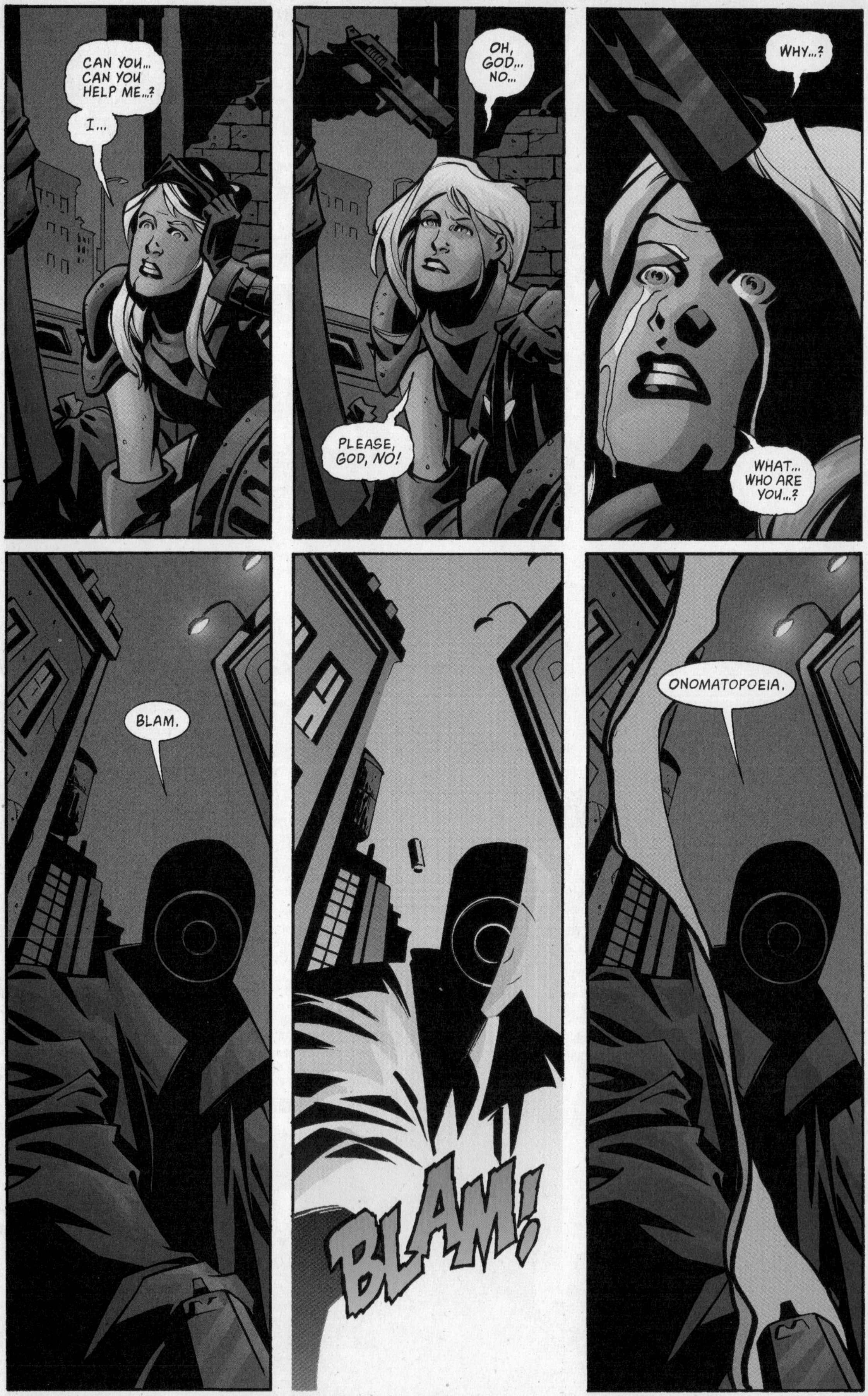
CAN YOU... CAN YOU HELP ME...?
I...
OH, GOD... NO...
PLEASE, GOD, NO!
WHY...?
WHAT... WHO ARE YOU...?
BLAM.
BLAM!
ONOMATOPOEIA.

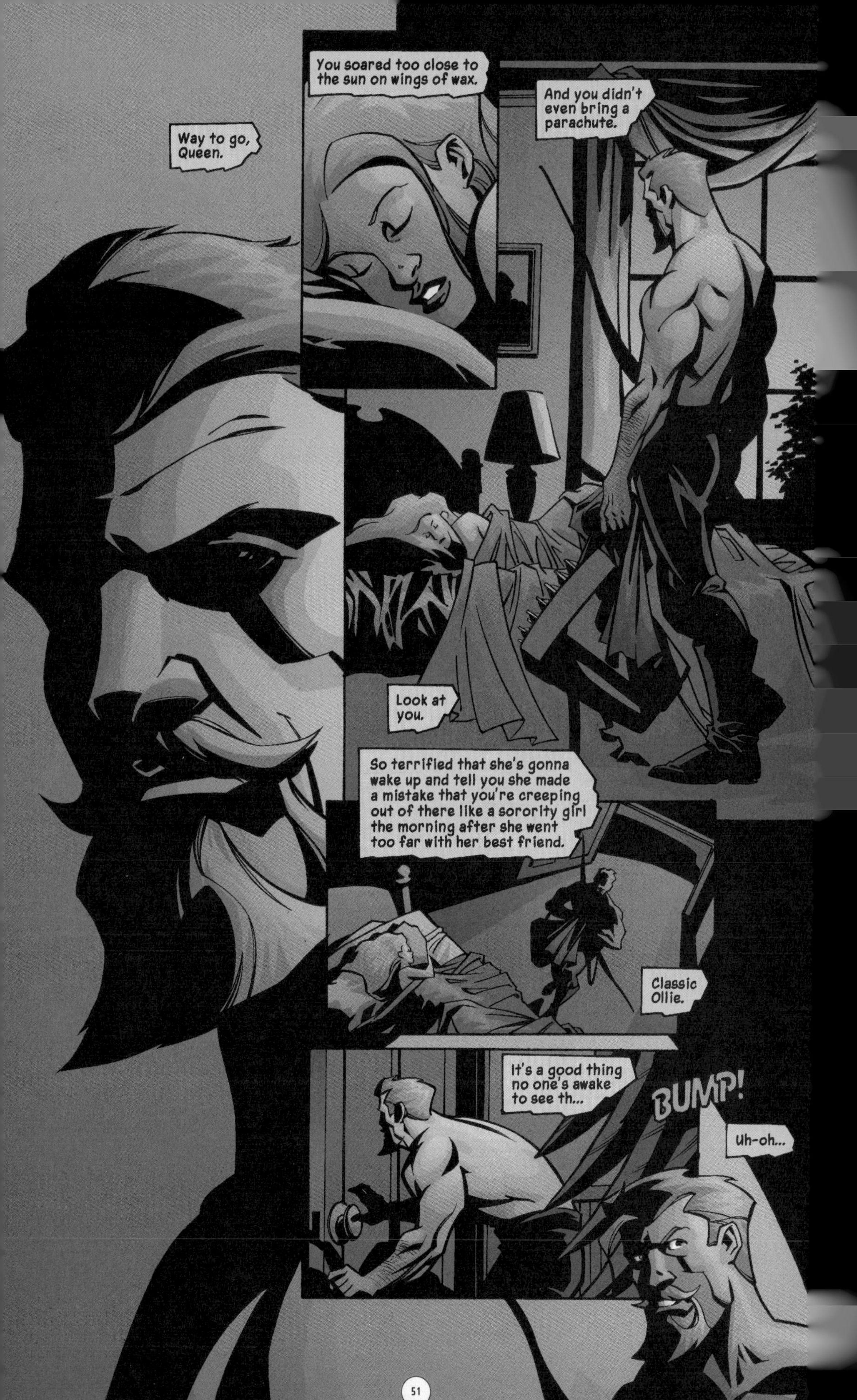
Way to go, Queen.
You soared too close to the sun on wings of wax.
And you didn't even bring a parachute.
Look at you.
So terrified that she's gonna wake up and tell you she made a mistake that you're creeping out of there like a sorority girl the morning after she went too far with her best friend.
Classic Ollie.
It's a good thing no one's awake to see th...
BUMP!
Uh-oh...

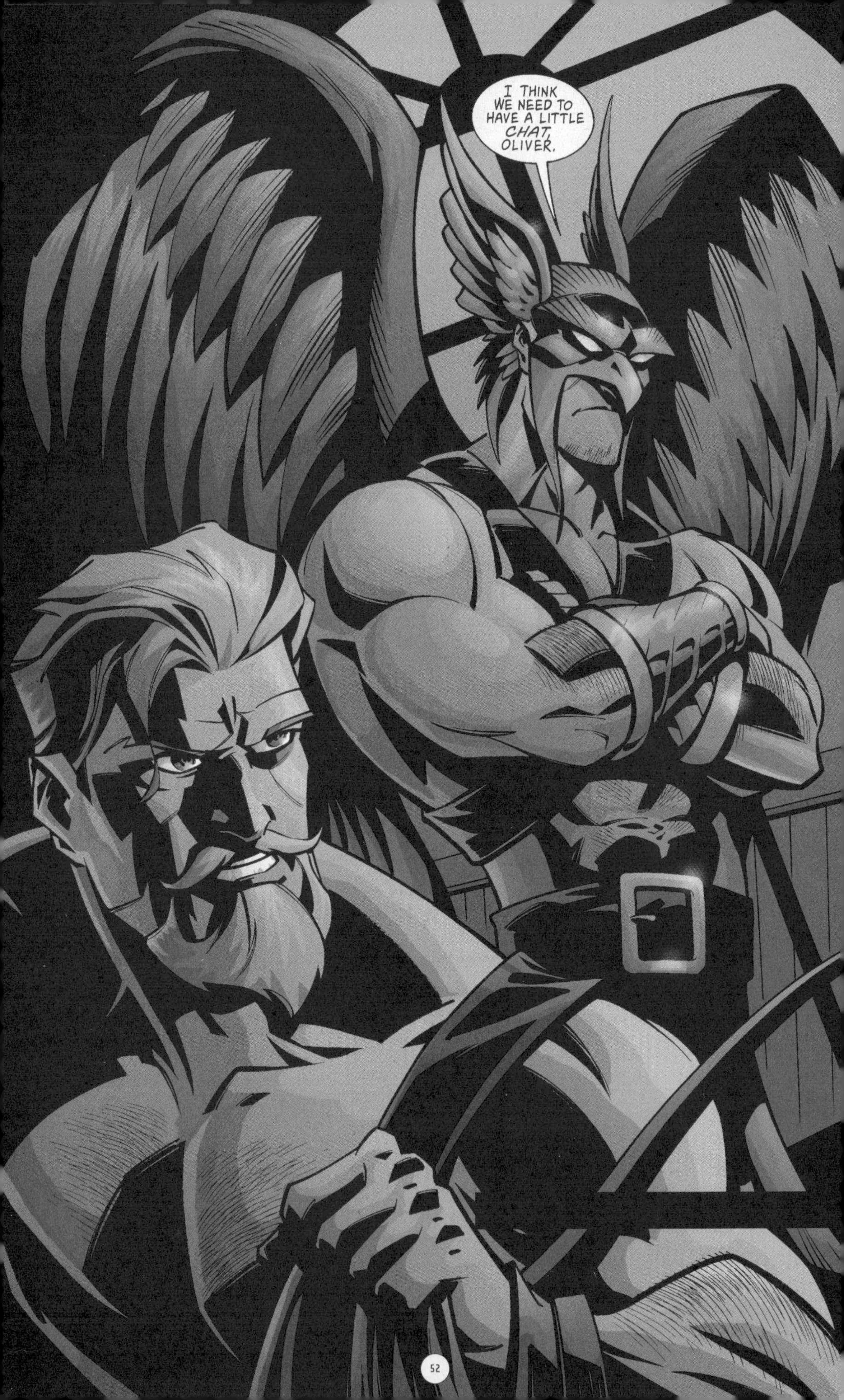
I THINK WE NEED TO HAVE A LITTLE *CHAT,* OLIVER.

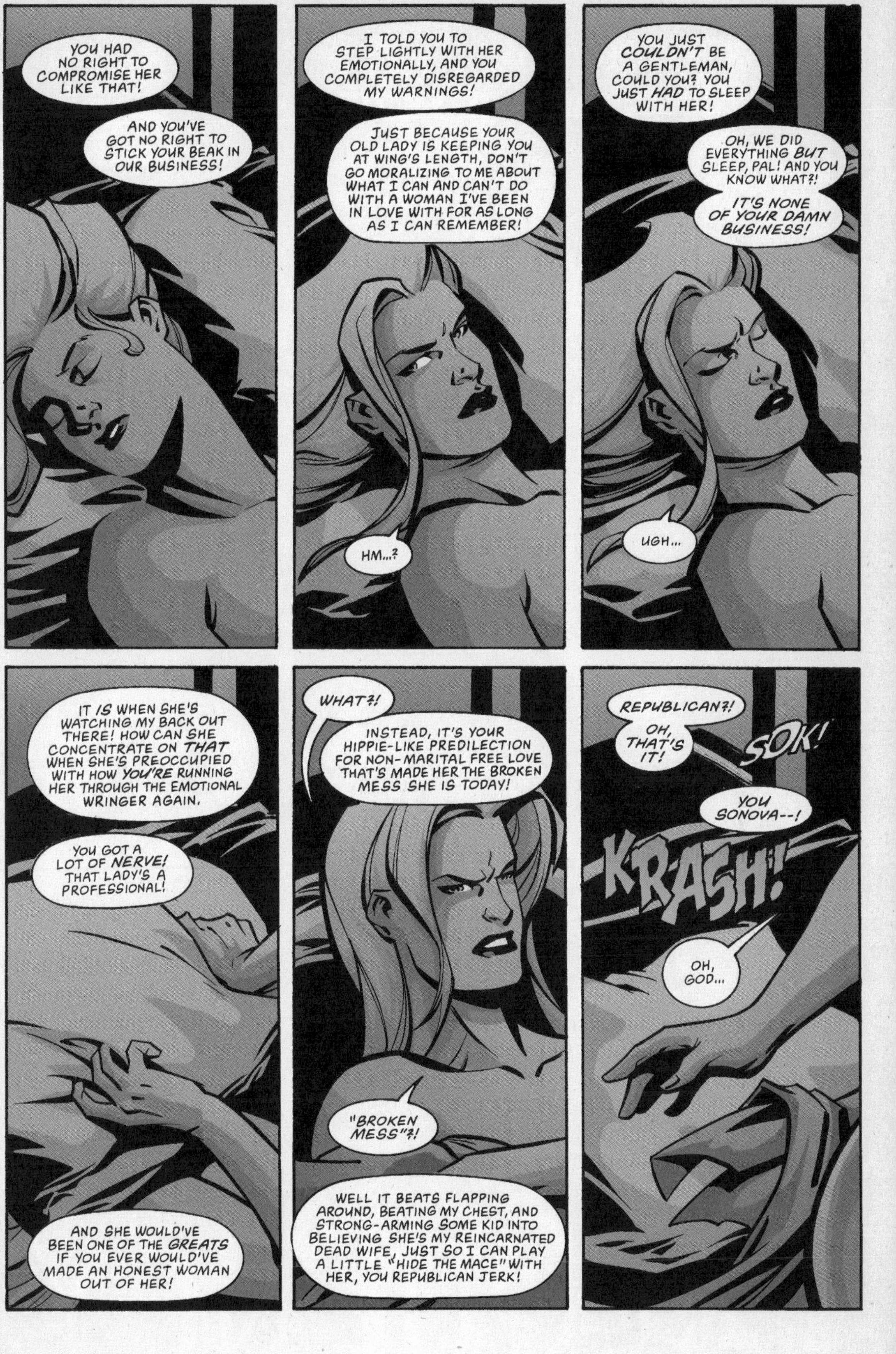
YOU HAD NO RIGHT TO COMPROMISE HER LIKE THAT!
AND YOU'VE GOT NO RIGHT TO STICK YOUR BEAK IN OUR BUSINESS!
I TOLD YOU TO STEP LIGHTLY WITH HER EMOTIONALLY, AND YOU COMPLETELY DISREGARDED MY WARNINGS!
JUST BECAUSE YOUR OLD LADY IS KEEPING YOU AT WING'S LENGTH, DON'T GO MORALIZING TO ME ABOUT WHAT I CAN AND CAN'T DO WITH A WOMAN I'VE BEEN IN LOVE WITH FOR AS LONG AS I CAN REMEMBER!
HM...?
YOU JUST COULDN'T BE A GENTLEMAN, COULD YOU? YOU JUST HAD TO SLEEP WITH HER!
OH, WE DID EVERYTHING BUT SLEEP, PAL! AND YOU KNOW WHAT?!
IT'S NONE OF YOUR DAMN BUSINESS!
UGH...
IT IS WHEN SHE'S WATCHING MY BACK OUT THERE! HOW CAN SHE CONCENTRATE ON THAT WHEN SHE'S PREOCCUPIED WITH HOW YOU'RE RUNNING HER THROUGH THE EMOTIONAL WRINGER AGAIN.
YOU GOT A LOT OF NERVE! THAT LADY'S A PROFESSIONAL!
AND SHE WOULD'VE BEEN ONE OF THE GREATS IF YOU EVER WOULD'VE MADE AN HONEST WOMAN OUT OF HER!
WHAT?!
INSTEAD, IT'S YOUR HIPPIE-LIKE PREDILECTION FOR NON-MARITAL FREE LOVE THAT'S MADE HER THE BROKEN MESS SHE IS TODAY!
"BROKEN MESS"?!
WELL IT BEATS FLAPPING AROUND, BEATING MY CHEST, AND STRONG-ARMING SOME KID INTO BELIEVING SHE'S MY REINCARNATED DEAD WIFE, JUST SO I CAN PLAY A LITTLE "HIDE THE MACE" WITH HER, YOU REPUBLICAN JERK!
REPUBLICAN?!
OH, THAT'S IT!
SOK!
YOU SONOVA--!
KRASH!
OH, GOD...

DC COMICS PRESENTS
THE SOUND OF VIOLENCE
YOU FLYING FASCIST!
PART ONE
FREQUENCY

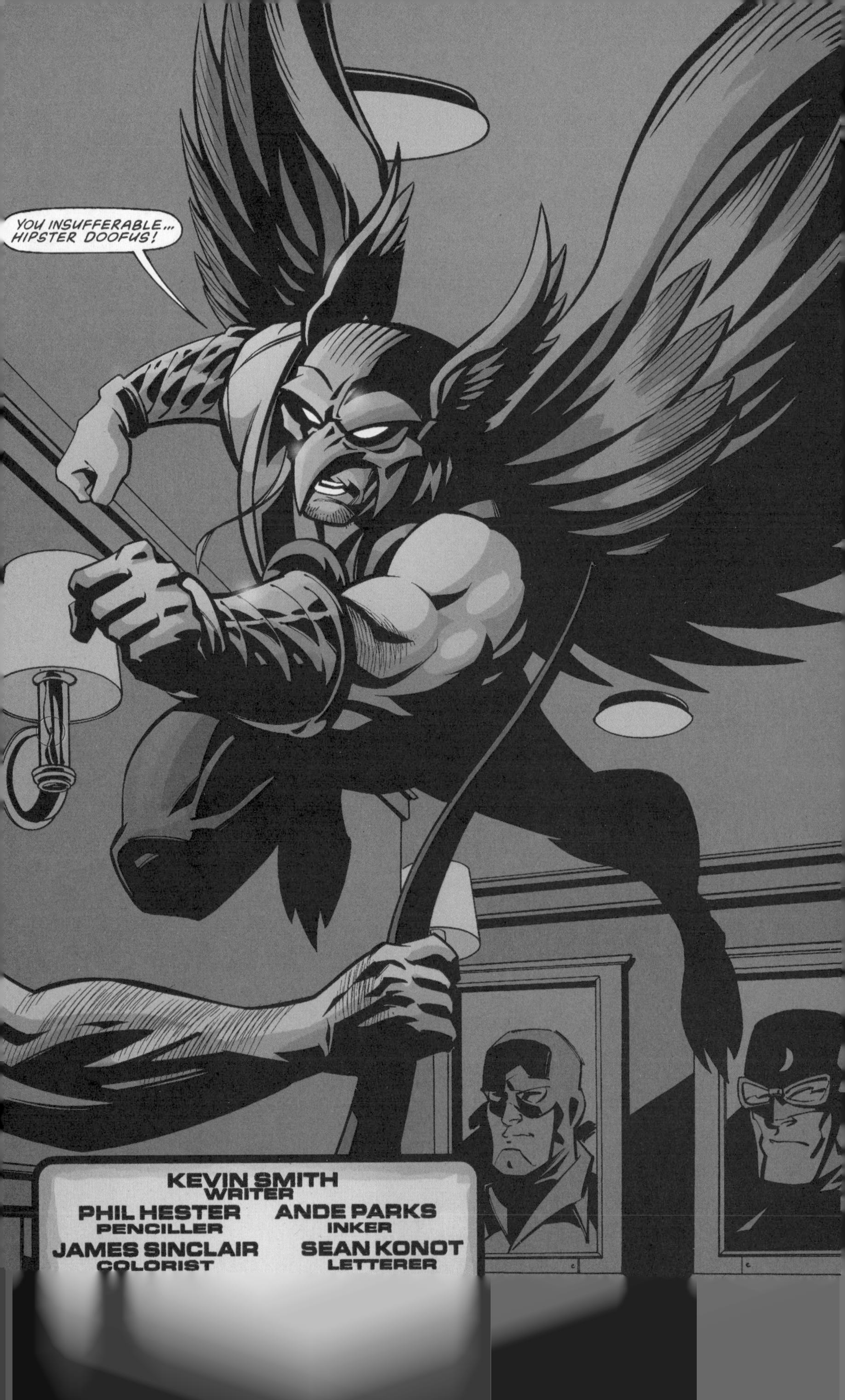
YOU INSUFFERABLE... HIPSTER DOOFUS!
KEVIN SMITH
WRITER
PHIL HESTER
PENCILLER
ANDE PARKS
INKER
JAMES SINCLAIR
COLORIST
SEAN KONOT
LETTERER

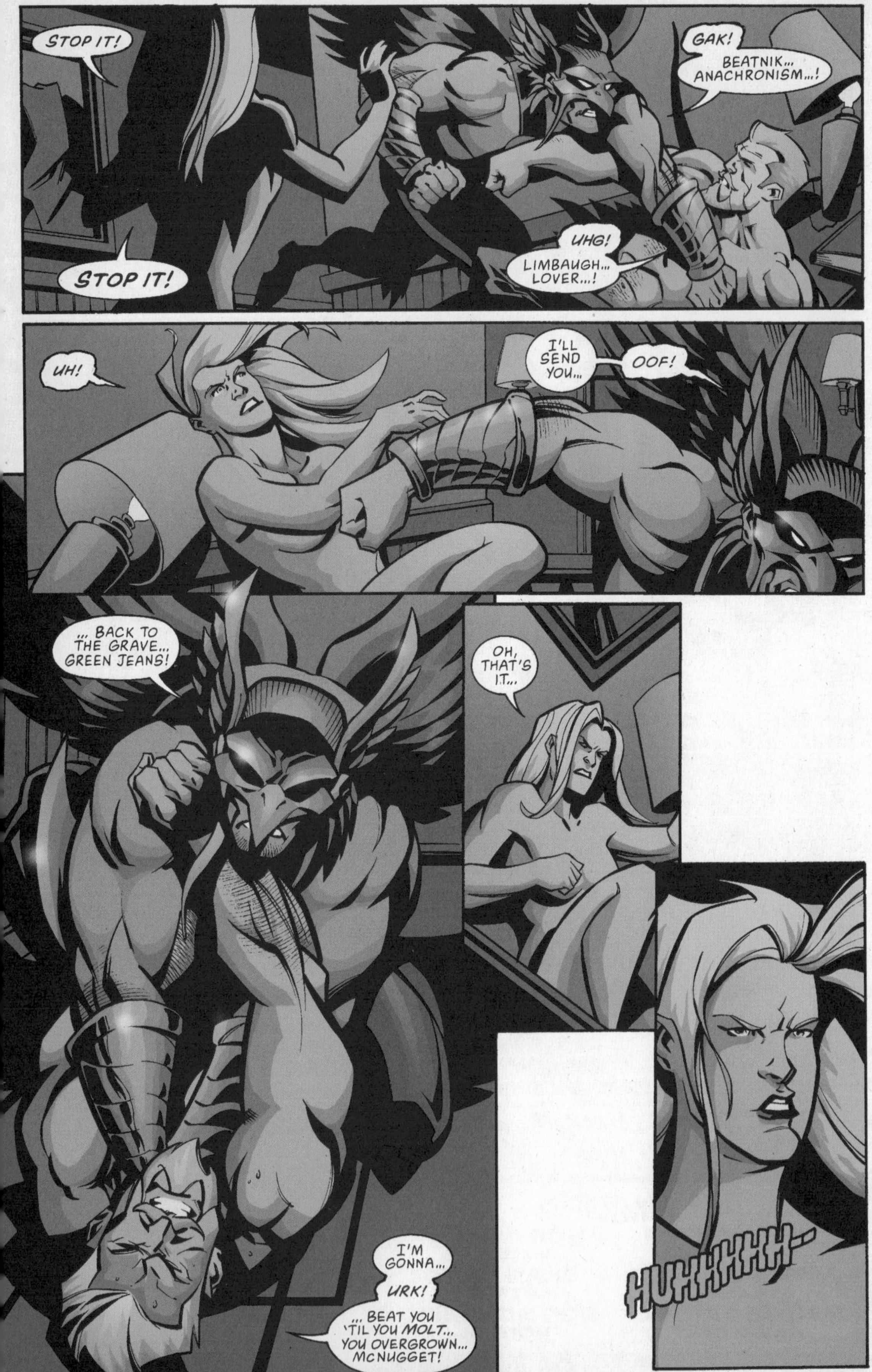
STOP IT!
STOP IT!
GAK!
BEATNIK... ANACHRONISM...!
UHG!
LIMBAUGH... LOVER...!
UH!
I'LL SEND YOU...
OOF!
... BACK TO THE GRAVE... GREEN JEANS!
OH, THAT'S IT...
I'M GONNA...
URK!
... BEAT YOU 'TIL YOU MOLT... YOU OVERGROWN... McNUGGET!
HUHHHHHH-

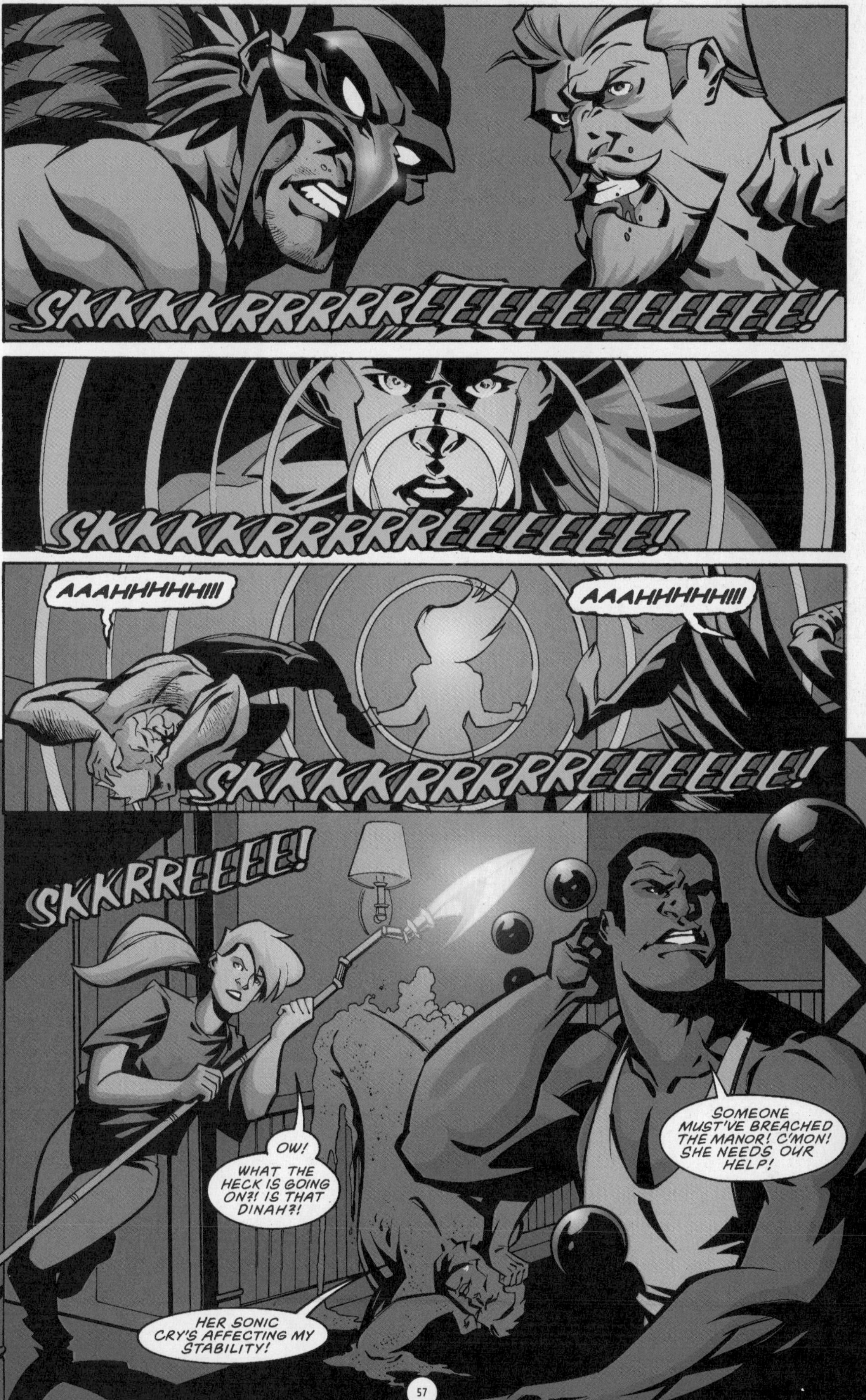
SKKKKRRRRRREEEEEEEEEEEEE!
SKKKKRRRRRREEEEEEE!
AAAHHHHH!!!
AAAHHHHH!!!
SKKKKKRRRRRREEEEEEE!
SKKRREEEE!
SOMEONE MUST'VE BREACHED THE MANOR! C'MON! SHE NEEDS OUR HELP!
OW! WHAT THE HECK IS GOING ON?! IS THAT DINAH?!
HER SONIC CRY'S AFFECTING MY STABILITY!

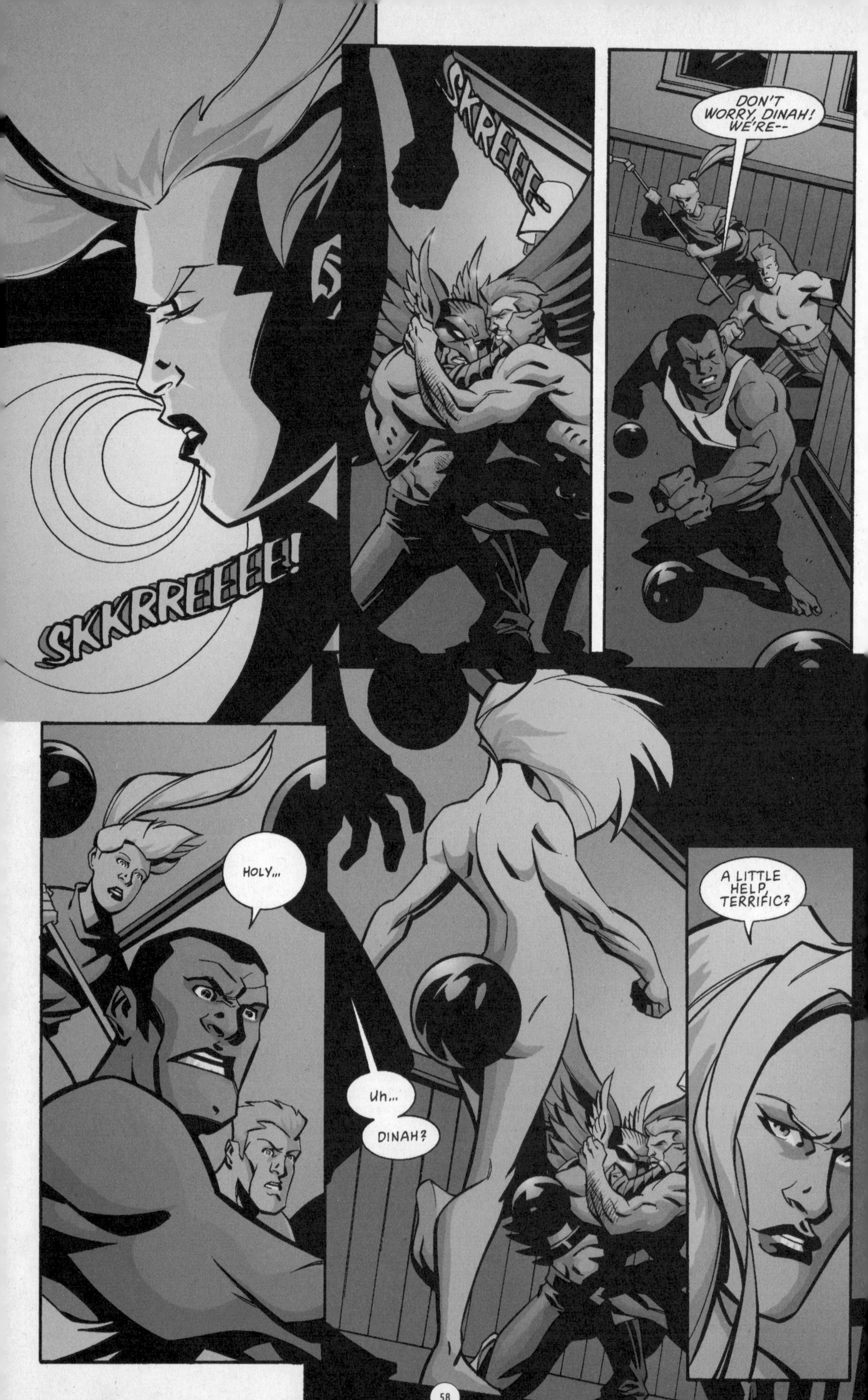
SKKRREEEE!
SKREEEE--
DON'T WORRY, DINAH! WE'RE--
HOLY...
Uh...
DINAH?
A LITTLE HELP, TERRIFIC?

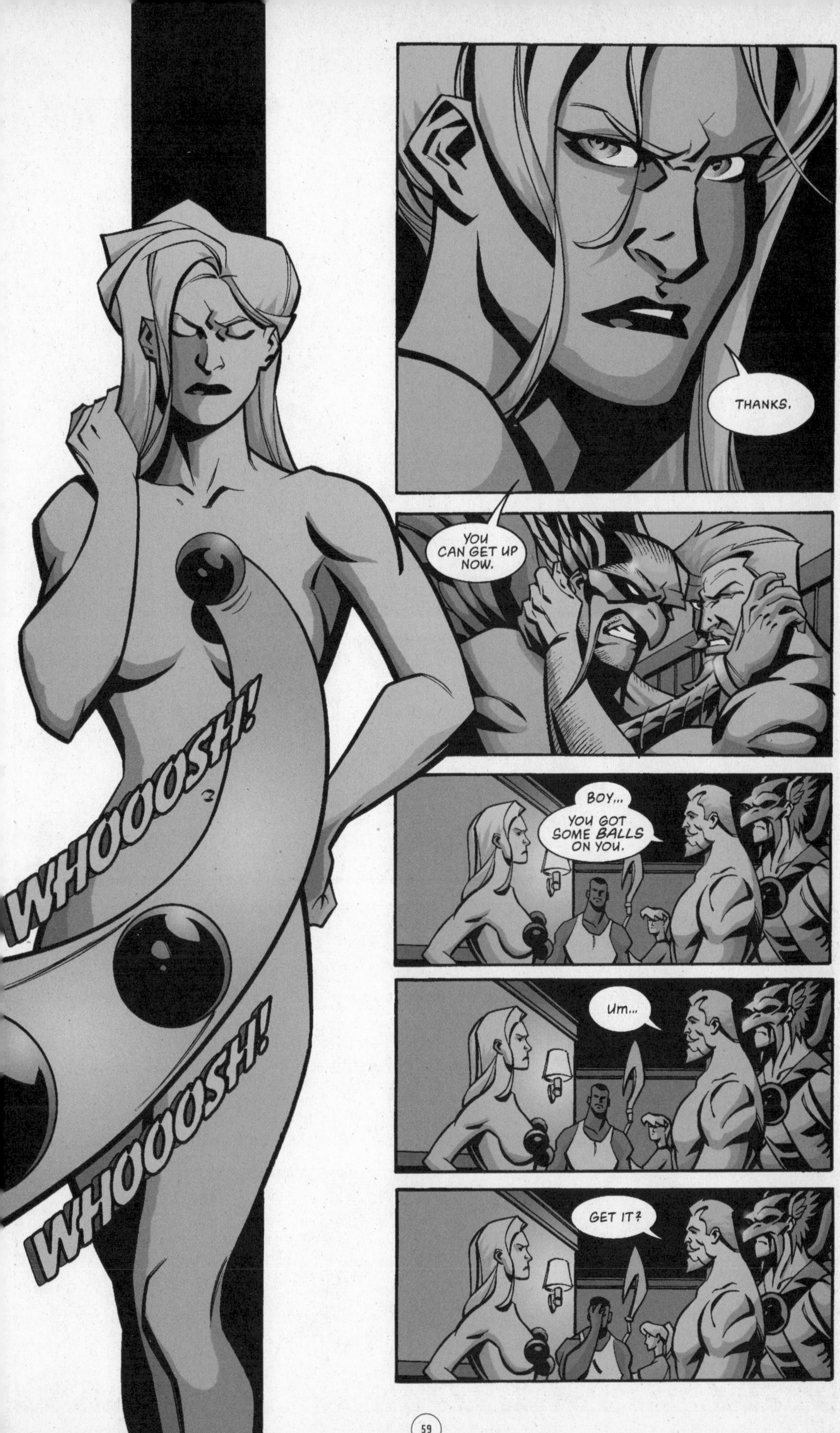
THANKS.
YOU CAN GET UP NOW.
WHOOOSH!
WHOOOSH!
BOY... YOU GOT SOME BALLS ON YOU.
Um...
GET IT?

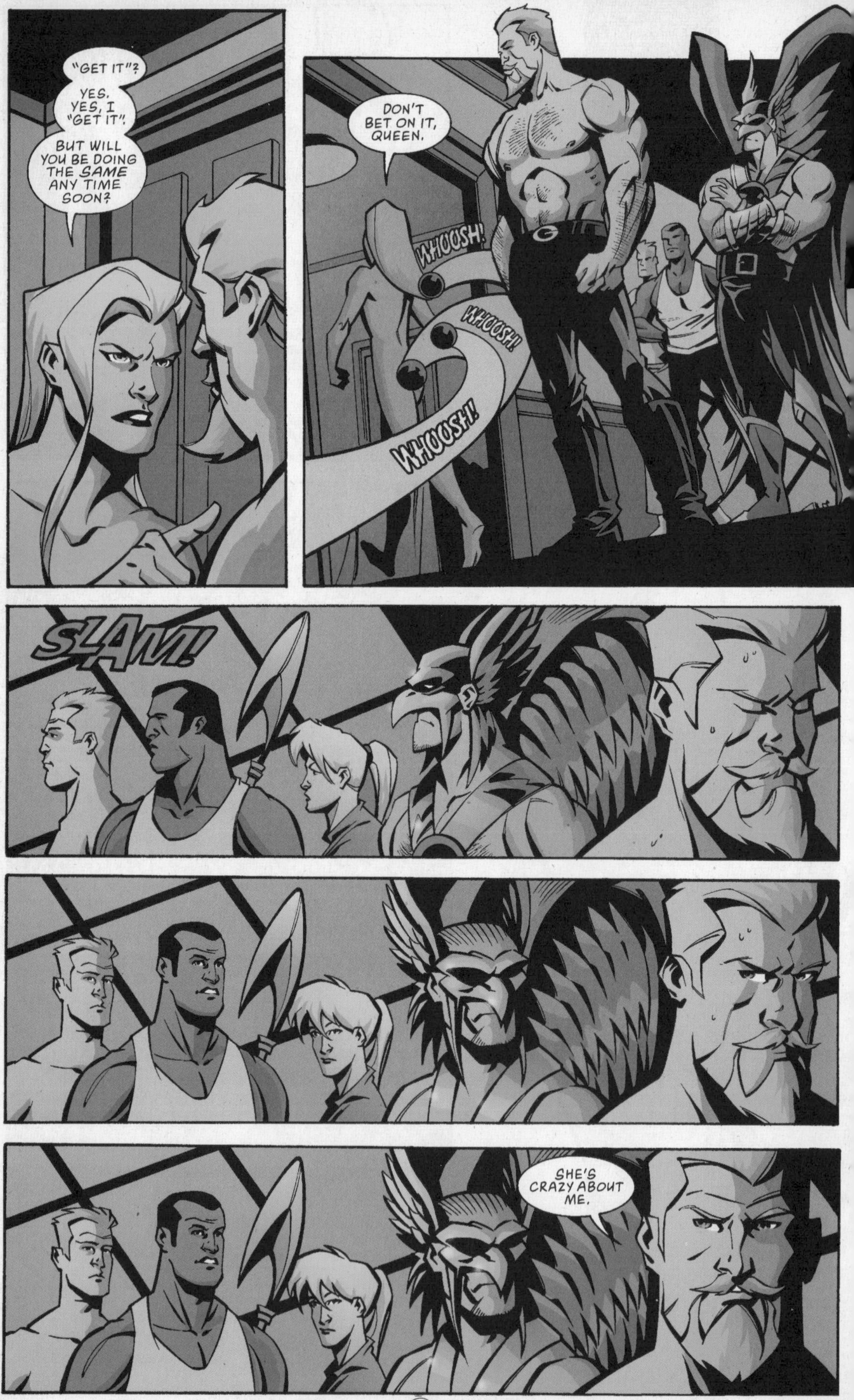
"GET IT"?
YES. YES, I "GET IT".
BUT WILL YOU BE DOING THE SAME ANY TIME SOON?
DON'T BET ON IT, QUEEN.
WHOOSH!
WHOOSH!
WHOOSH!
SLAM!
SHE'S CRAZY ABOUT ME.

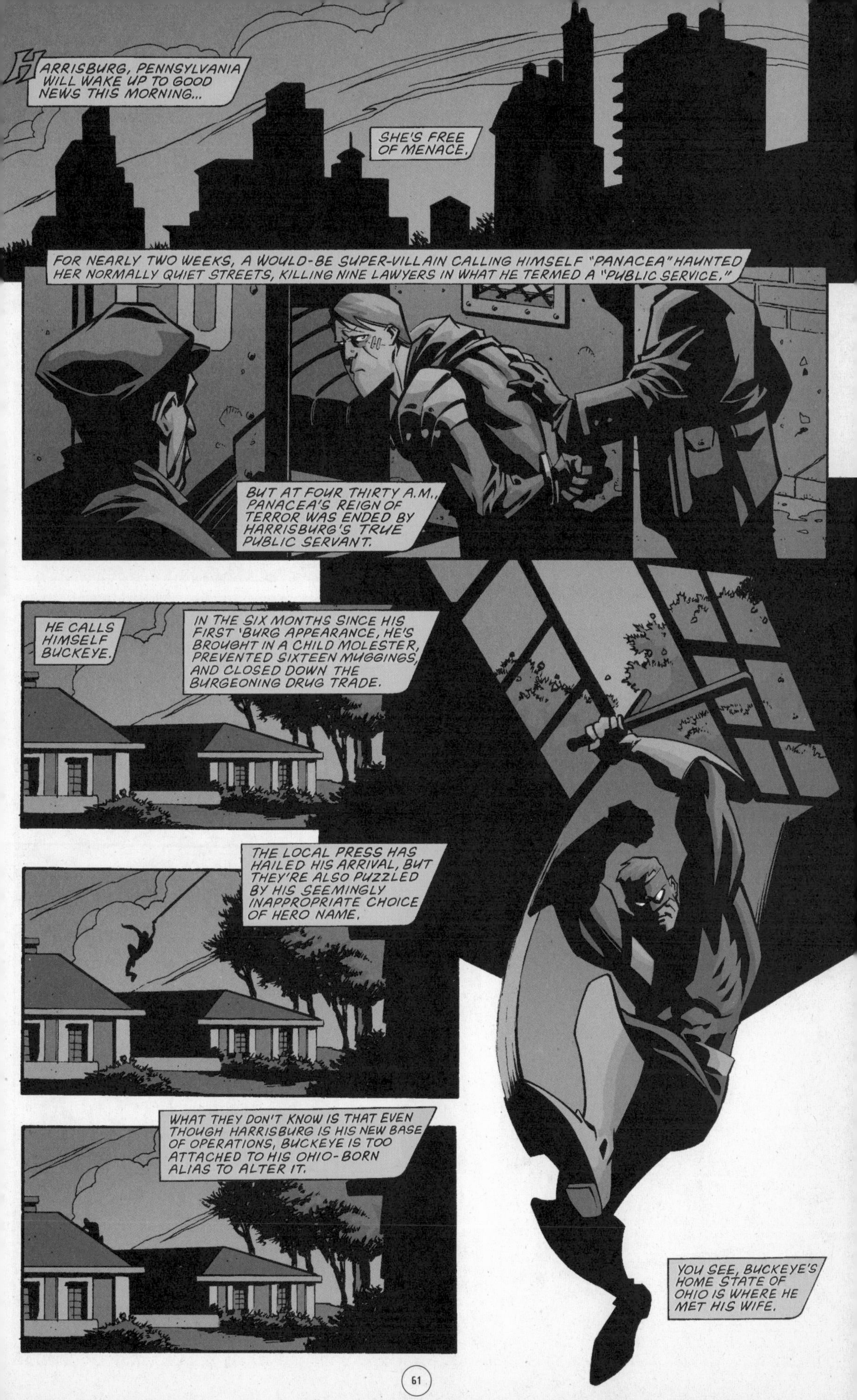
HARRISBURG, PENNSYLVANIA WILL WAKE UP TO GOOD NEWS THIS MORNING...
SHE'S FREE OF MENACE.
FOR NEARLY TWO WEEKS, A WOULD-BE SUPER-VILLAIN CALLING HIMSELF "PANACEA" HAUNTED HER NORMALLY QUIET STREETS, KILLING NINE LAWYERS IN WHAT HE TERMED A "PUBLIC SERVICE."
BUT AT FOUR THIRTY A.M., PANACEA'S REIGN OF TERROR WAS ENDED BY HARRISBURG'S TRUE PUBLIC SERVANT.
HE CALLS HIMSELF BUCKEYE.
IN THE SIX MONTHS SINCE HIS FIRST 'BURG APPEARANCE, HE'S BROUGHT IN A CHILD MOLESTER, PREVENTED SIXTEEN MUGGINGS, AND CLOSED DOWN THE BURGEONING DRUG TRADE.
THE LOCAL PRESS HAS HAILED HIS ARRIVAL, BUT THEY'RE ALSO PUZZLED BY HIS SEEMINGLY INAPPROPRIATE CHOICE OF HERO NAME.
WHAT THEY DON'T KNOW IS THAT EVEN THOUGH HARRISBURG IS HIS NEW BASE OF OPERATIONS, BUCKEYE IS TOO ATTACHED TO HIS OHIO-BORN ALIAS TO ALTER IT.
YOU SEE, BUCKEYE'S HOME STATE OF OHIO IS WHERE HE MET HIS WIFE.

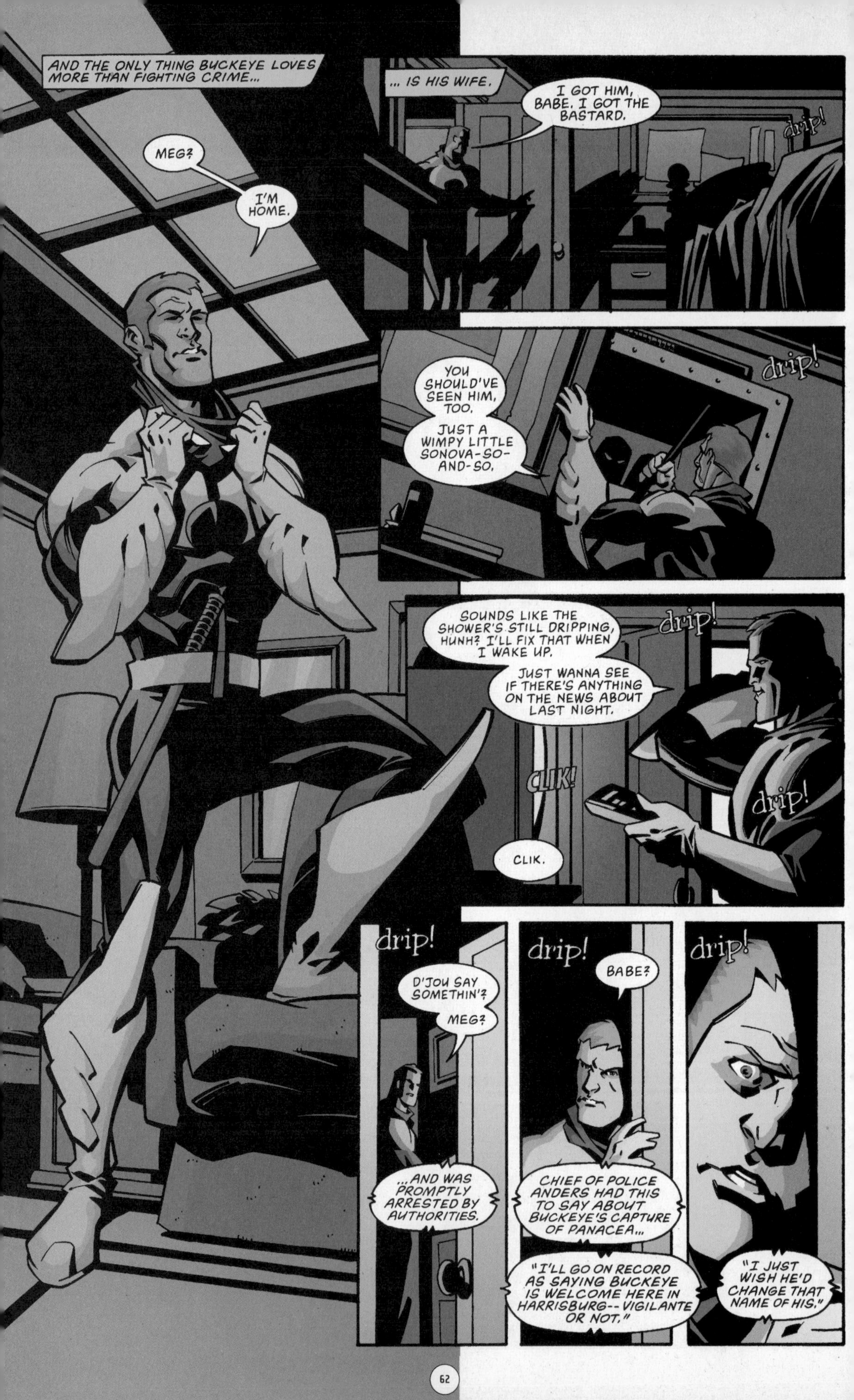
AND THE ONLY THING BUCKEYE LOVES MORE THAN FIGHTING CRIME...
MEG?
I'M HOME.
... IS HIS WIFE.
I GOT HIM, BABE. I GOT THE BASTARD.
drip!
YOU SHOULD'VE SEEN HIM, TOO.
JUST A WIMPY LITTLE SONOVA-SO-AND-SO.
drip!
SOUNDS LIKE THE SHOWER'S STILL DRIPPING, HUNH? I'LL FIX THAT WHEN I WAKE UP.
drip!
JUST WANNA SEE IF THERE'S ANYTHING ON THE NEWS ABOUT LAST NIGHT.
CLIK!
drip!
CLIK.
drip!
D'JOU SAY SOMETHIN'?
MEG?
...AND WAS PROMPTLY ARRESTED BY AUTHORITIES.
drip!
BABE?
CHIEF OF POLICE ANDERS HAD THIS TO SAY ABOUT BUCKEYE'S CAPTURE OF PANACEA...
"I'LL GO ON RECORD AS SAYING BUCKEYE IS WELCOME HERE IN HARRISBURG-- VIGILANTE OR NOT."
drip!
"I JUST WISH HE'D CHANGE THAT NAME OF HIS."

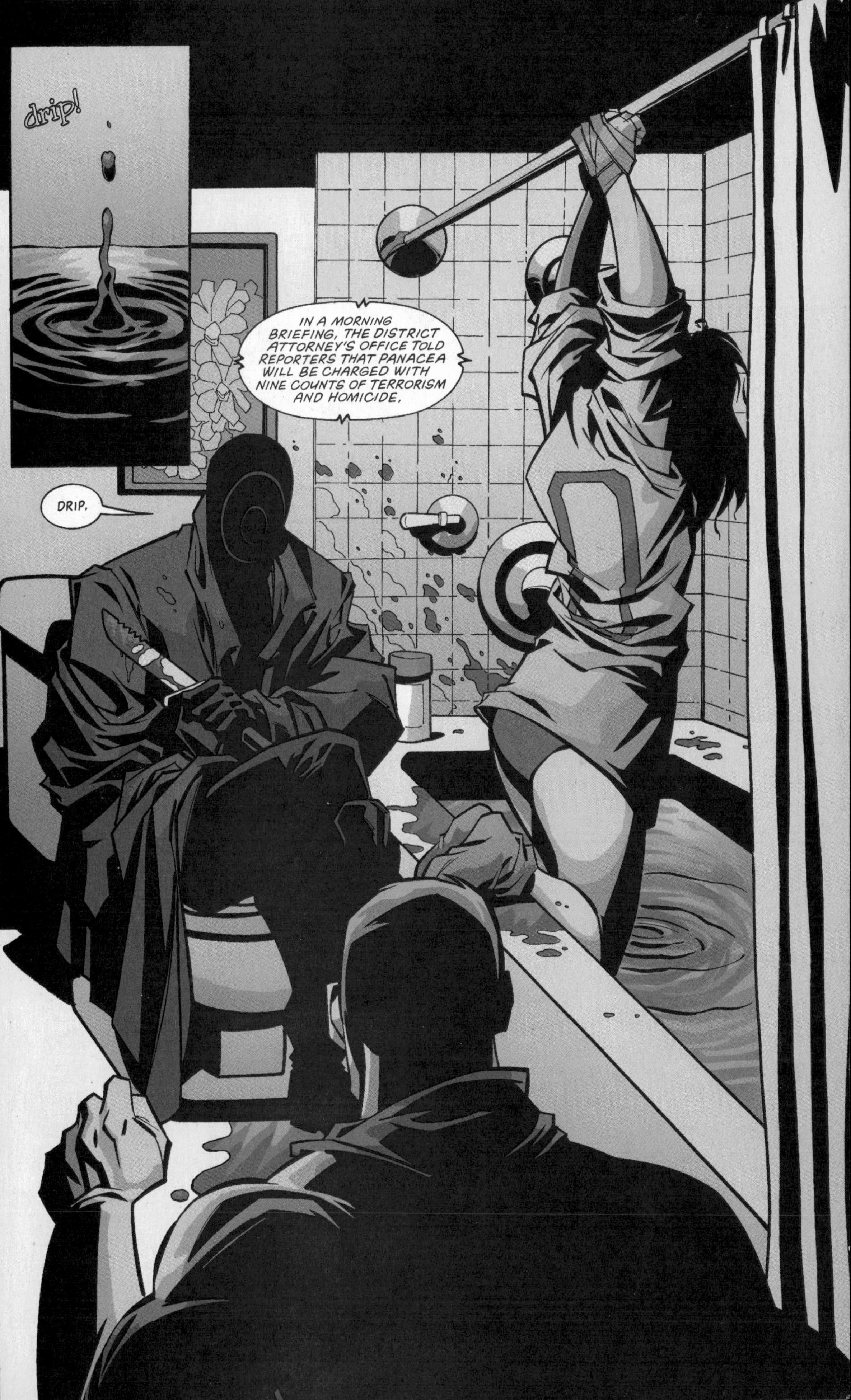
drip!
IN A MORNING BRIEFING, THE DISTRICT ATTORNEY'S OFFICE TOLD REPORTERS THAT PANACEA WILL BE CHARGED WITH NINE COUNTS OF TERRORISM AND HOMICIDE.
DRIP.

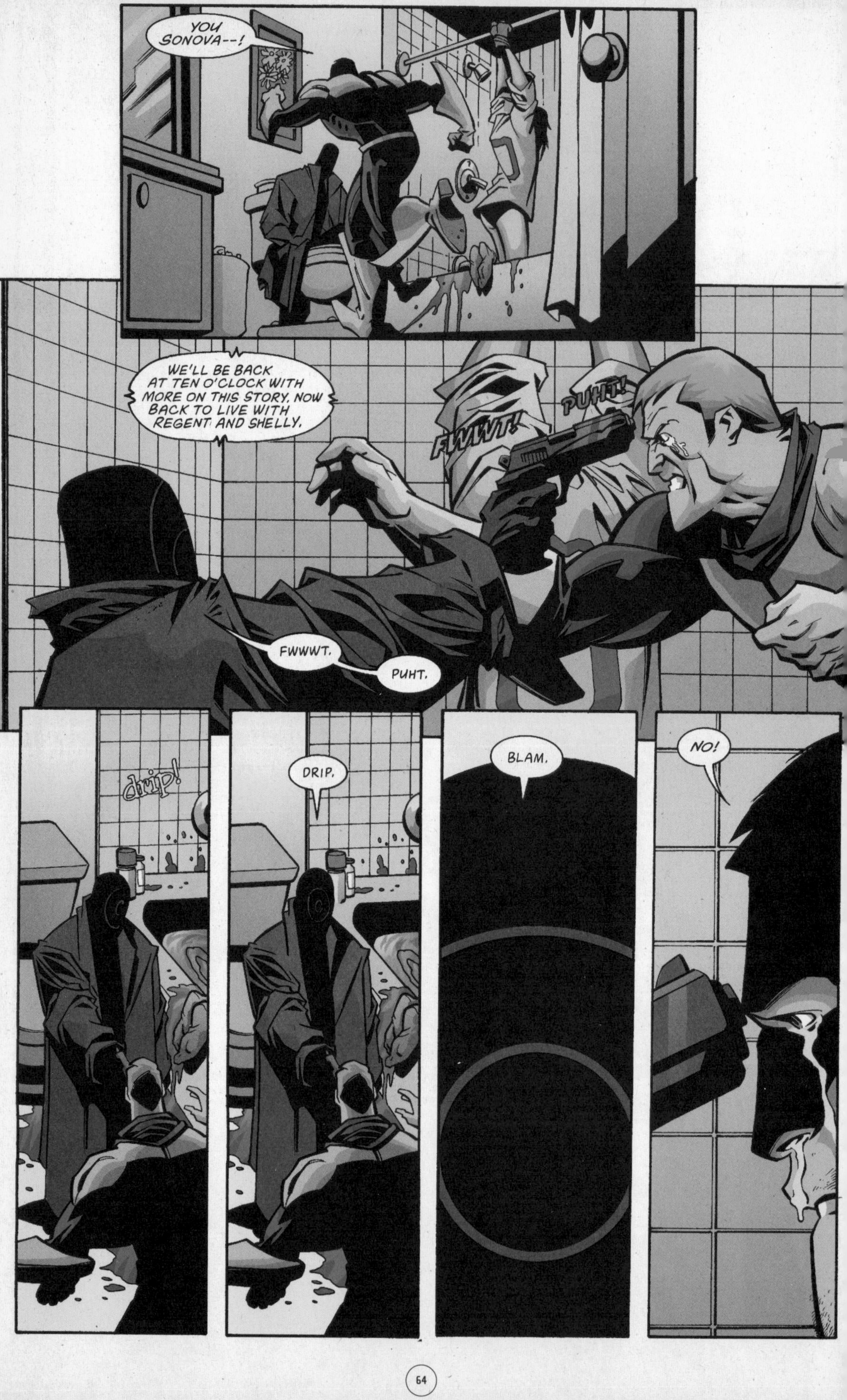
YOU SONOVA--!
WE'LL BE BACK AT TEN O'CLOCK WITH MORE ON THIS STORY. NOW BACK TO LIVE WITH REGENT AND SHELLY.
PUHT!
FWWT!
FWWWT.
PUHT.
drip!
DRIP.
BLAM.
NO!

BLAM!

LATER ON THE SHOW, BEN AFFLECK WILL BE HERE TO TALK ABOUT HIS NEW MOVIE.

OOO! I LOVE HIM.

FORGET HIM-- HOW ABOUT THIS: AT THAT NEW HOT-SPOT, THE CHEEZ HAUS, BLACK CANARY AND THE RECENTLY RETURNED GREEN ARROW PUT THE HURT ON REGULAR FIXTURE OF THE GOTHAM VILLAIN SET, THE RIDDLER.

WASN'T THAT GREAT? I HEARD NEITHER OF THEM WERE IN COSTUME, EITHER.

LET 'EM ALL TAKE OFF THE COSTUMES, I SAY.

FOR THE LAST TIME, REEGE: I'M SURE BATMAN DOESN'T WATCH THIS SHOW.

WHAT BATMAN? I WAS TALKING ABOUT WONDER WOMAN!

HAHAHAHA!

BUT THAT'S WHAT I LIKE ABOUT HIM. HE'S JUST A GUY RUNNING AROUND WITH A BOW AND ARROW, THE BLACK CANARY'S GOT THAT YELLING THING, BUT WHAT DOES THIS GUY HAVE? HE DOESN'T HAVE ANY SUPER-POWERS OR ANYTHING. HE'S JUST A NORMAL GUY IN A FUNNY SUIT.

I'LL TAKE THAT PLASTIC MAN. HE CAN STRETCH INTO THOSE HARD TO REACH PLACES.

BUT SERIOUSLY, I LIKE THIS GREEN ARROW GUY.

HE'S NO SUPERMAN.

HAHAHAHA!

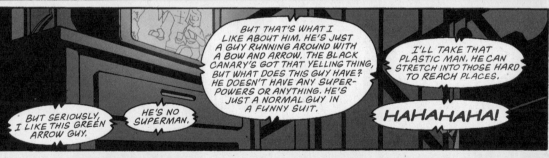

GIVE ME GREEN ARROW. HECK, ANYONE COULD BE GREEN ARROW, RIGHT? THAT'S WHAT'S SO APPEALING ABOUT HIM. I MEAN, HE'S JUST A NORMAL GUY RUNNING AROUND WITH A BOW AND ARROW!

YEAH-- THAT'S A NORMAL GUY, ALL RIGHT.

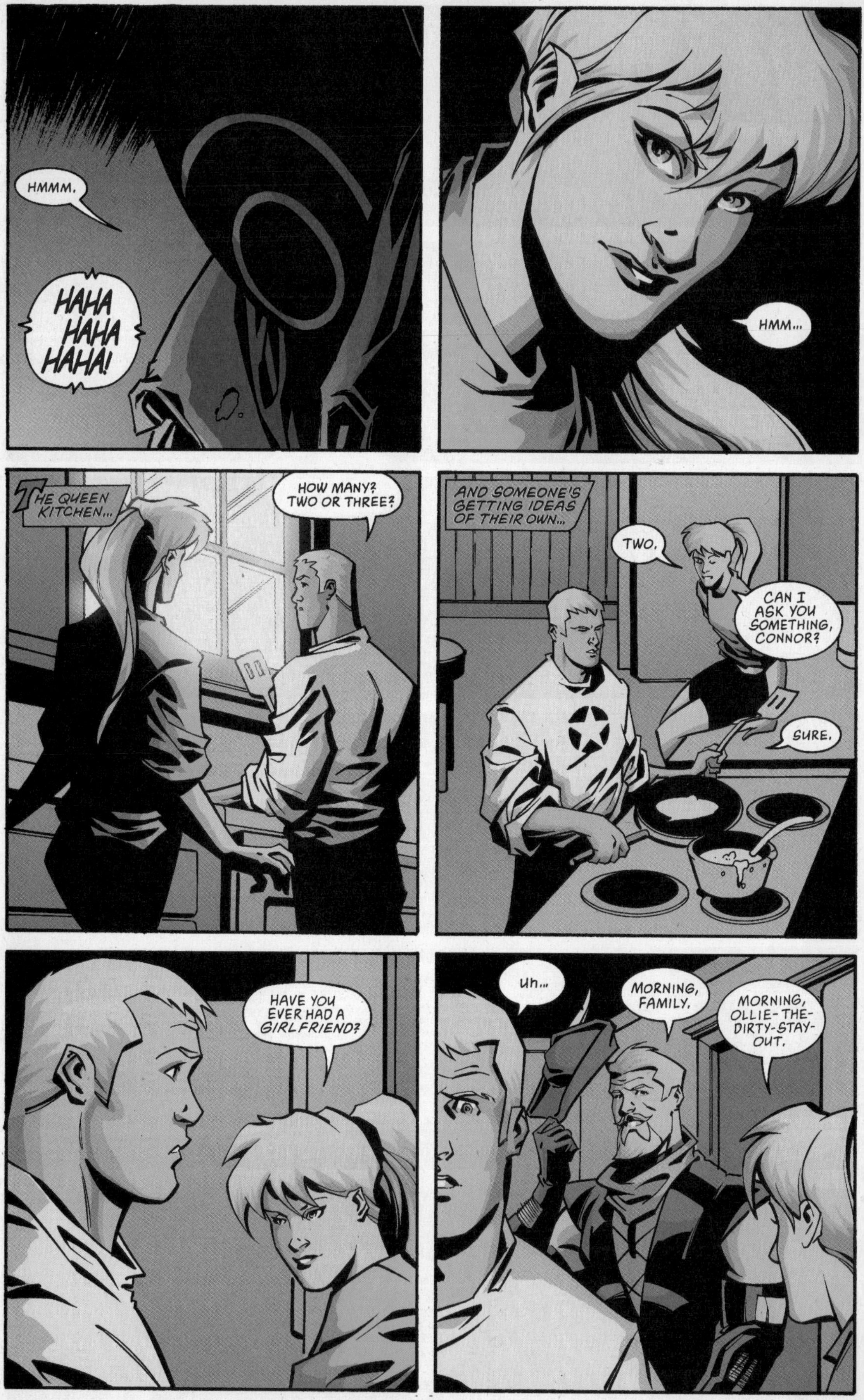
HMMM.
HAHA HAHA HAHA!
HMM...
THE QUEEN KITCHEN...
HOW MANY? TWO OR THREE?
AND SOMEONE'S GETTING IDEAS OF THEIR OWN...
TWO.
CAN I ASK YOU SOMETHING, CONNOR?
SURE.
HAVE YOU EVER HAD A GIRLFRIEND?
Uh...
MORNING, FAMILY.
MORNING, OLLIE-THE-DIRTY-STAY-OUT.

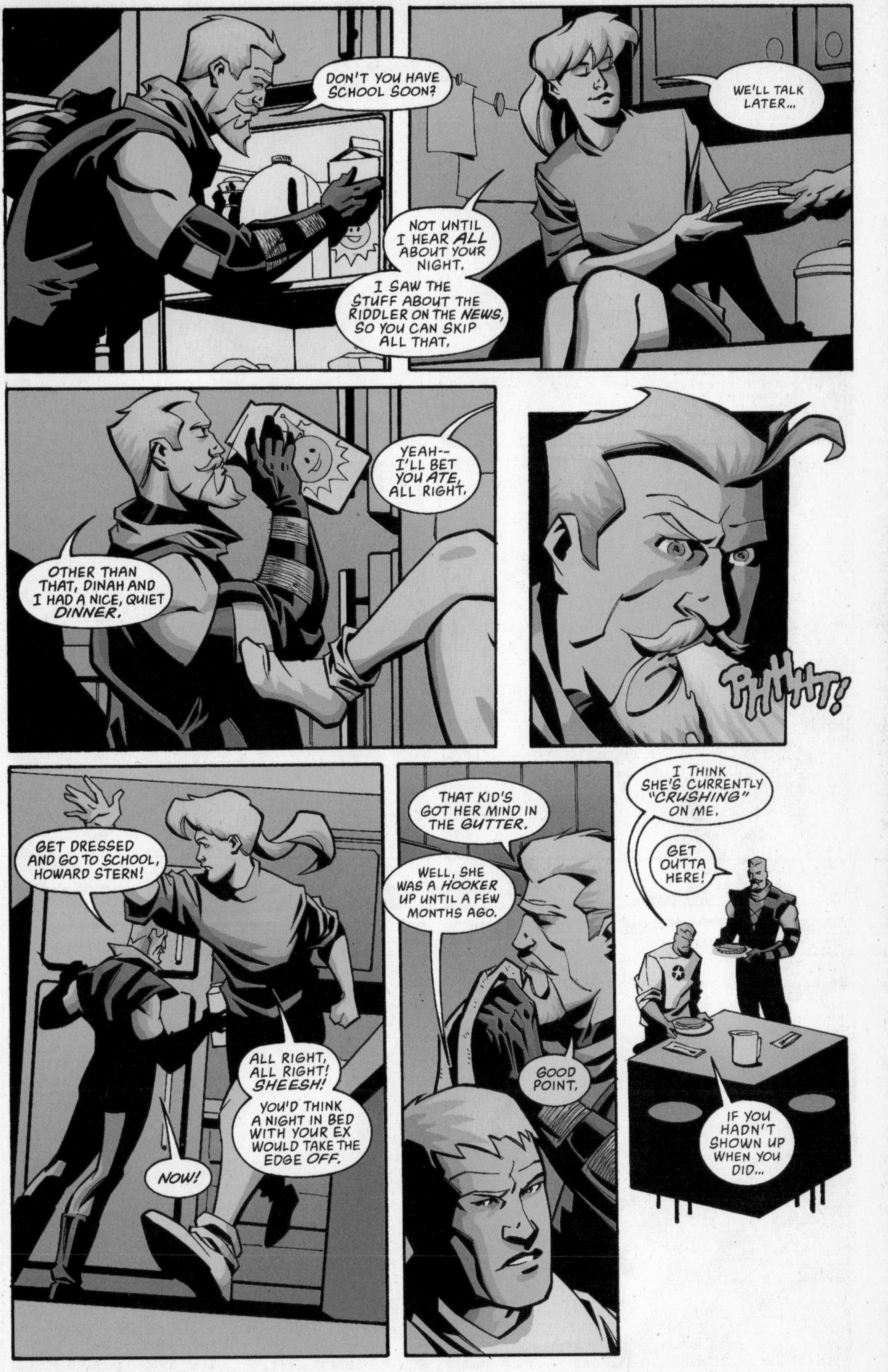
DON'T YOU HAVE SCHOOL SOON?
WE'LL TALK LATER...
NOT UNTIL I HEAR ALL ABOUT YOUR NIGHT.
I SAW THE STUFF ABOUT THE RIDDLER ON THE NEWS, SO YOU CAN SKIP ALL THAT.
OTHER THAN THAT, DINAH AND I HAD A NICE, QUIET DINNER.
YEAH-- I'LL BET YOU ATE, ALL RIGHT.
PHHHT!
GET DRESSED AND GO TO SCHOOL, HOWARD STERN!
ALL RIGHT, ALL RIGHT! SHEESH!
YOU'D THINK A NIGHT IN BED WITH YOUR EX WOULD TAKE THE EDGE OFF.
NOW!
THAT KID'S GOT HER MIND IN THE GUTTER.
WELL, SHE WAS A HOOKER UP UNTIL A FEW MONTHS AGO.
GOOD POINT.
I THINK SHE'S CURRENTLY "CRUSHING" ON ME.
GET OUTTA HERE!
IF YOU HADN'T SHOWN UP WHEN YOU DID...

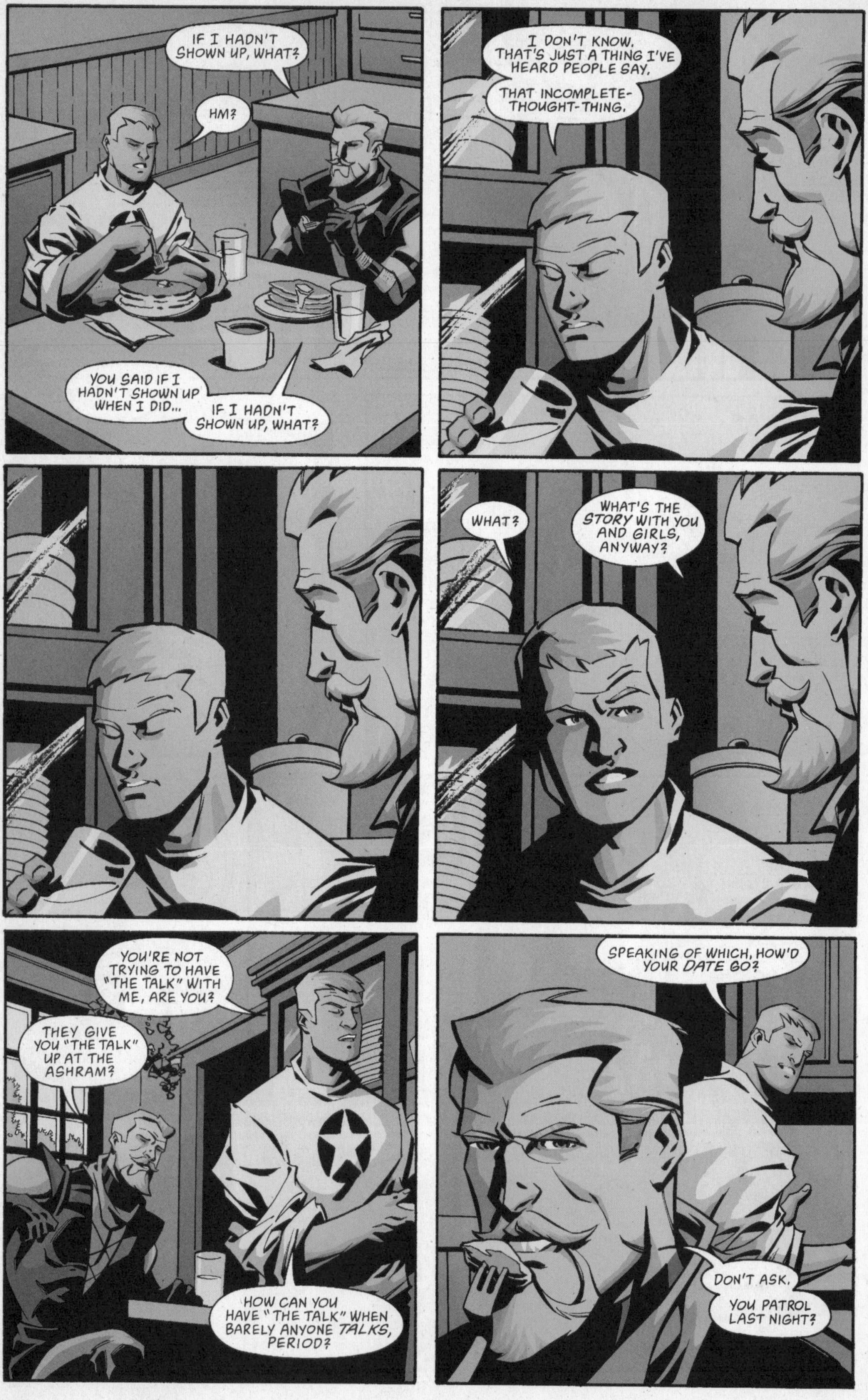
IF I HADN'T SHOWN UP, WHAT?
HM?
YOU SAID IF I HADN'T SHOWN UP WHEN I DID...
IF I HADN'T SHOWN UP, WHAT?
I DON'T KNOW. THAT'S JUST A THING I'VE HEARD PEOPLE SAY.
THAT INCOMPLETE-THOUGHT-THING.
WHAT'S THE *STORY* WITH YOU AND GIRLS, ANYWAY?
WHAT?
YOU'RE NOT TRYING TO HAVE "THE TALK" WITH ME, ARE YOU?
THEY GIVE YOU "THE TALK" UP AT THE ASHRAM?
HOW CAN YOU HAVE "THE TALK" WHEN BARELY ANYONE *TALKS*, PERIOD?
SPEAKING OF WHICH, HOW'D YOUR *DATE* GO?
DON'T ASK.
YOU PATROL LAST NIGHT?

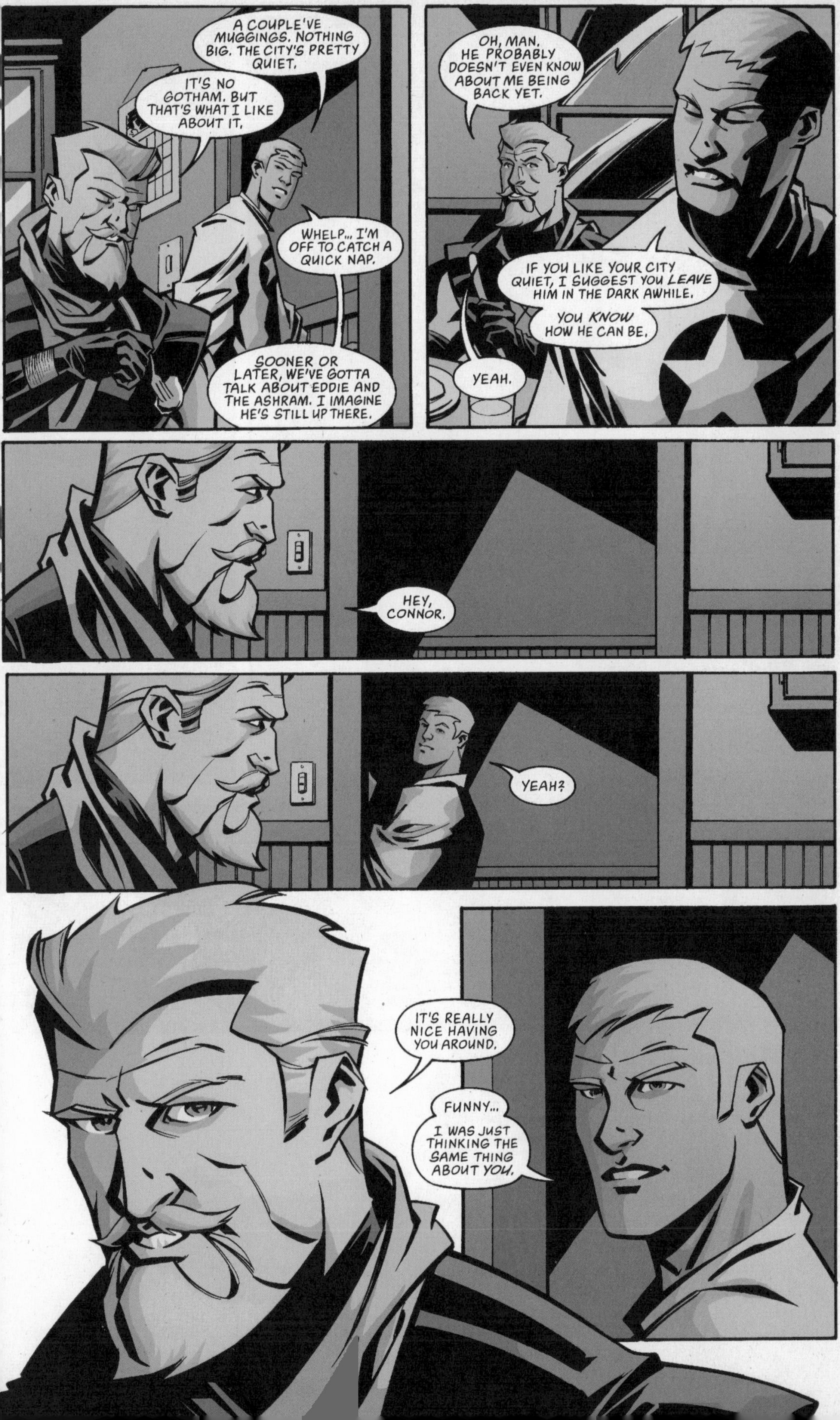
A COUPLE'VE MUGGINGS. NOTHING BIG. THE CITY'S PRETTY QUIET.
IT'S NO GOTHAM. BUT THAT'S WHAT I LIKE ABOUT IT.
WHELP... I'M OFF TO CATCH A QUICK NAP.
SOONER OR LATER, WE'VE GOTTA TALK ABOUT EDDIE AND THE ASHRAM. I IMAGINE HE'S STILL UP THERE.
OH, MAN. HE PROBABLY DOESN'T EVEN KNOW ABOUT ME BEING BACK YET.
IF YOU LIKE YOUR CITY QUIET, I SUGGEST YOU LEAVE HIM IN THE DARK AWHILE.
YOU KNOW HOW HE CAN BE.
YEAH.
HEY, CONNOR.
YEAH?
IT'S REALLY NICE HAVING YOU AROUND.
FUNNY...
I WAS JUST THINKING THE SAME THING ABOUT YOU.

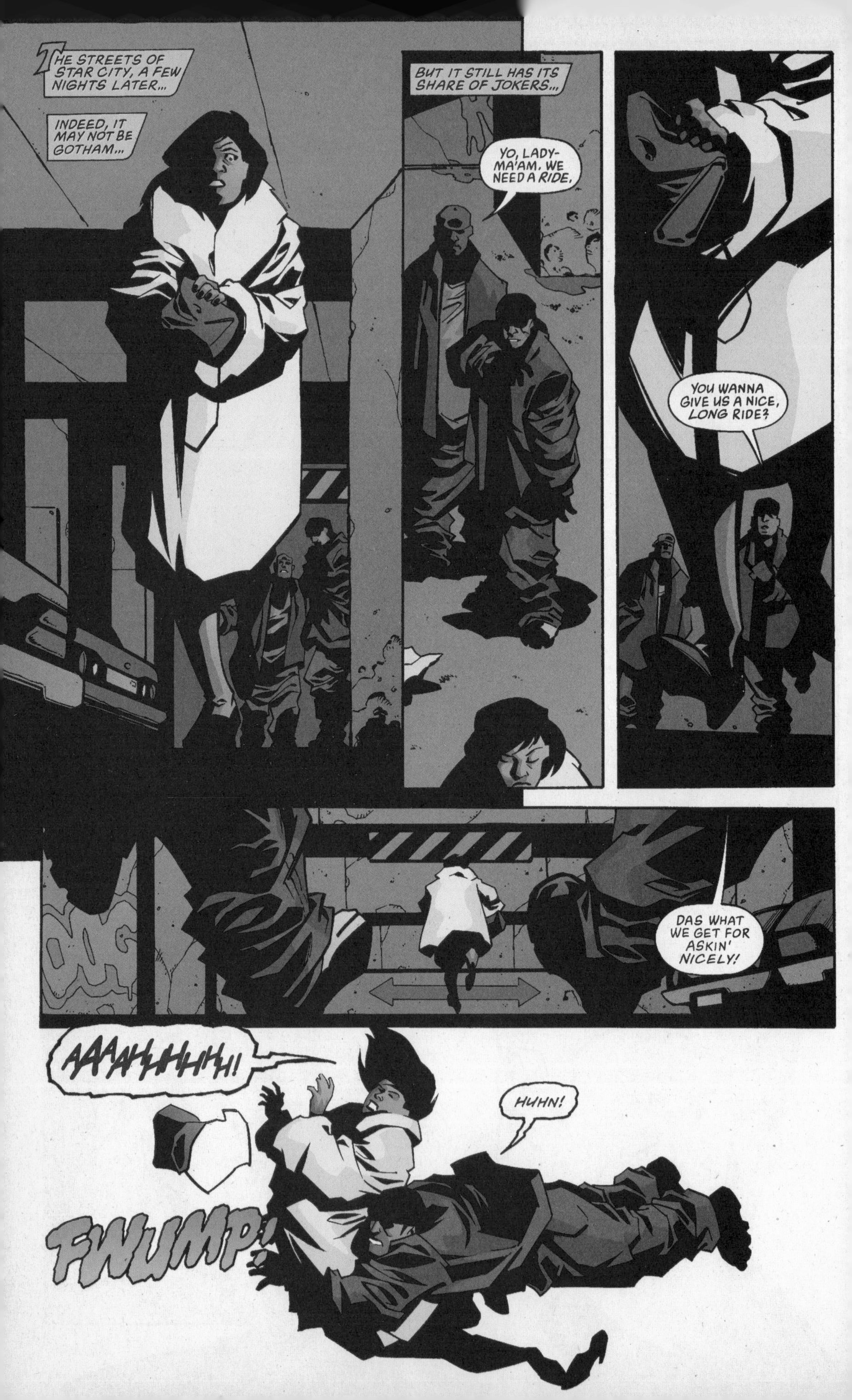
THE STREETS OF STAR CITY, A FEW NIGHTS LATER...
INDEED, IT MAY NOT BE GOTHAM...
BUT IT STILL HAS ITS SHARE OF JOKERS...
YO, LADY-MA'AM. WE NEED A RIDE.
YOU WANNA GIVE US A NICE, LONG RIDE?
DAS WHAT WE GET FOR ASKIN' NICELY!
AAAAHHHHHH!
HUHN!
FWUMP!

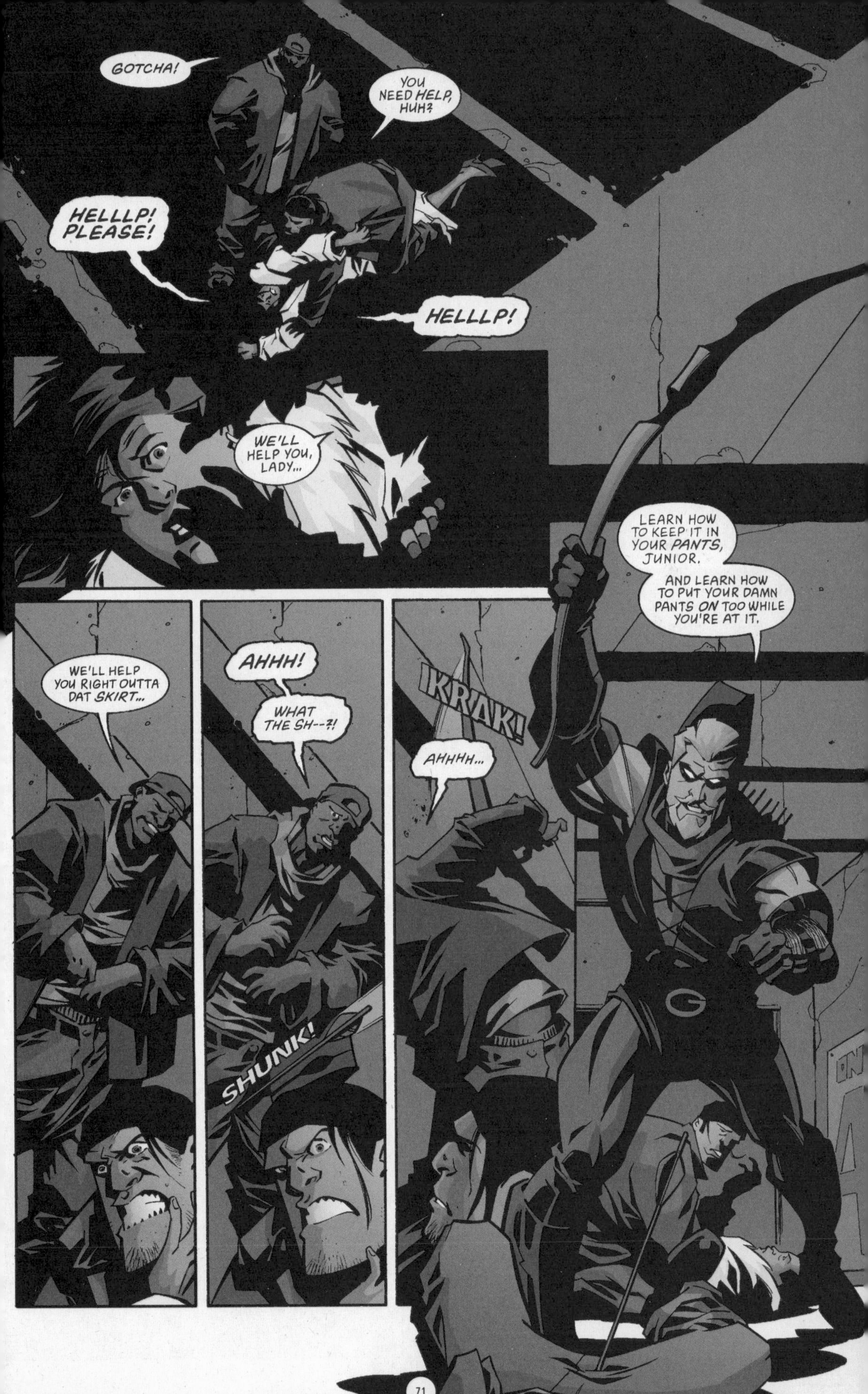
GOTCHA!
YOU NEED HELP, HUH?
HELLLP! PLEASE!
HELLLP!
WE'LL HELP YOU, LADY...
WE'LL HELP YOU RIGHT OUTTA DAT SKIRT...
AHHH!
WHAT THE SH--?!
SHUNK!
KRAK!
AHHHH...
LEARN HOW TO KEEP IT IN YOUR PANTS, JUNIOR.
AND LEARN HOW TO PUT YOUR DAMN PANTS ON TOO WHILE YOU'RE AT IT.

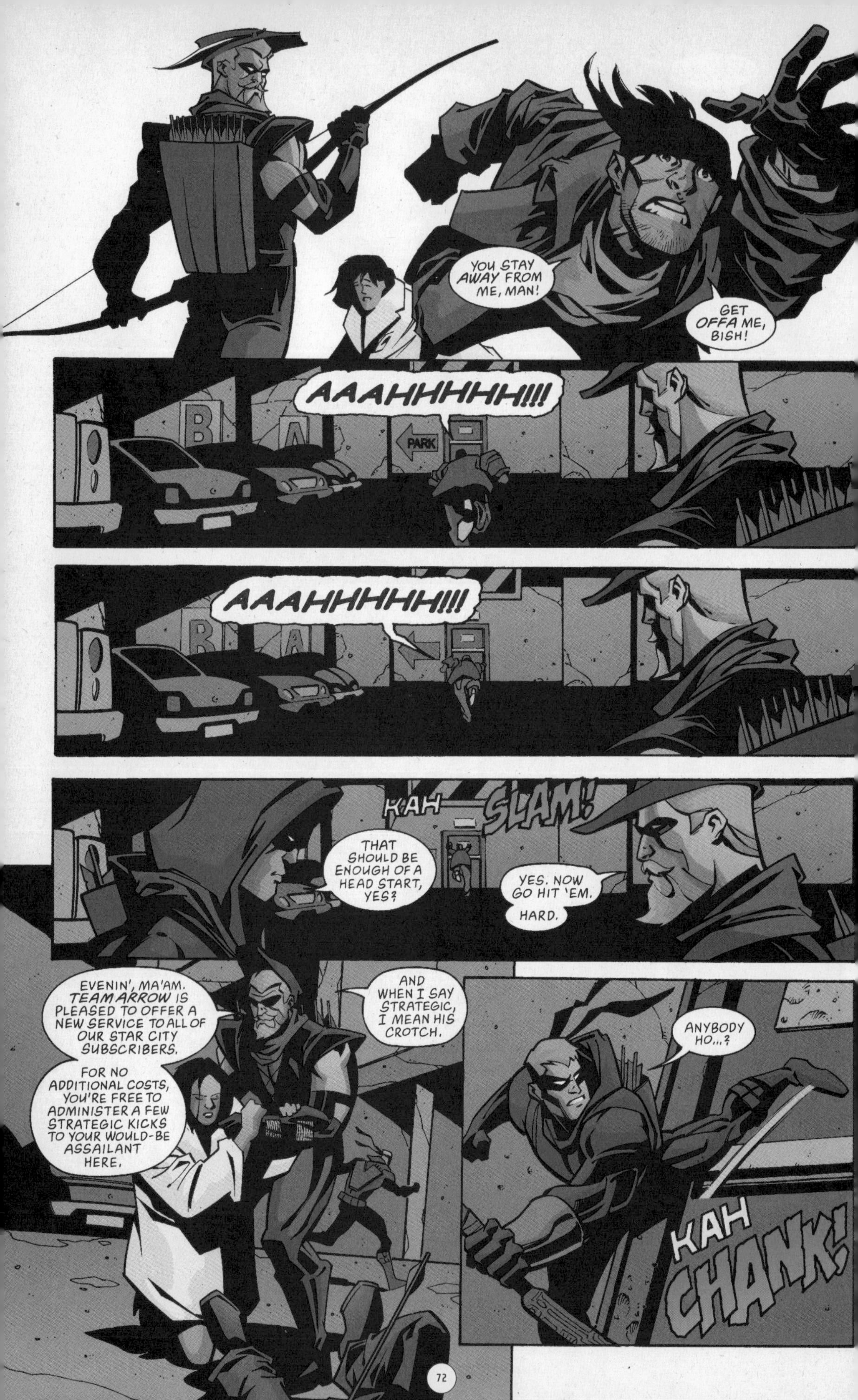
YOU STAY AWAY FROM ME, MAN!
GET OFFA ME, BISH!
AAAHHHHH!!!
PARK
AAAHHHHH!!!
KAH SLAM!
THAT SHOULD BE ENOUGH OF A HEAD START, YES?
YES. NOW GO HIT 'EM.
HARD.
EVENIN', MA'AM. TEAM ARROW IS PLEASED TO OFFER A NEW SERVICE TO ALL OF OUR STAR CITY SUBSCRIBERS.
FOR NO ADDITIONAL COSTS, YOU'RE FREE TO ADMINISTER A FEW STRATEGIC KICKS TO YOUR WOULD-BE ASSAILANT HERE.
AND WHEN I SAY STRATEGIC, I MEAN HIS CROTCH.
ANYBODY HO...?
KAH CHANK!

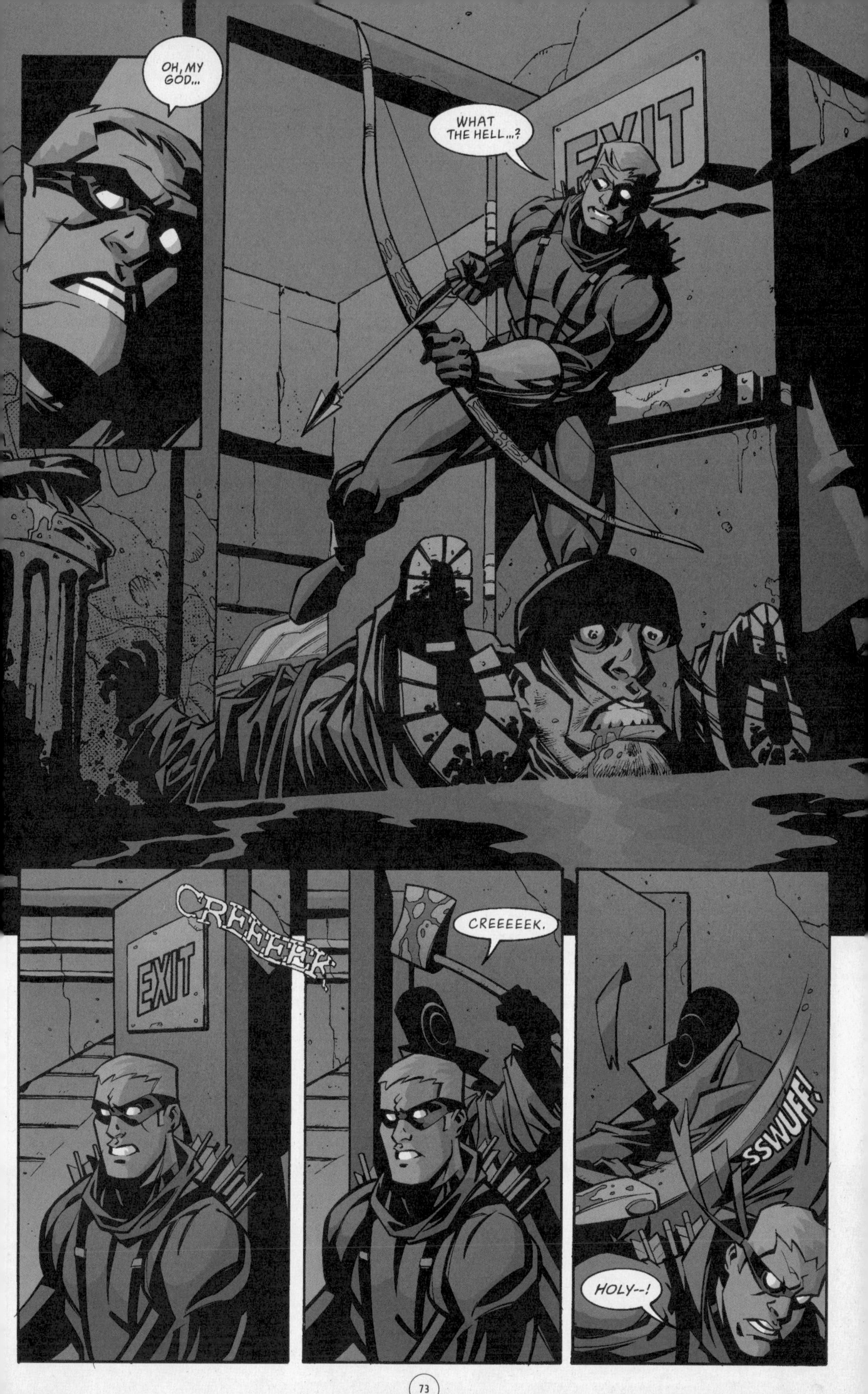
OH, MY GOD...
WHAT THE HELL...?
EXIT
EXIT
CREEEEEK
CREEEEEK.
SSWUFF!
HOLY--!

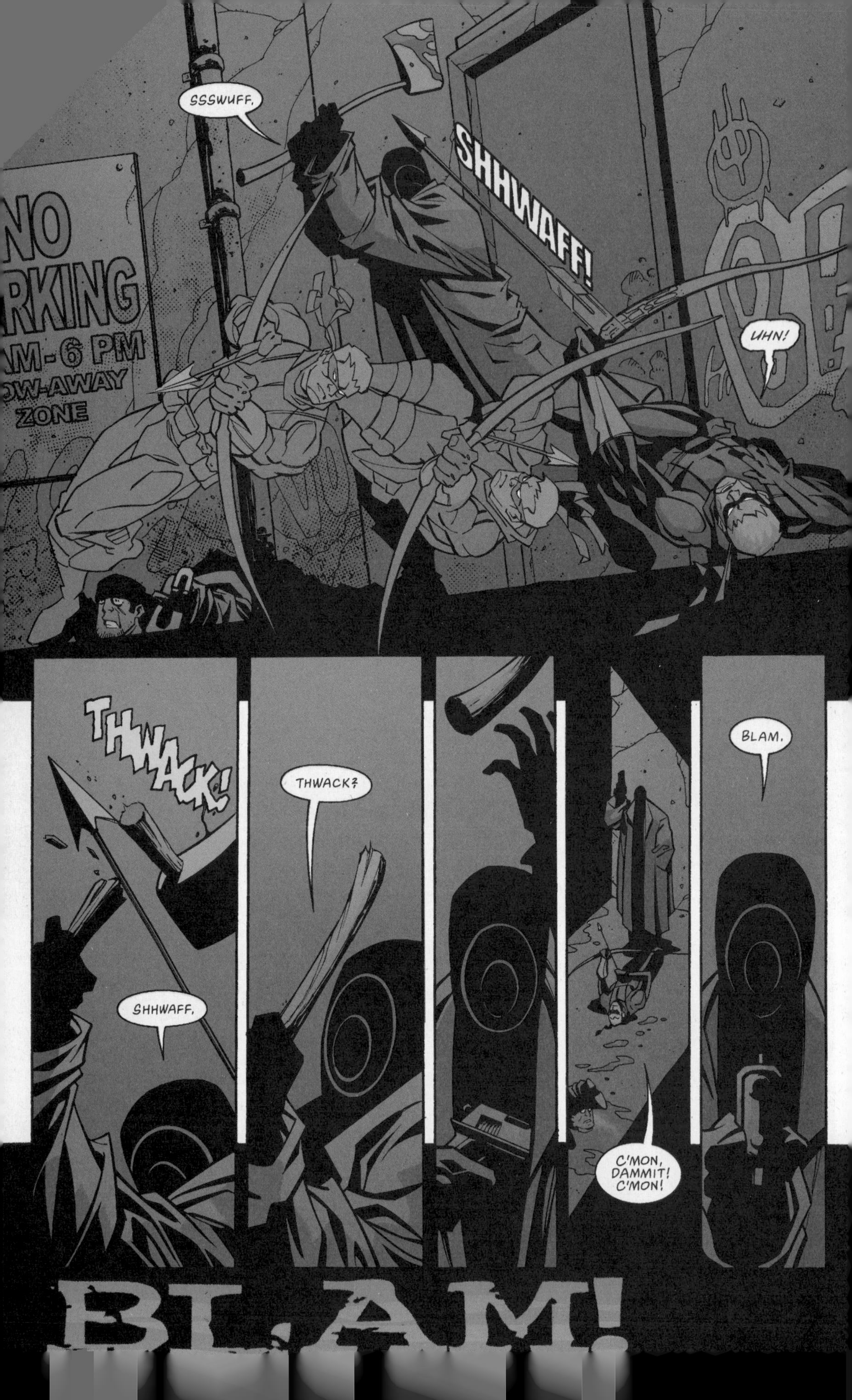

SSSWUFF.
SHHWAFF!
NO
RKING
AM - 6 PM
OW-AWAY
ZONE
UHN!
THWACK!
SHHWAFF.
THWACK?
C'MON, DAMMIT! C'MON!
BLAM.
BLAM!

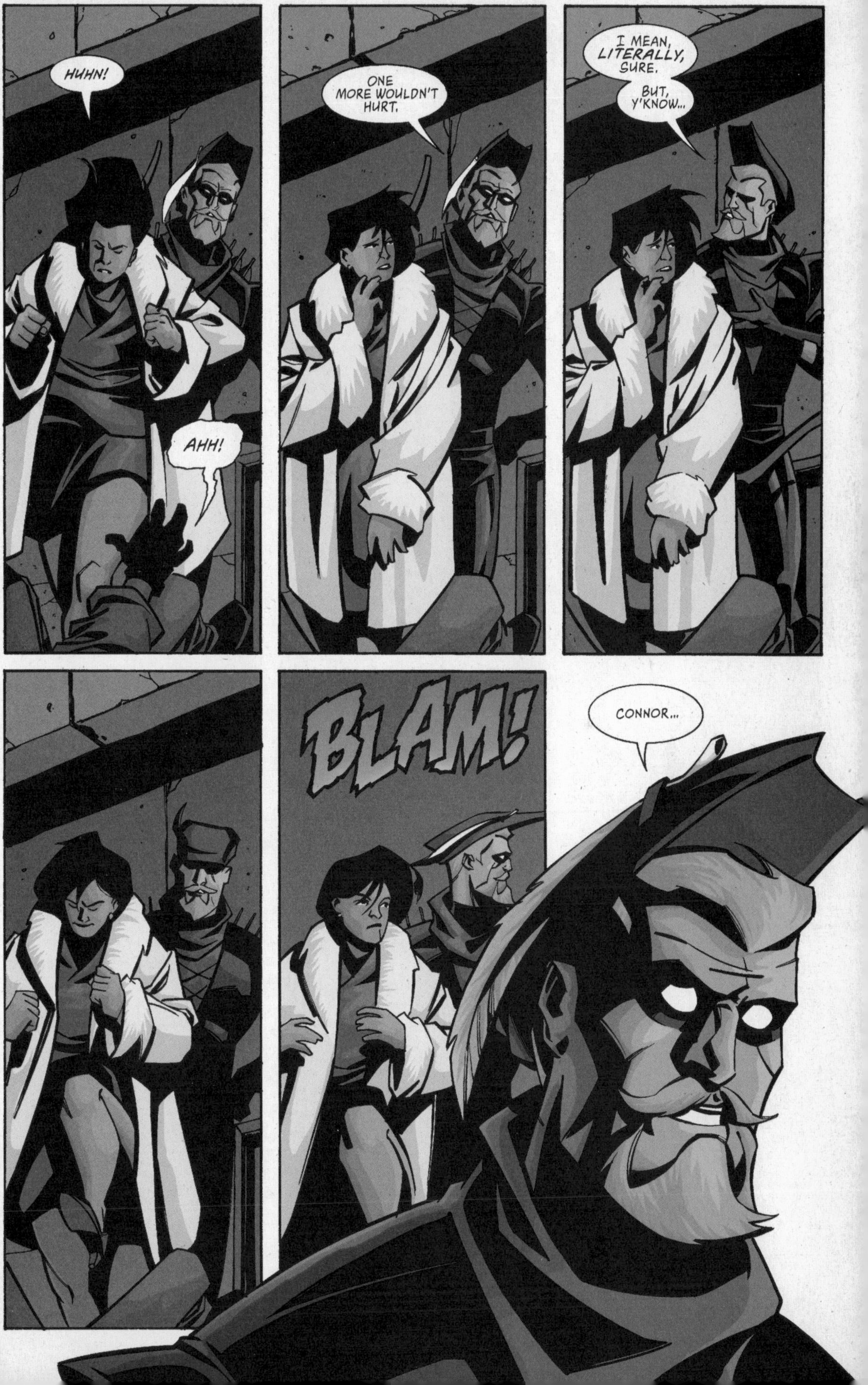
HUHN!
AHH!
ONE MORE WOULDN'T HURT.
I MEAN, LITERALLY, SURE.
BUT, Y'KNOW...
BLAM!
CONNOR...

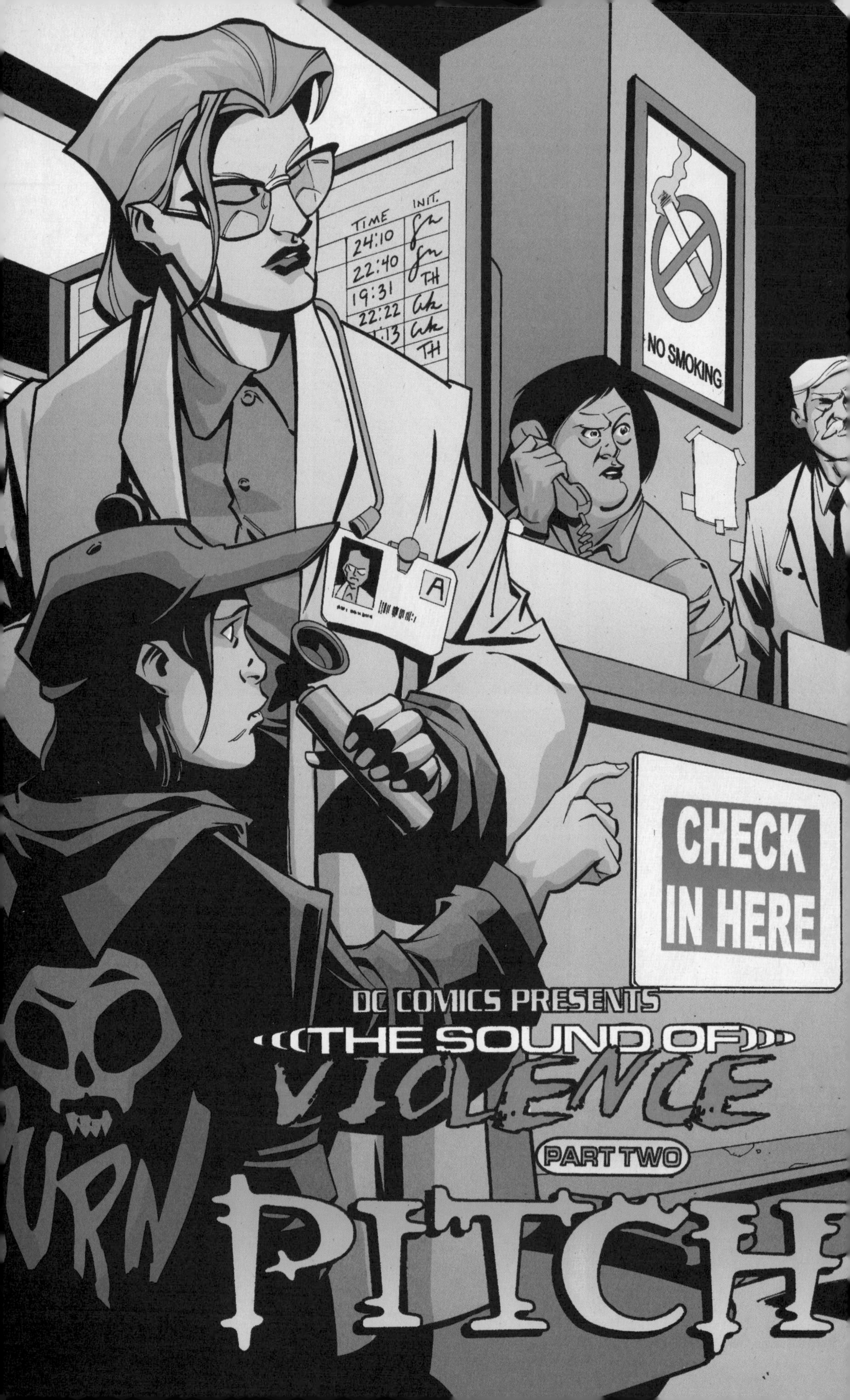
TIME
INIT.
24:10
22:40
19:31
22:22
TH
TH
NO SMOKING
A
CHECK IN HERE
DC COMICS PRESENTS
((THE SOUND OF))
VIOLENCE
PART TWO
PITCH

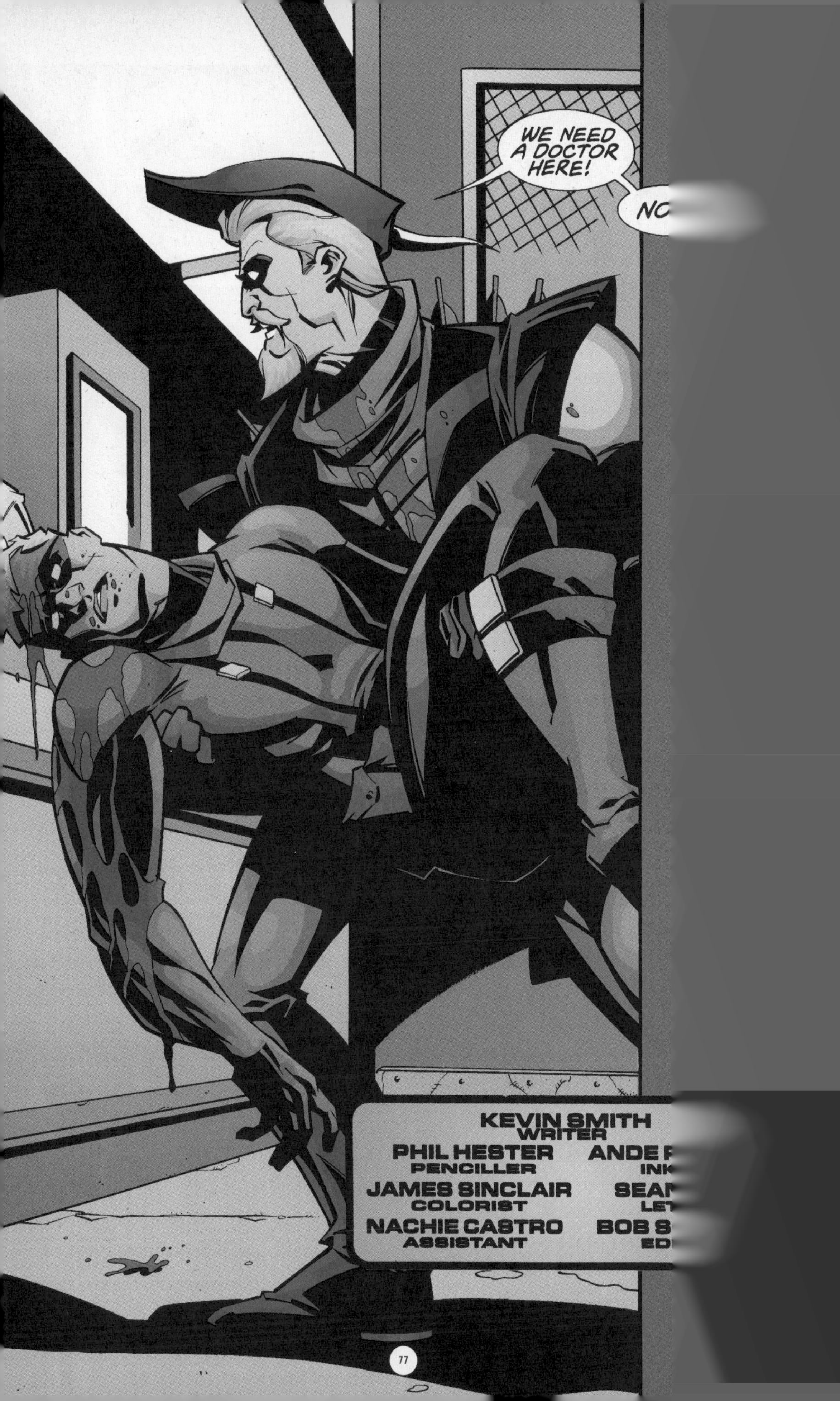
WE NEED A DOCTOR HERE!
NO
KEVIN SMITH
WRITER
PHIL HESTER
PENCILLER
JAMES SINCLAIR
COLORIST
NACHIE CASTRO
ASSISTANT

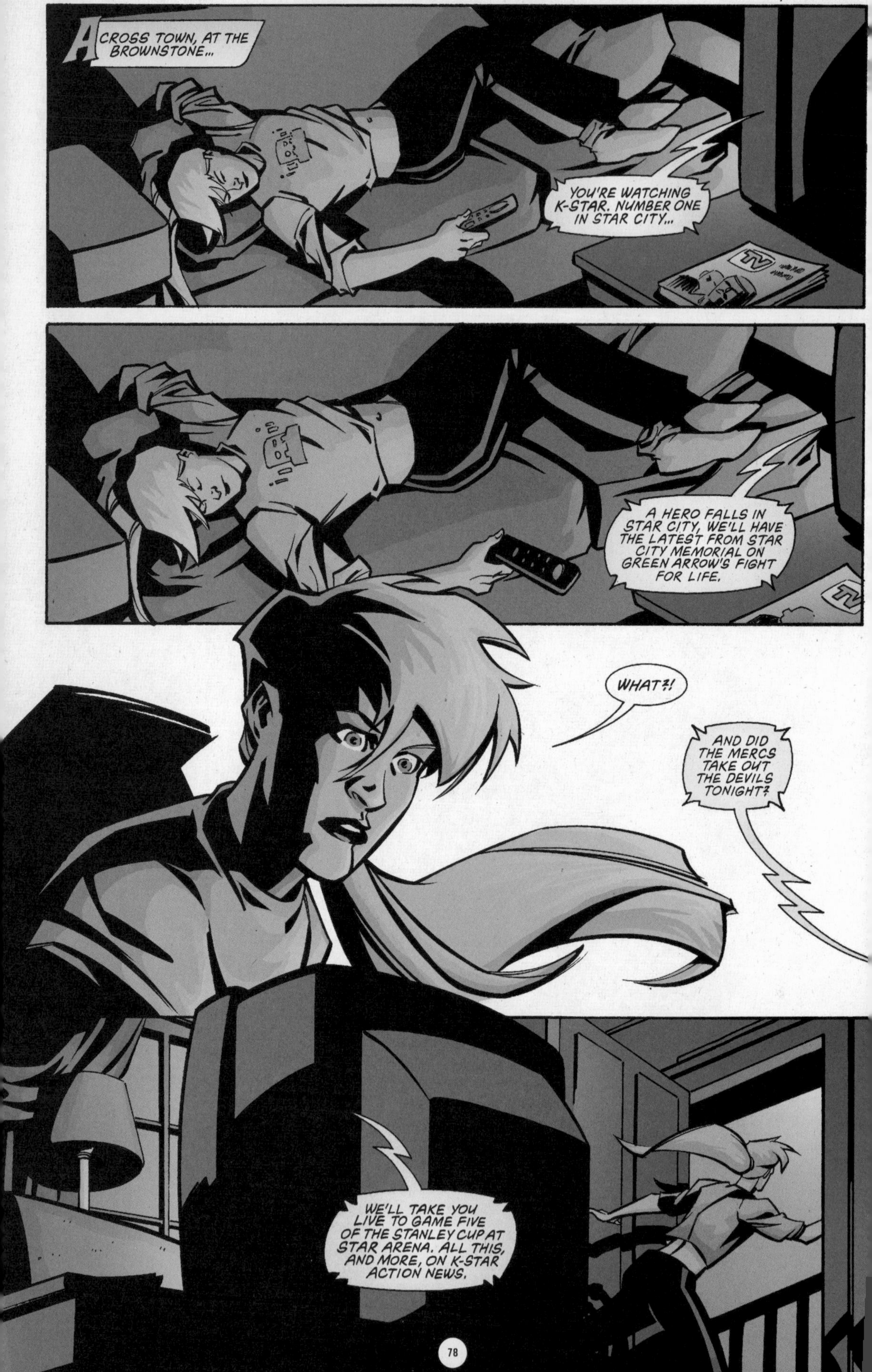
ACROSS TOWN, AT THE BROWNSTONE...
YOU'RE WATCHING K-STAR. NUMBER ONE IN STAR CITY...
A HERO FALLS IN STAR CITY, WE'LL HAVE THE LATEST FROM STAR CITY MEMORIAL ON GREEN ARROW'S FIGHT FOR LIFE.
WHAT?!
AND DID THE MERCS TAKE OUT THE DEVILS TONIGHT?
WE'LL TAKE YOU LIVE TO GAME FIVE OF THE STANLEY CUP AT STAR ARENA. ALL THIS, AND MORE, ON K-STAR ACTION NEWS.

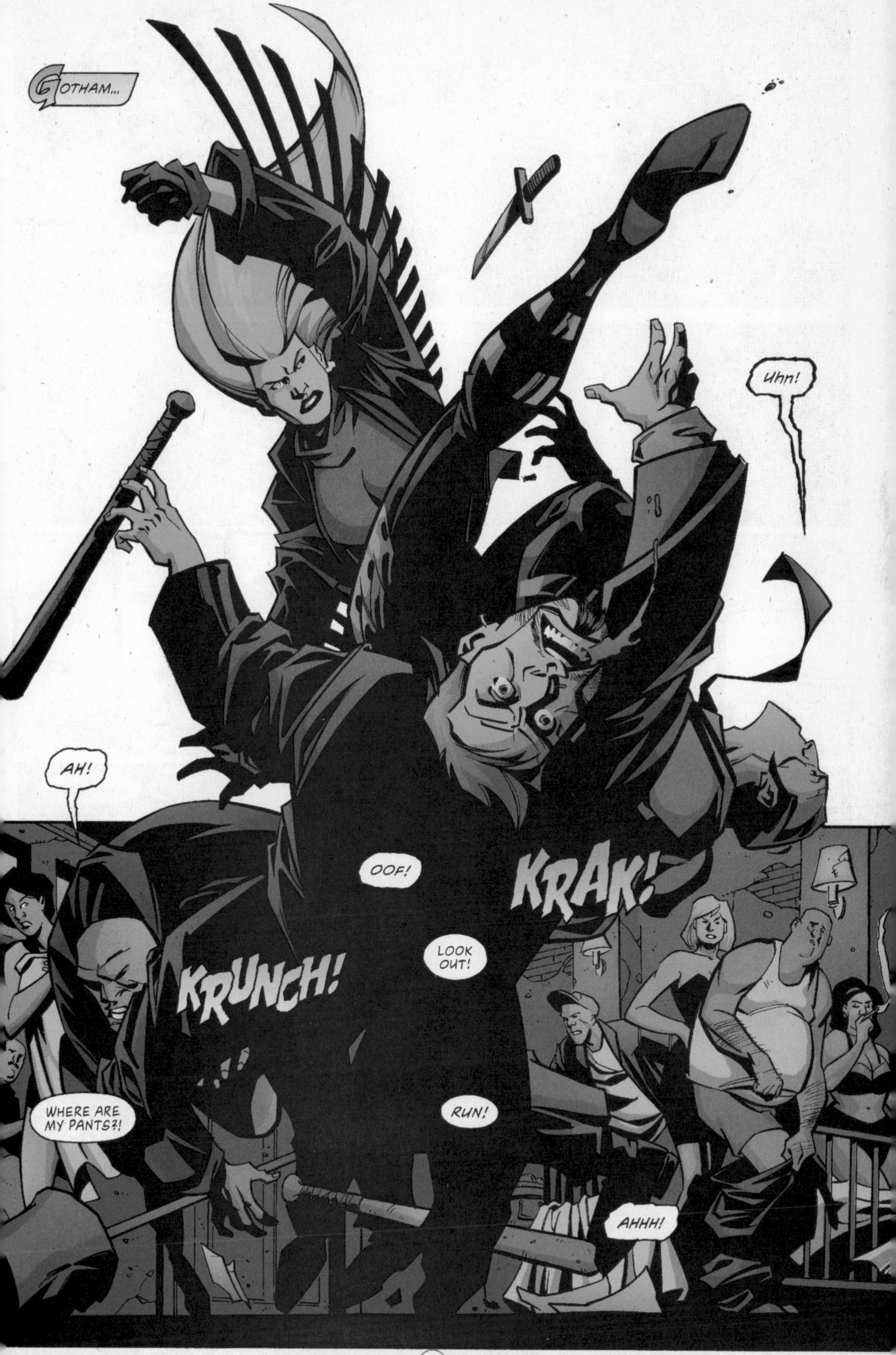
GOTHAM...
Uhn!
AH!
OOF!
KRAK!
LOOK OUT!
KRUNCH!
WHERE ARE MY PANTS?!
RUN!
AHHH!

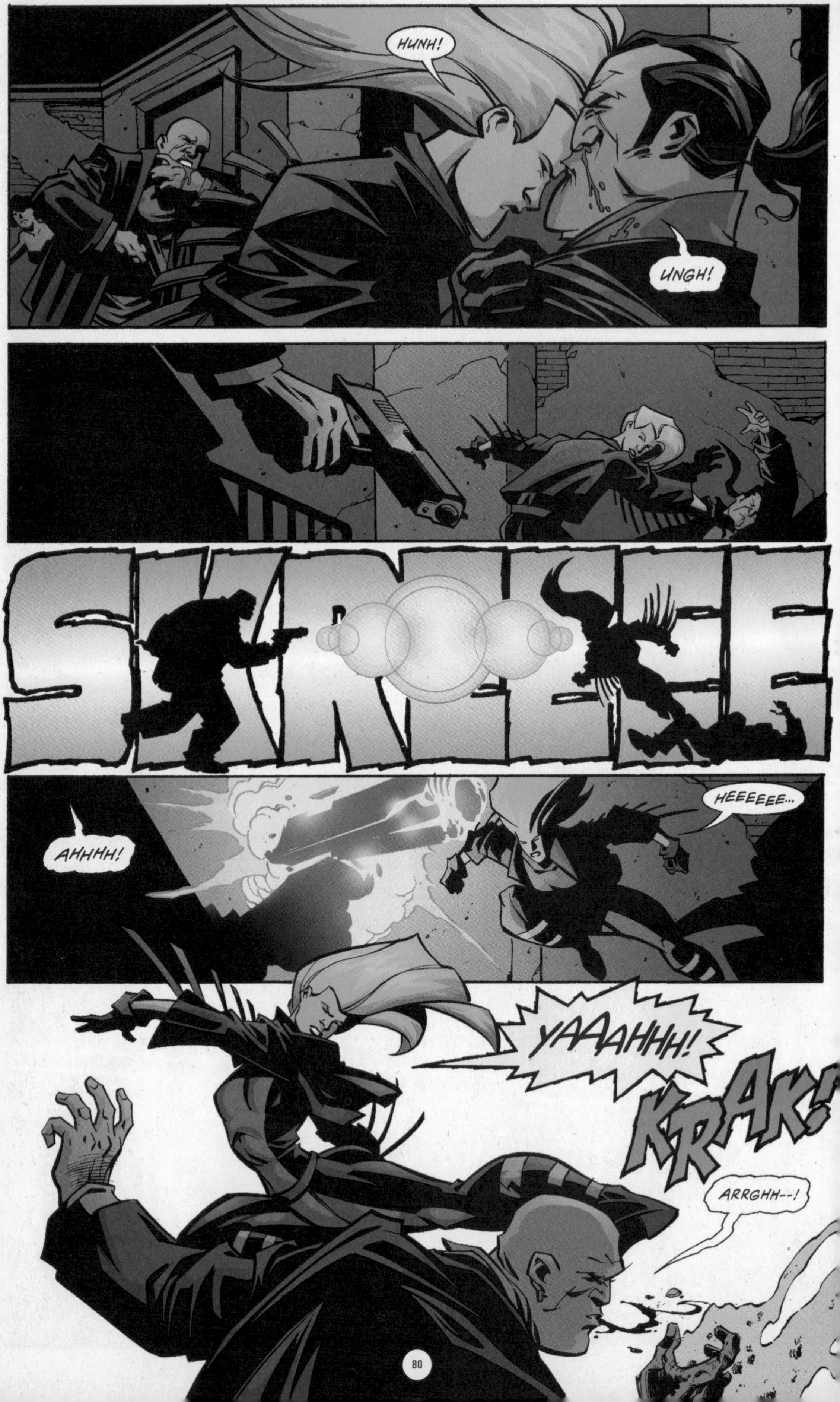
HUNH!
UNGH!
SKREEE
AHHHH!
HEEEEEE...
YAAAHHH!
KRAK!
ARRGHH--!

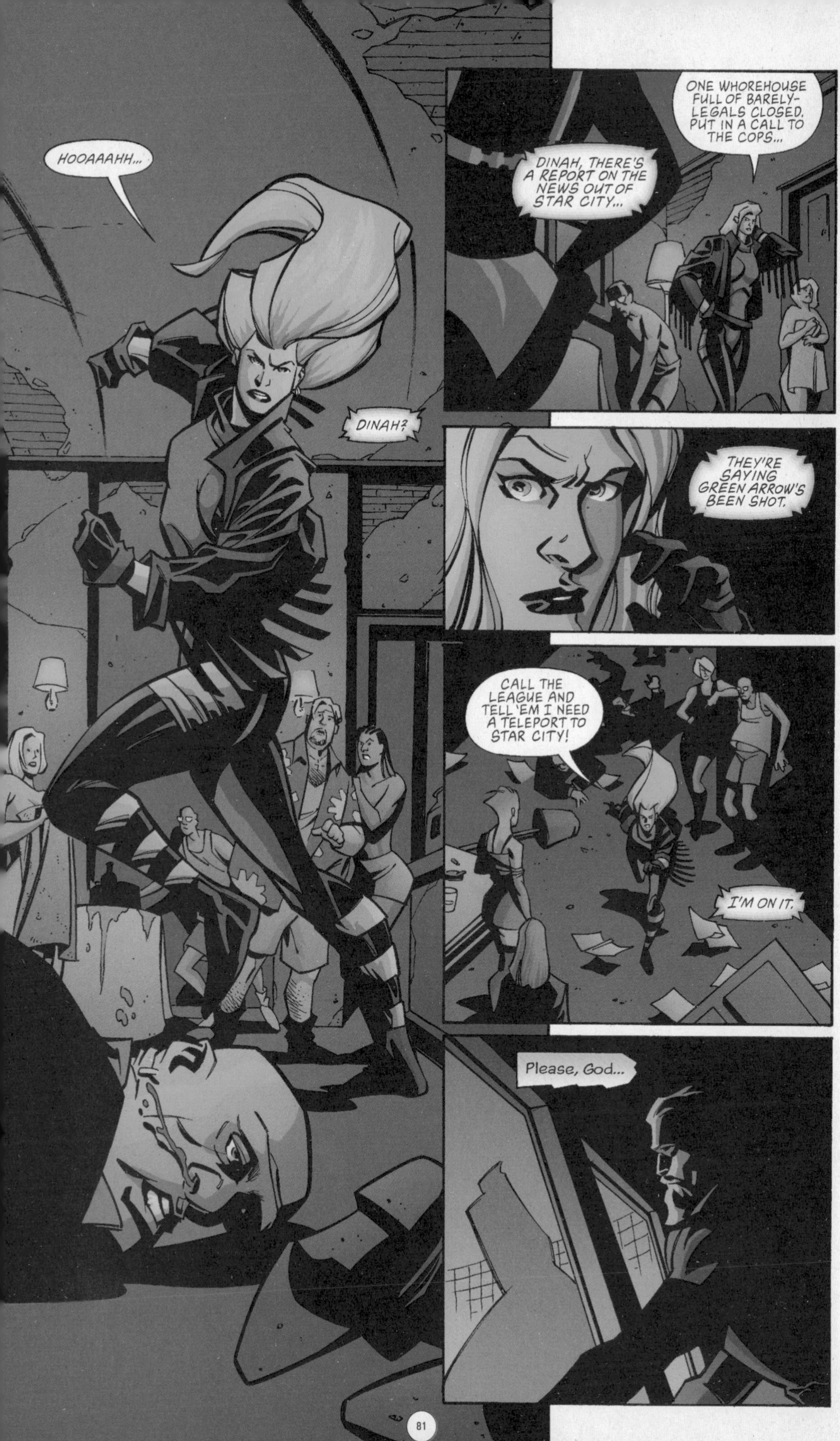

HOOAAAAHH...
DINAH?
DINAH, THERE'S A REPORT ON THE NEWS OUT OF STAR CITY...
ONE WHOREHOUSE FULL OF BARELY-LEGALS CLOSED. PUT IN A CALL TO THE COPS...
THEY'RE SAYING GREEN ARROW'S BEEN SHOT.
CALL THE LEAGUE AND TELL 'EM I NEED A TELEPORT TO STAR CITY!
I'M ON IT.
Please, God...

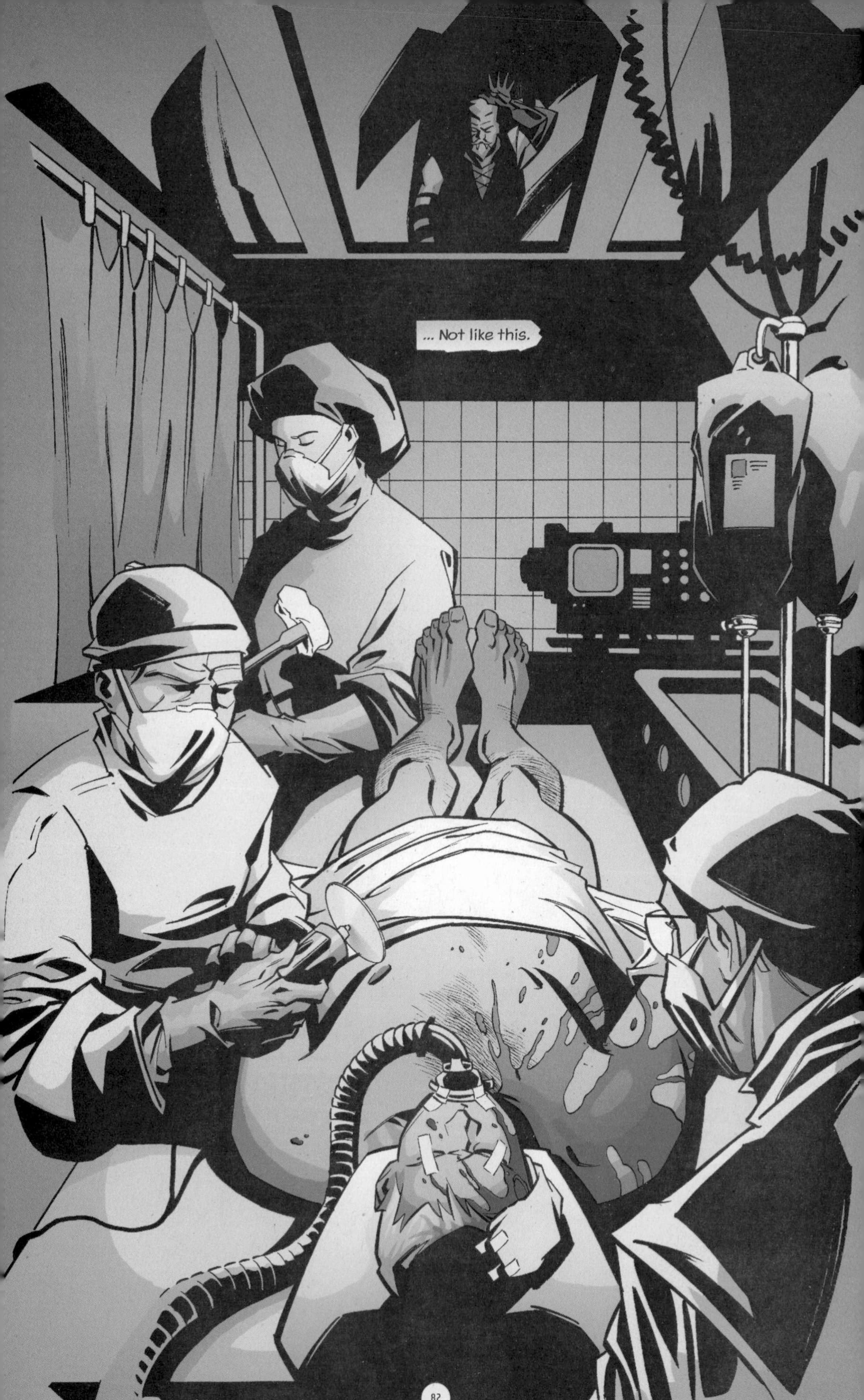
... Not like this.

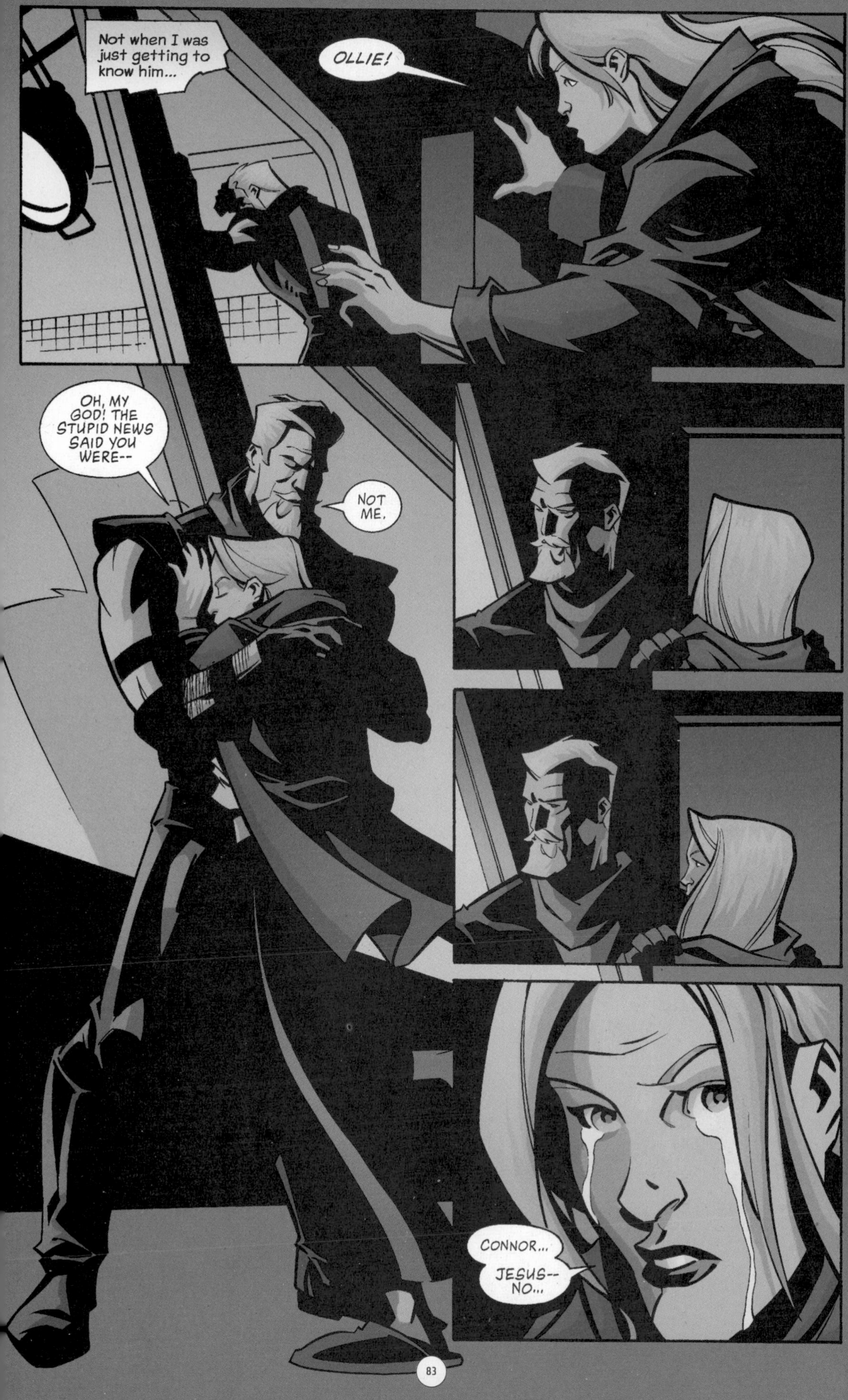
Not when I was just getting to know him...
OLLIE!
OH, MY GOD! THE STUPID NEWS SAID YOU WERE--
NOT ME.
CONNOR...
JESUS-- NO...

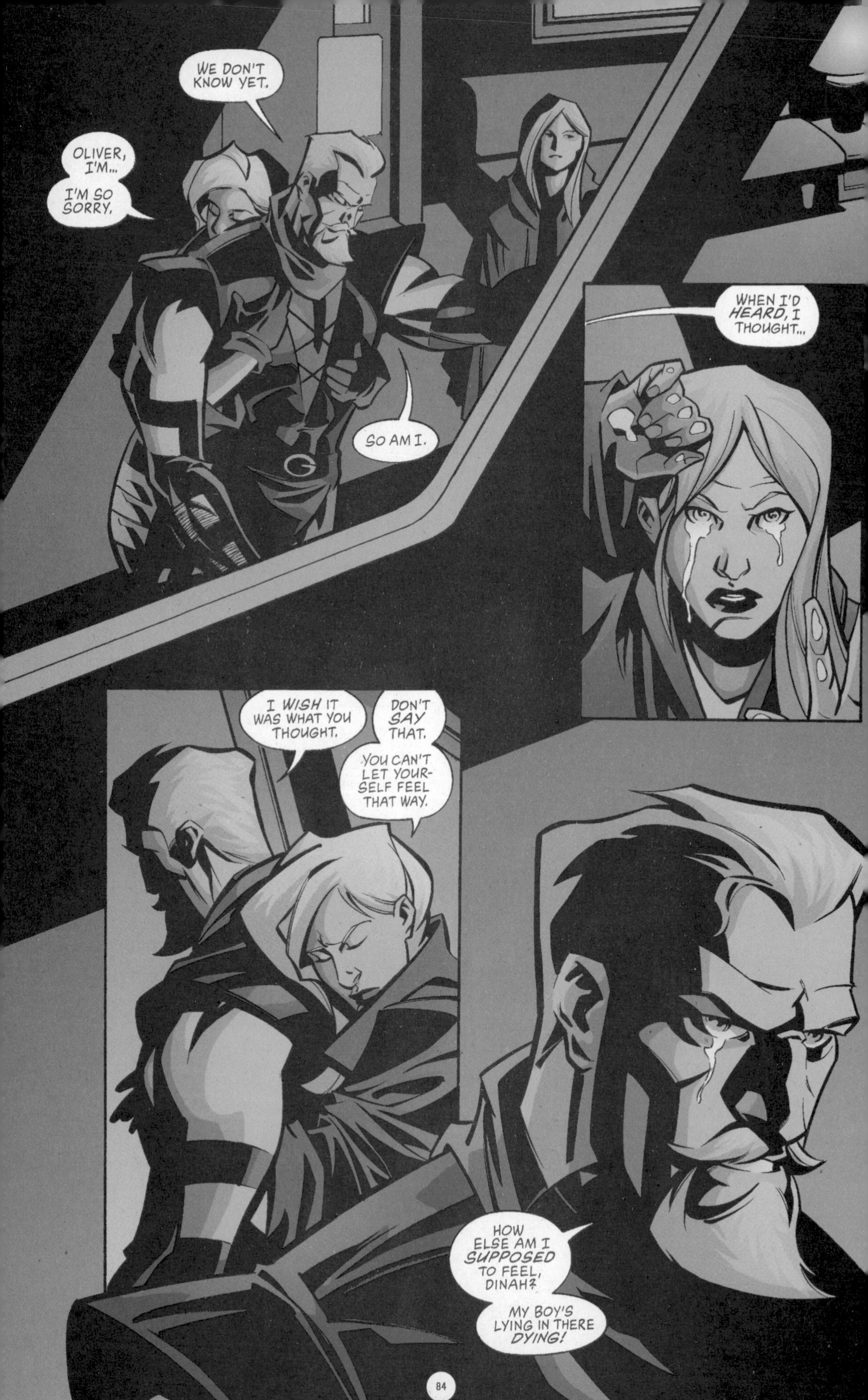

OLIVER, I'M...
I'M SO SORRY.
WE DON'T KNOW YET.
SO AM I.
WHEN I'D HEARD, I THOUGHT...
I WISH IT WAS WHAT YOU THOUGHT.
DON'T SAY THAT.
YOU CAN'T LET YOURSELF FEEL THAT WAY.
HOW ELSE AM I SUPPOSED TO FEEL, DINAH?
MY BOY'S LYING IN THERE DYING!

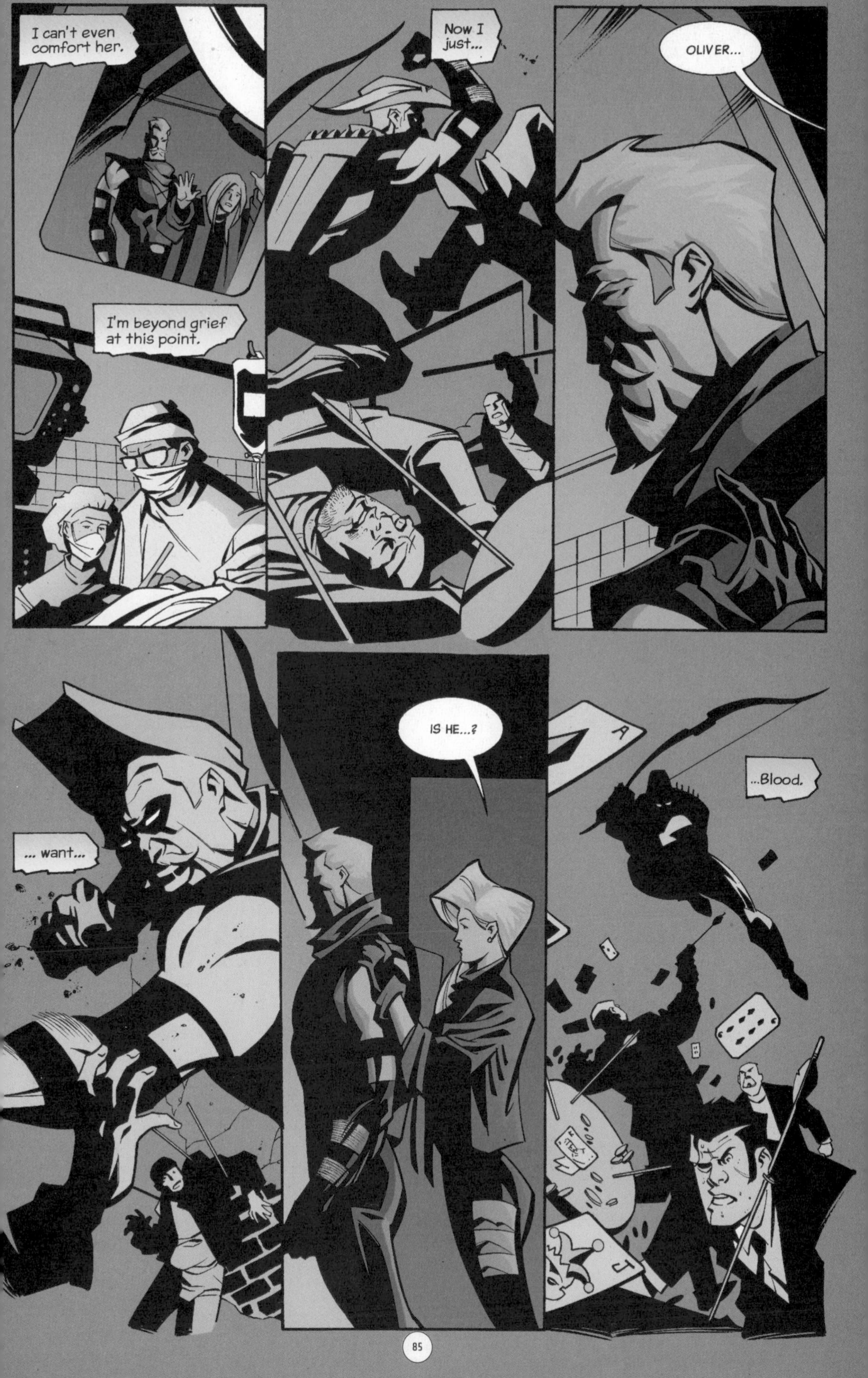
I can't even comfort her.
I'm beyond grief at this point.
Now I just...
OLIVER...
... want...
IS HE...?
...Blood.

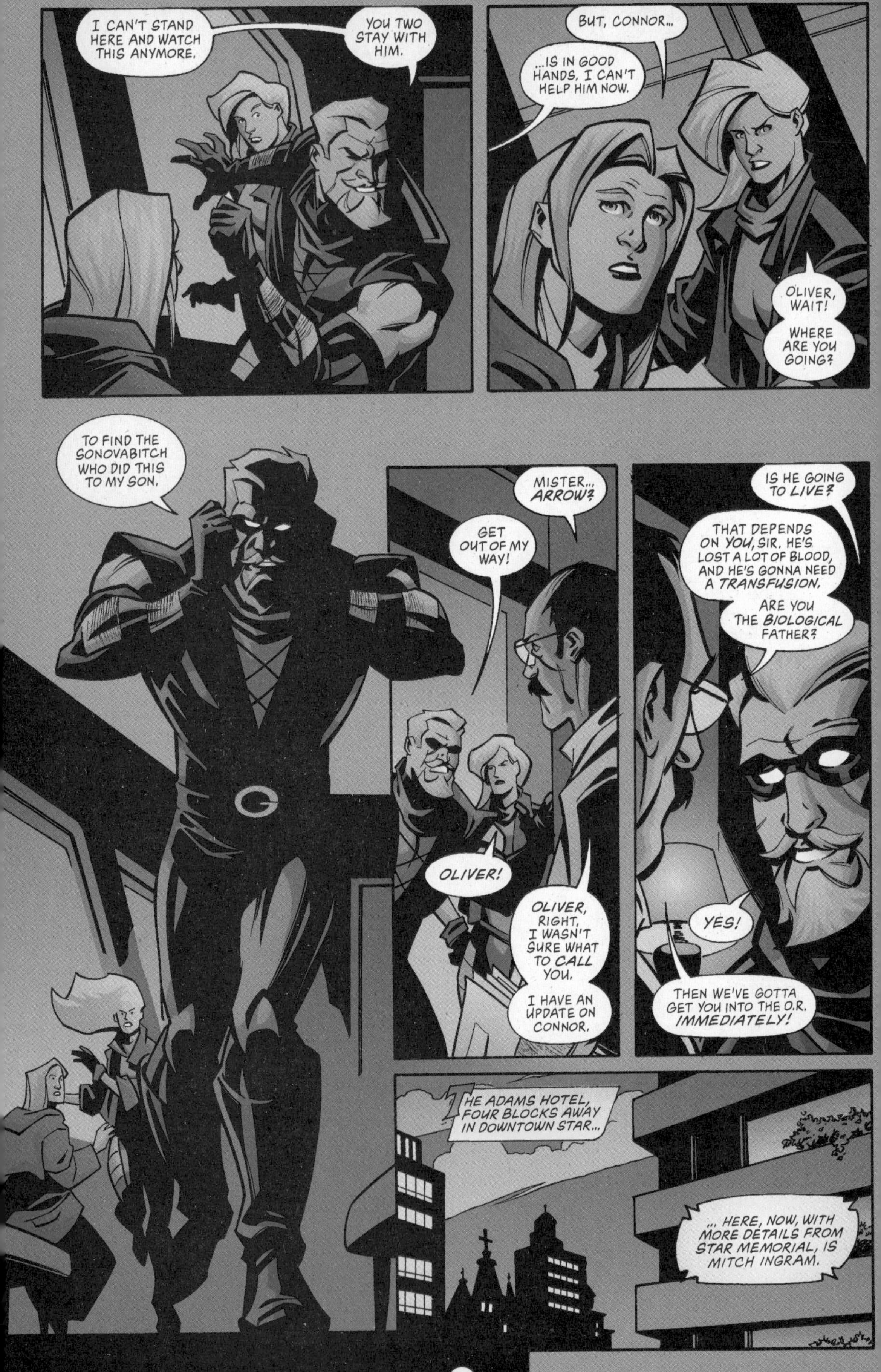

I CAN'T STAND HERE AND WATCH THIS ANYMORE.
YOU TWO STAY WITH HIM.
BUT, CONNOR...
...IS IN GOOD HANDS. I CAN'T HELP HIM NOW.
OLIVER, WAIT!
WHERE ARE YOU GOING?
TO FIND THE SONOVABITCH WHO DID THIS TO MY SON.
MISTER... ARROW?
GET OUT OF MY WAY!
OLIVER!
OLIVER, RIGHT, I WASN'T SURE WHAT TO CALL YOU.
I HAVE AN UPDATE ON CONNOR.
IS HE GOING TO LIVE?
THAT DEPENDS ON YOU, SIR. HE'S LOST A LOT OF BLOOD, AND HE'S GONNA NEED A TRANSFUSION.
ARE YOU THE BIOLOGICAL FATHER?
YES!
THEN WE'VE GOTTA GET YOU INTO THE O.R. IMMEDIATELY!
THE ADAMS HOTEL, FOUR BLOCKS AWAY IN DOWNTOWN STAR...
... HERE, NOW, WITH MORE DETAILS FROM STAR MEMORIAL, IS MITCH INGRAM.

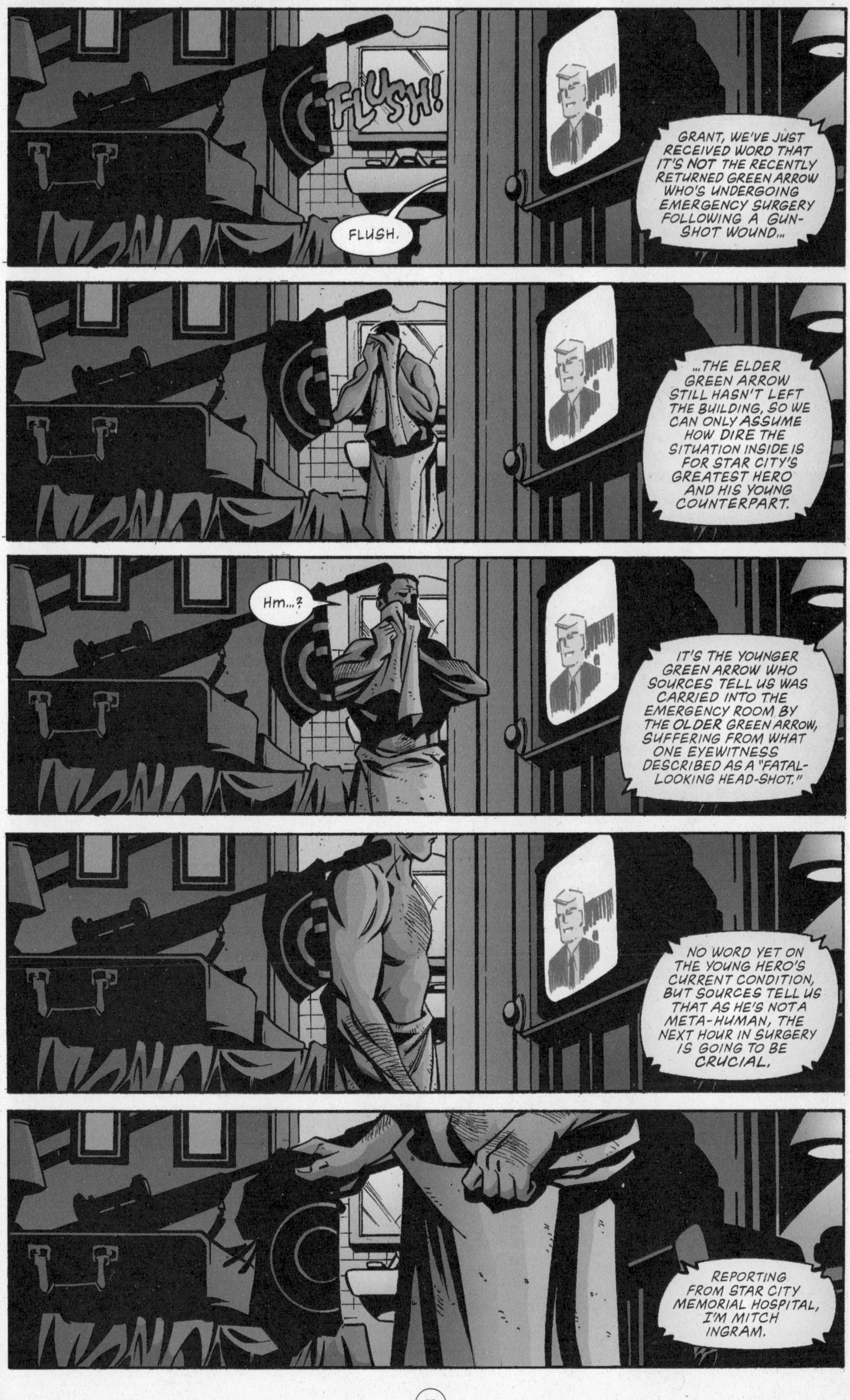
FLUSH!
FLUSH.
GRANT, WE'VE JUST RECEIVED WORD THAT IT'S NOT THE RECENTLY RETURNED GREEN ARROW WHO'S UNDERGOING EMERGENCY SURGERY FOLLOWING A GUN-SHOT WOUND...
...THE ELDER GREEN ARROW STILL HASN'T LEFT THE BUILDING, SO WE CAN ONLY ASSUME HOW DIRE THE SITUATION INSIDE IS FOR STAR CITY'S GREATEST HERO AND HIS YOUNG COUNTERPART.
Hm...?
IT'S THE YOUNGER GREEN ARROW WHO SOURCES TELL US WAS CARRIED INTO THE EMERGENCY ROOM BY THE OLDER GREEN ARROW, SUFFERING FROM WHAT ONE EYEWITNESS DESCRIBED AS A "FATAL-LOOKING HEAD-SHOT."
NO WORD YET ON THE YOUNG HERO'S CURRENT CONDITION, BUT SOURCES TELL US THAT AS HE'S NOT A META-HUMAN, THE NEXT HOUR IN SURGERY IS GOING TO BE CRUCIAL.
REPORTING FROM STAR CITY MEMORIAL HOSPITAL, I'M MITCH INGRAM.

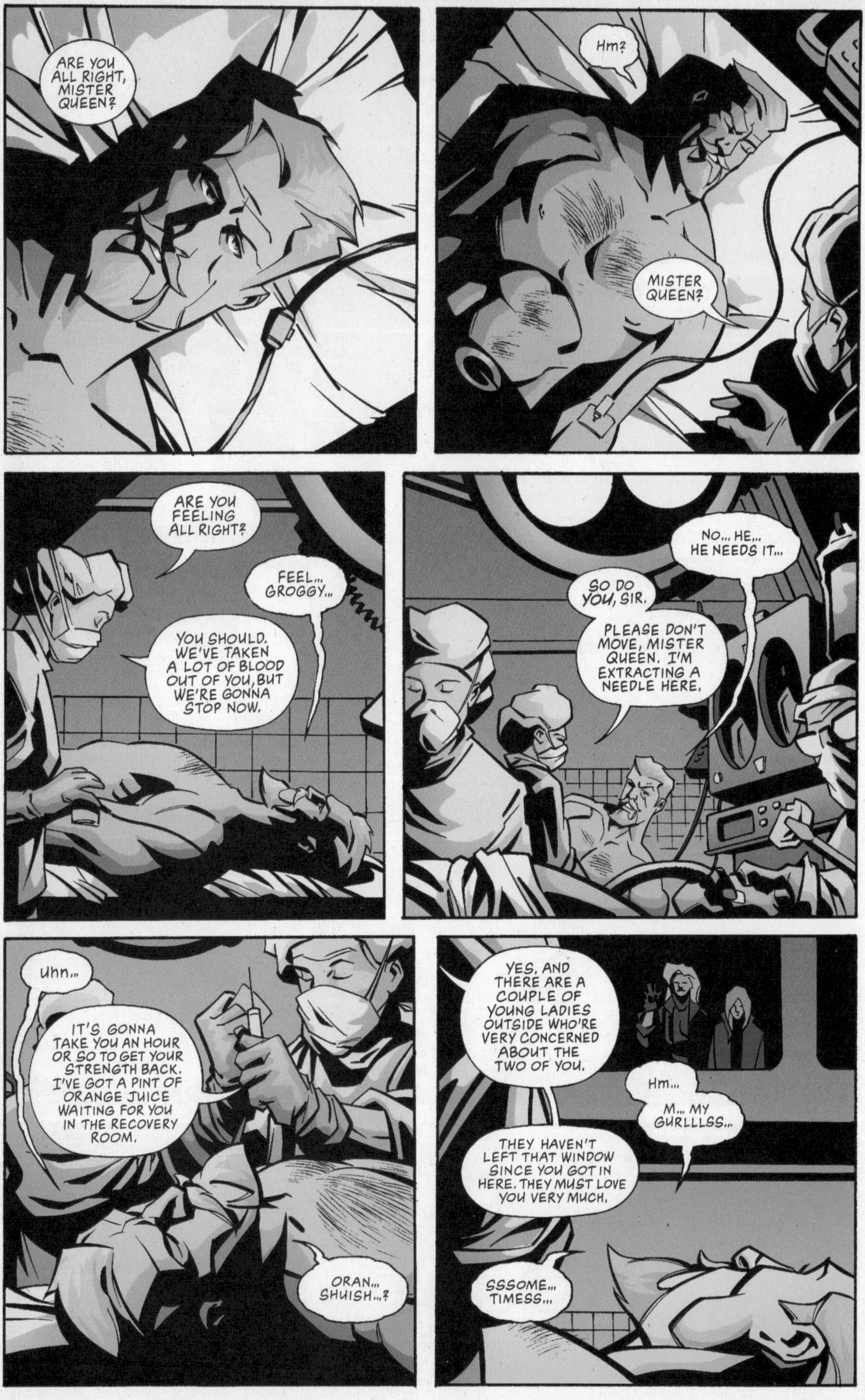
ARE YOU ALL RIGHT, MISTER QUEEN?
Hm?
MISTER QUEEN?
ARE YOU FEELING ALL RIGHT?
FEEL... GROGGY...
YOU SHOULD. WE'VE TAKEN A LOT OF BLOOD OUT OF YOU, BUT WE'RE GONNA STOP NOW.
NO... HE... HE NEEDS IT...
SO DO YOU, SIR.
PLEASE DON'T MOVE, MISTER QUEEN. I'M EXTRACTING A NEEDLE HERE.
Uhn...
IT'S GONNA TAKE YOU AN HOUR OR SO TO GET YOUR STRENGTH BACK. I'VE GOT A PINT OF ORANGE JUICE WAITING FOR YOU IN THE RECOVERY ROOM.
ORAN... SHUISH...?
YES, AND THERE ARE A COUPLE OF YOUNG LADIES OUTSIDE WHO'RE VERY CONCERNED ABOUT THE TWO OF YOU.
Hm...
M... MY GURLLLSS...
THEY HAVEN'T LEFT THAT WINDOW SINCE YOU GOT IN HERE. THEY MUST LOVE YOU VERY MUCH.
SSSOME... TIMESS...

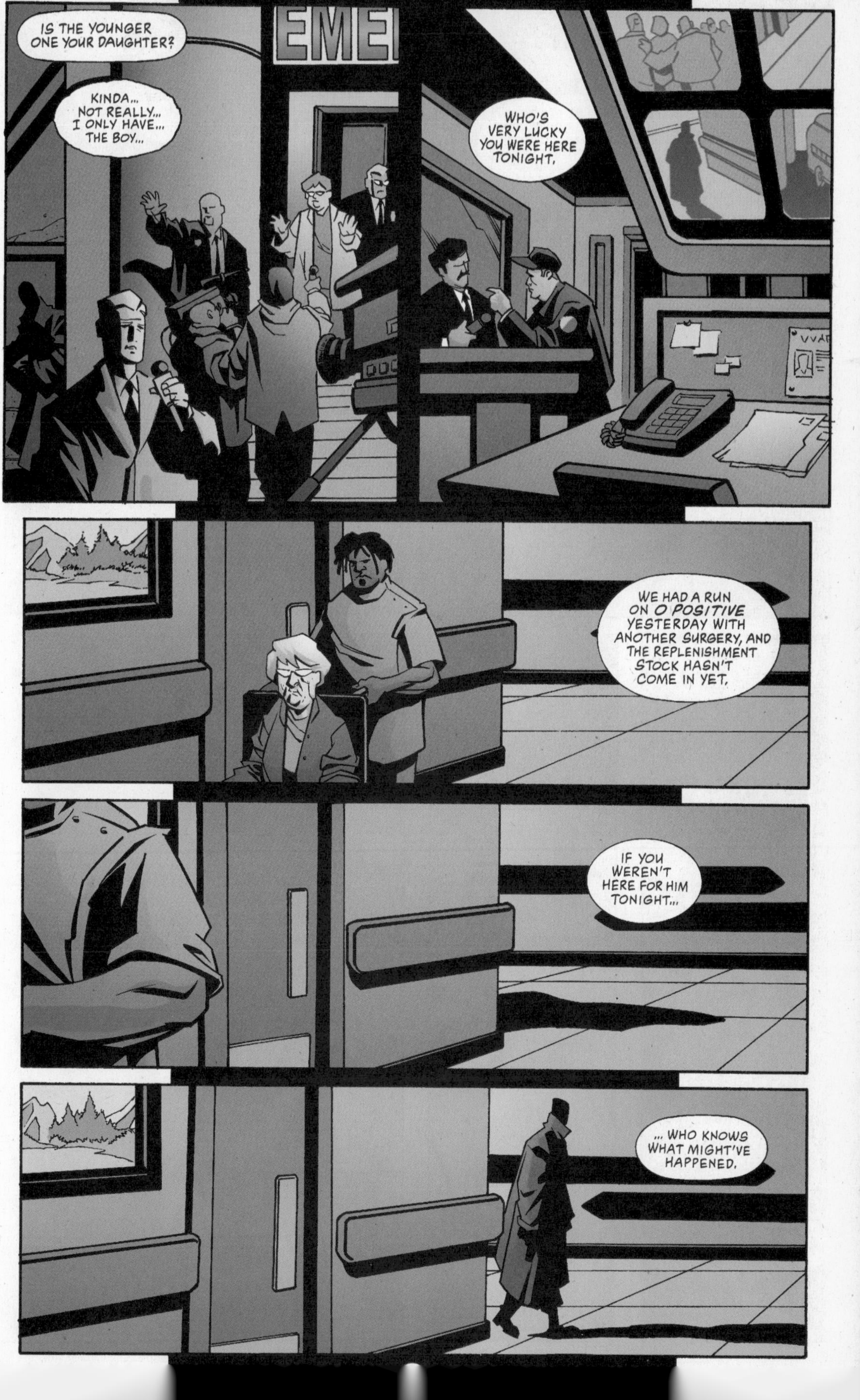
IS THE YOUNGER ONE YOUR DAUGHTER?
KINDA... NOT REALLY... I ONLY HAVE... THE BOY...
EME
WHO'S VERY LUCKY YOU WERE HERE TONIGHT.
WE HAD A RUN ON O POSITIVE YESTERDAY WITH ANOTHER SURGERY, AND THE REPLENISHMENT STOCK HASN'T COME IN YET.
IF YOU WEREN'T HERE FOR HIM TONIGHT...
... WHO KNOWS WHAT MIGHT'VE HAPPENED.

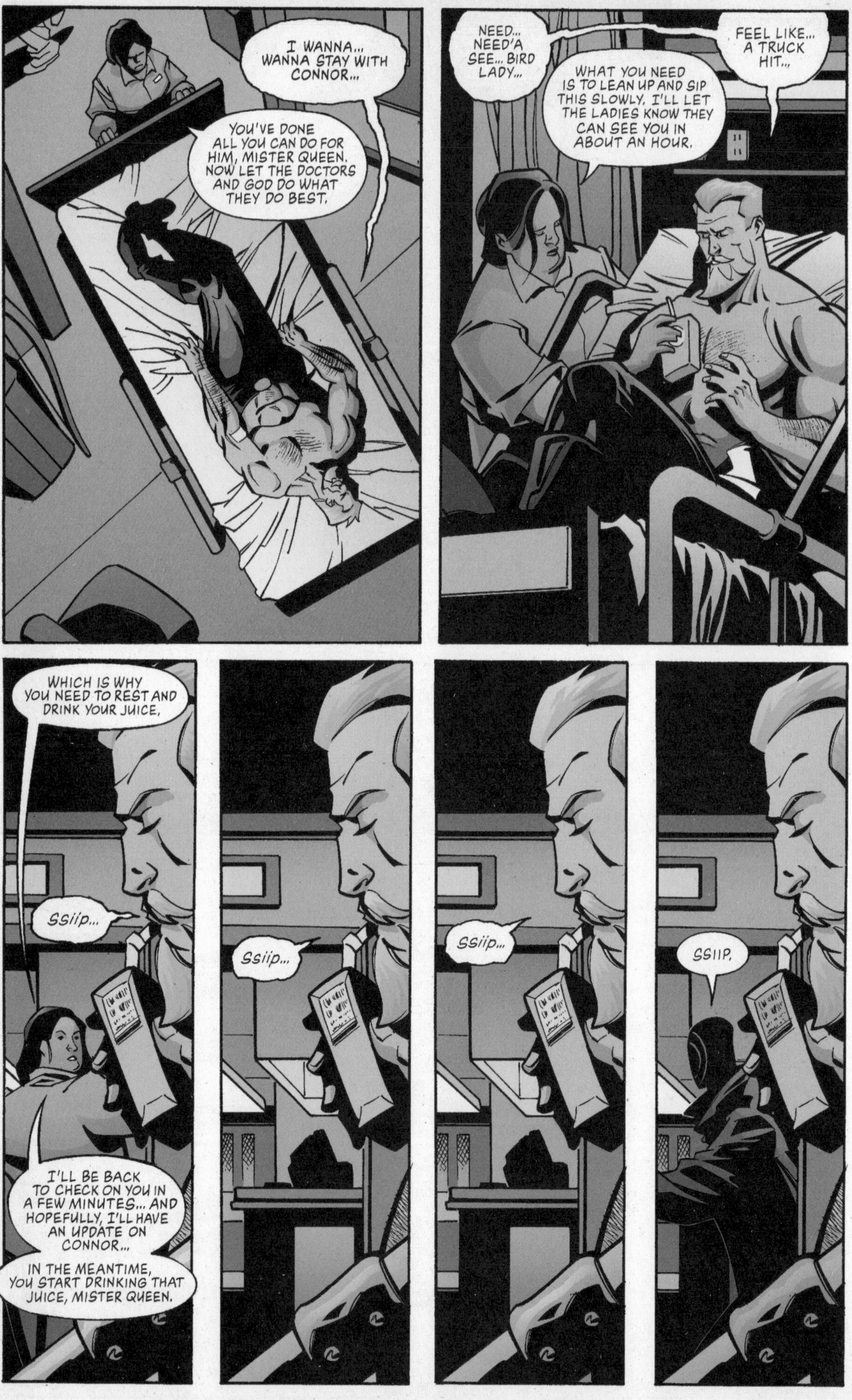
I WANNA... WANNA STAY WITH CONNOR...
YOU'VE DONE ALL YOU CAN DO FOR HIM, MISTER QUEEN. NOW LET THE DOCTORS AND GOD DO WHAT THEY DO BEST.
NEED... NEED'A SEE... BIRD LADY...
FEEL LIKE... A TRUCK HIT...
WHAT YOU NEED IS TO LEAN UP AND SIP THIS SLOWLY. I'LL LET THE LADIES KNOW THEY CAN SEE YOU IN ABOUT AN HOUR.
WHICH IS WHY YOU NEED TO REST AND DRINK YOUR JUICE.
Ssiip...
I'LL BE BACK TO CHECK ON YOU IN A FEW MINUTES... AND HOPEFULLY, I'LL HAVE AN UPDATE ON CONNOR...
IN THE MEANTIME, YOU START DRINKING THAT JUICE, MISTER QUEEN.
Ssiip...
Ssiip...
SSIIP.

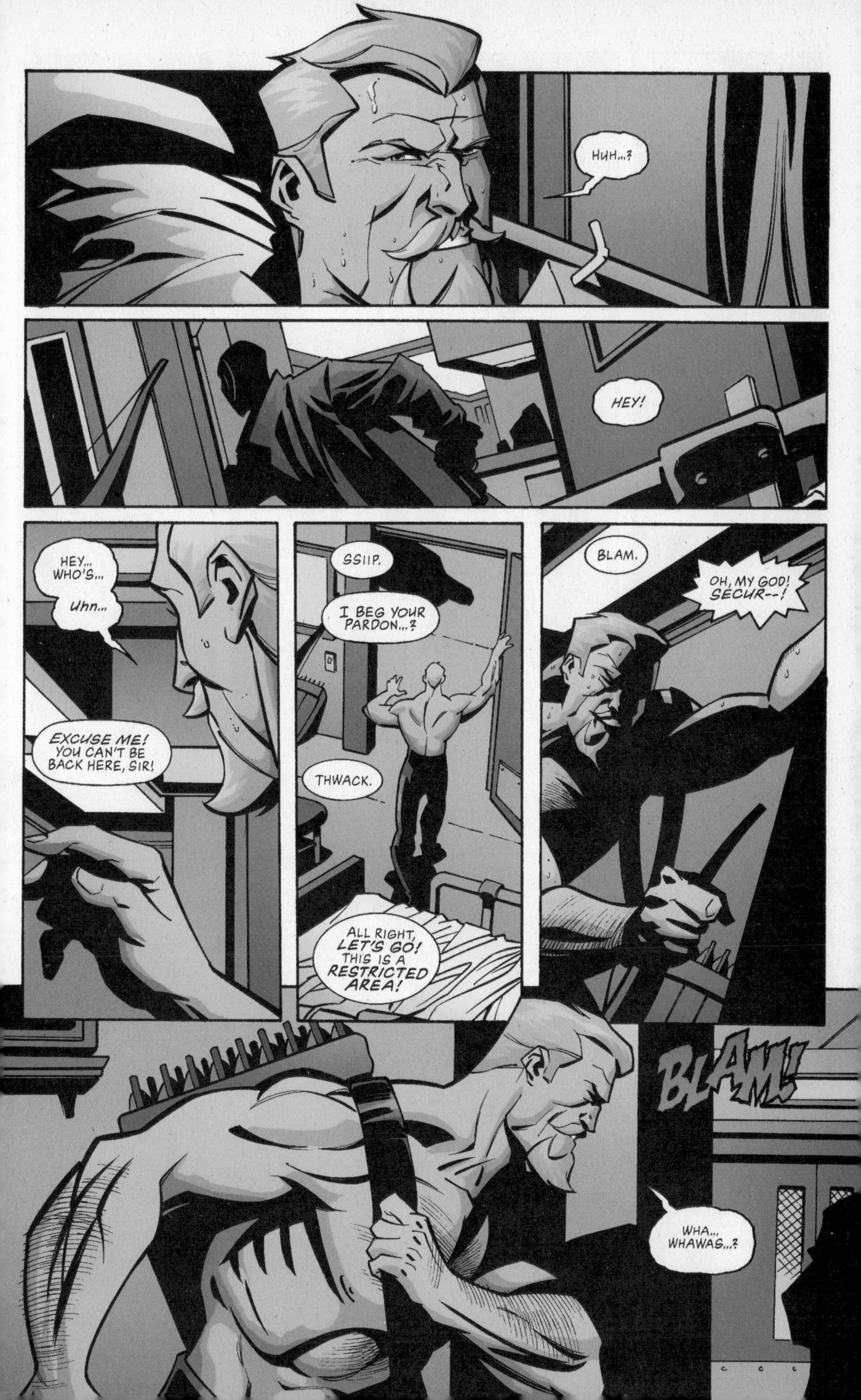
HUH...?
HEY!
HEY... WHO'S...
Uhn...
EXCUSE ME! YOU CAN'T BE BACK HERE, SIR!
SSIIP.
I BEG YOUR PARDON...?
THWACK.
ALL RIGHT, LET'S GO! THIS IS A RESTRICTED AREA!
BLAM.
OH, MY GOD! SECUR--!
BLAM!
WHA... WHAWAS...?

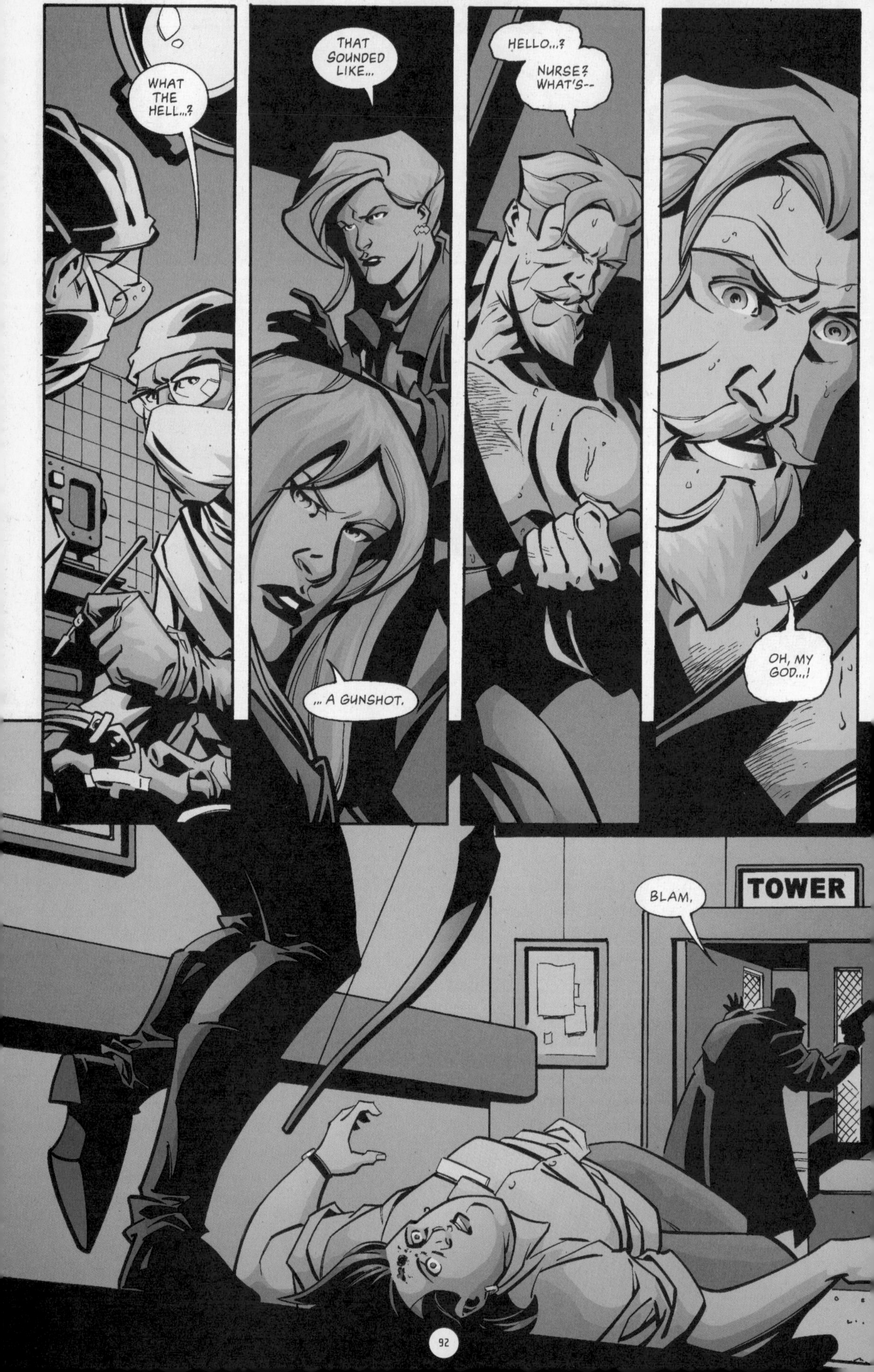
WHAT THE HELL...?
THAT SOUNDED LIKE...
... A GUNSHOT.
HELLO...?
NURSE? WHAT'S--
OH, MY GOD...!
TOWER
BLAM.

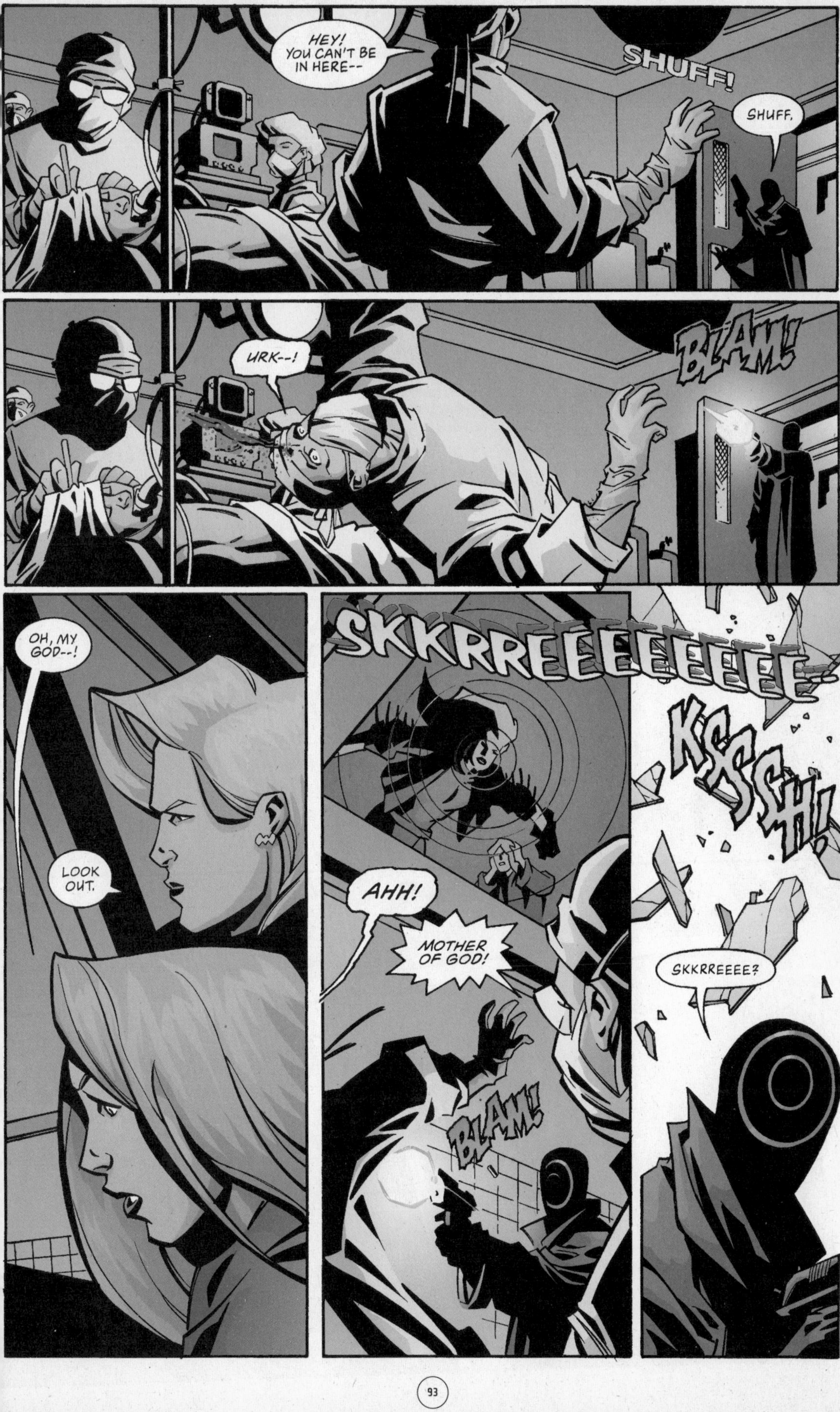

HEY! YOU CAN'T BE IN HERE--
SHUFF!
SHUFF.
URK--!
BLAM!
OH, MY GOD--!
LOOK OUT.
SKKRREEEEEEEEEE-
KSSSH!
AHH!
MOTHER OF GOD!
SKKRREEEE?
BLAM!

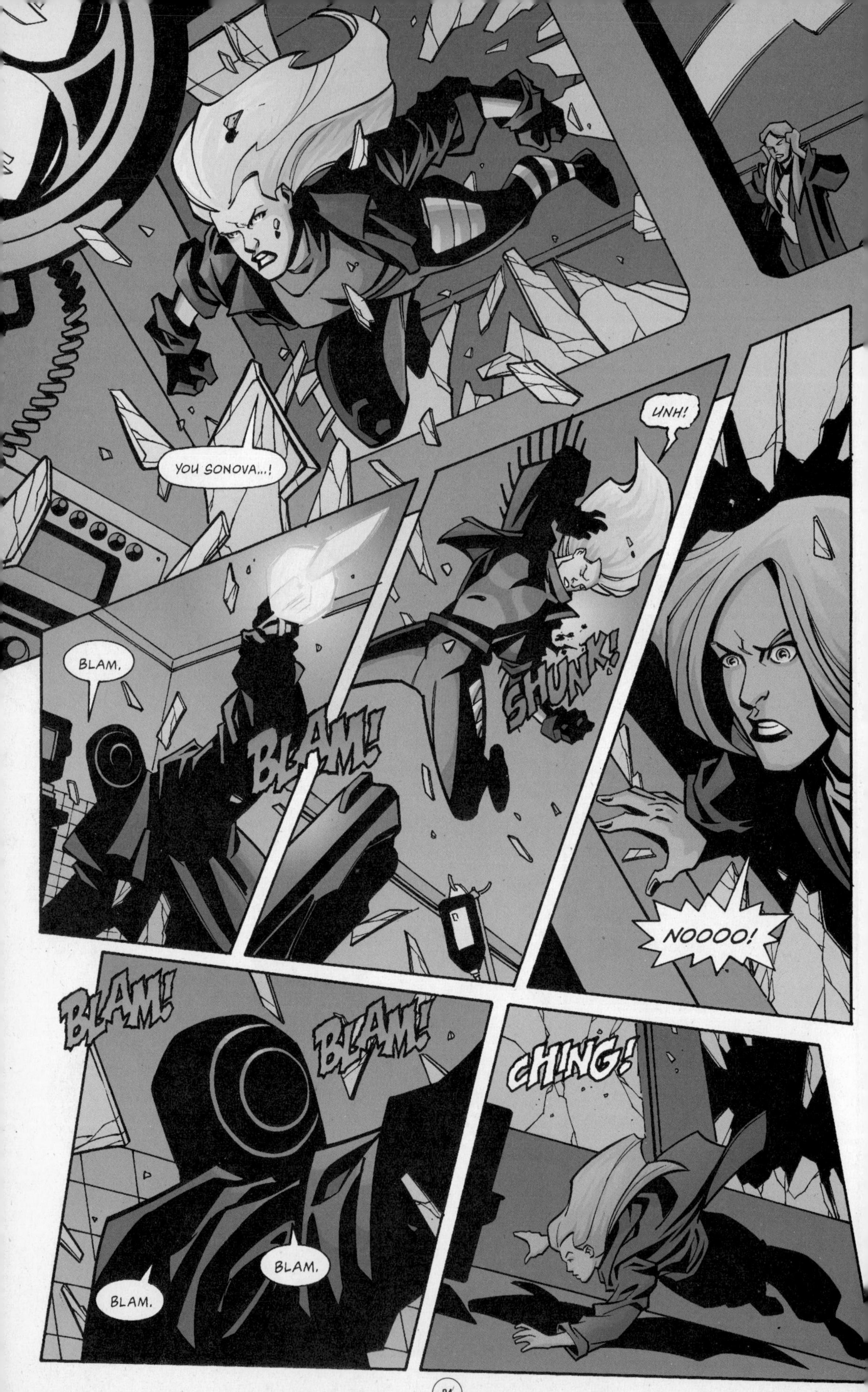

YOU SONOVA...!
BLAM.
BLAM!
UNH!
SHUNK!
NOOOO!
BLAM!
BLAM!
BLAM.
BLAM.
CHING!

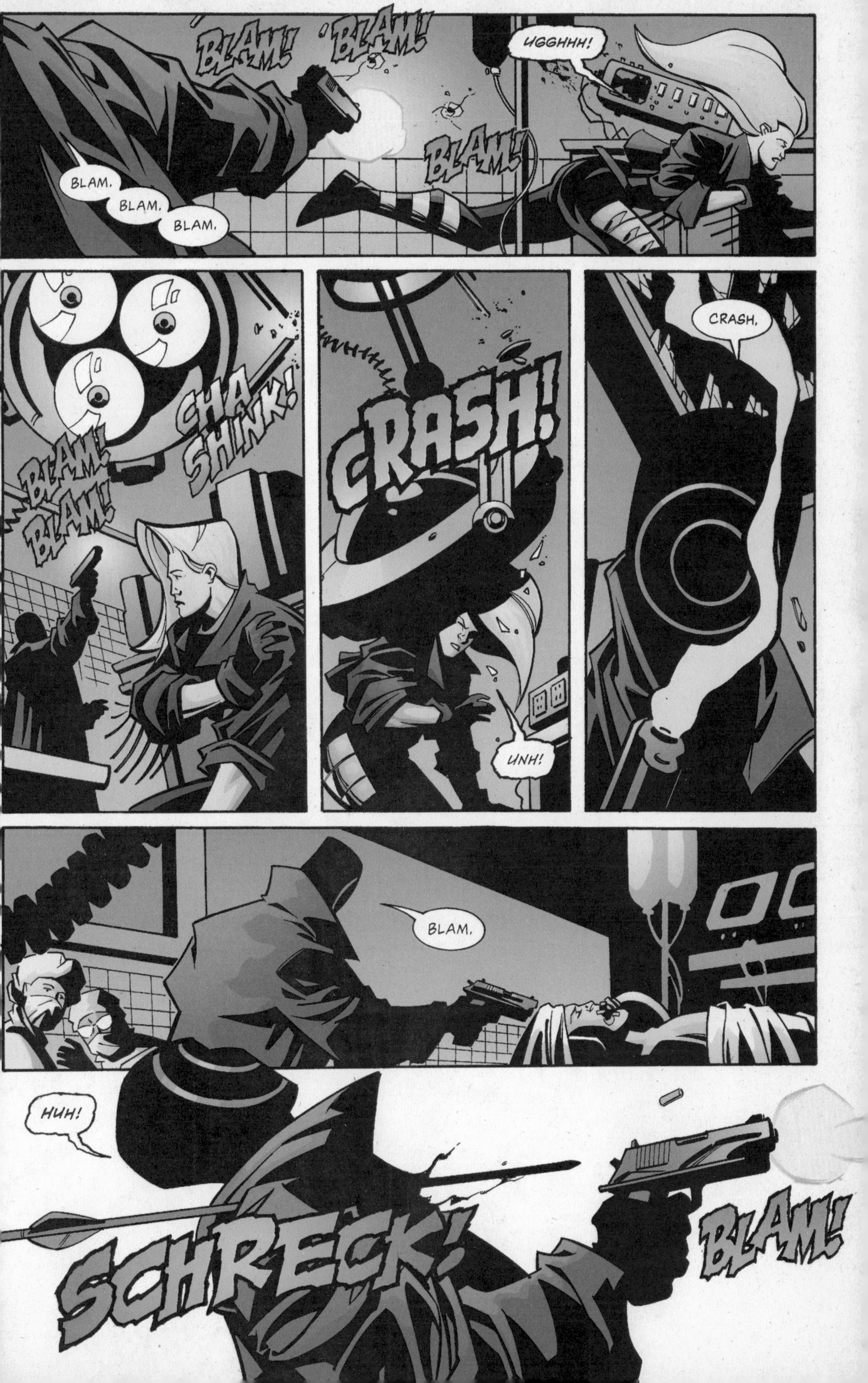
BLAM!
BLAM!
UGGHHH!
BLAM!
BLAM.
BLAM.
BLAM.
CHA SHINK!
BLAM! BLAM!
CRASH!
UNH!
CRASH.
BLAM.
HUH!
SCHRECK!
BLAM!

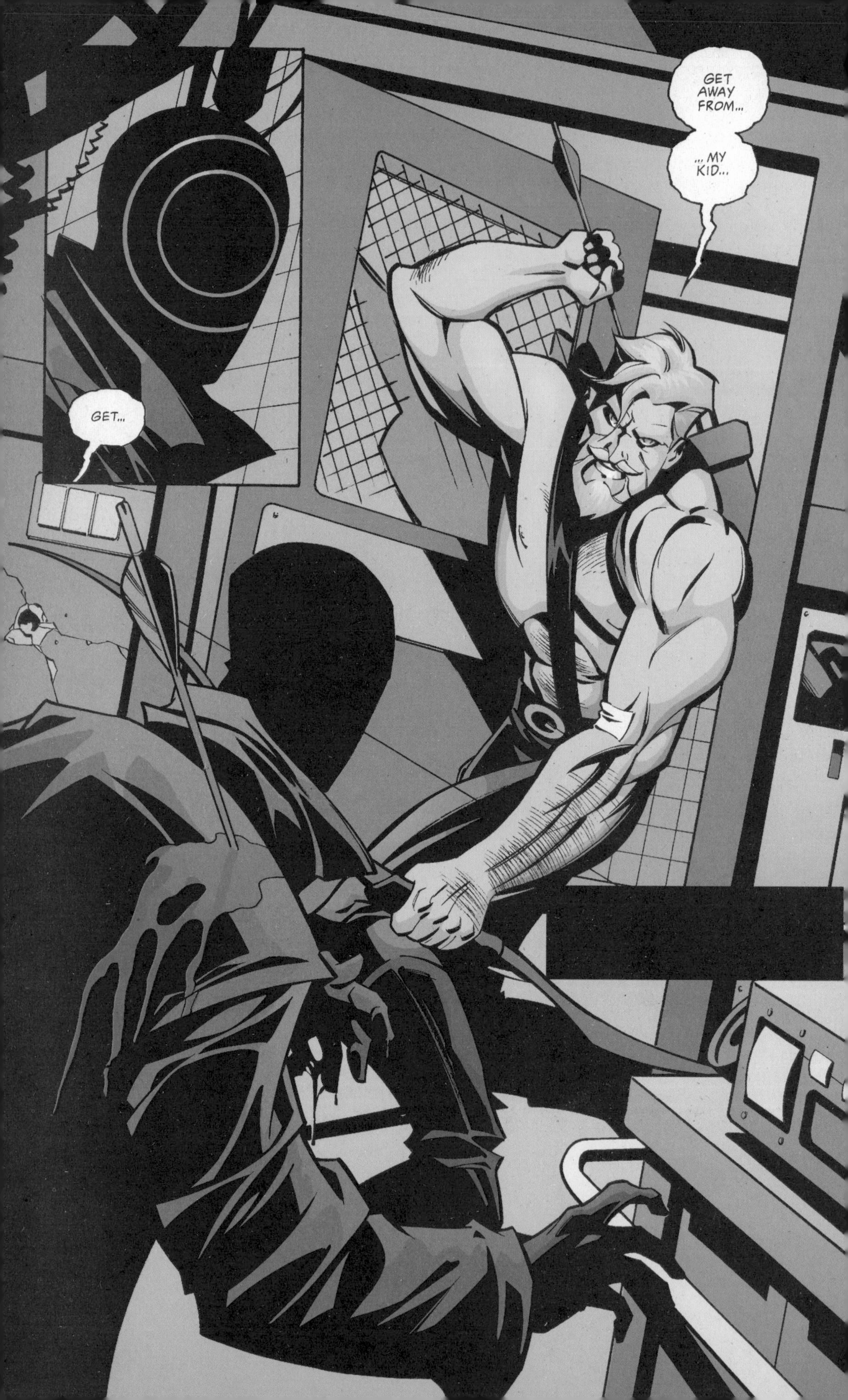
GET AWAY FROM...
... MY KID...
GET...

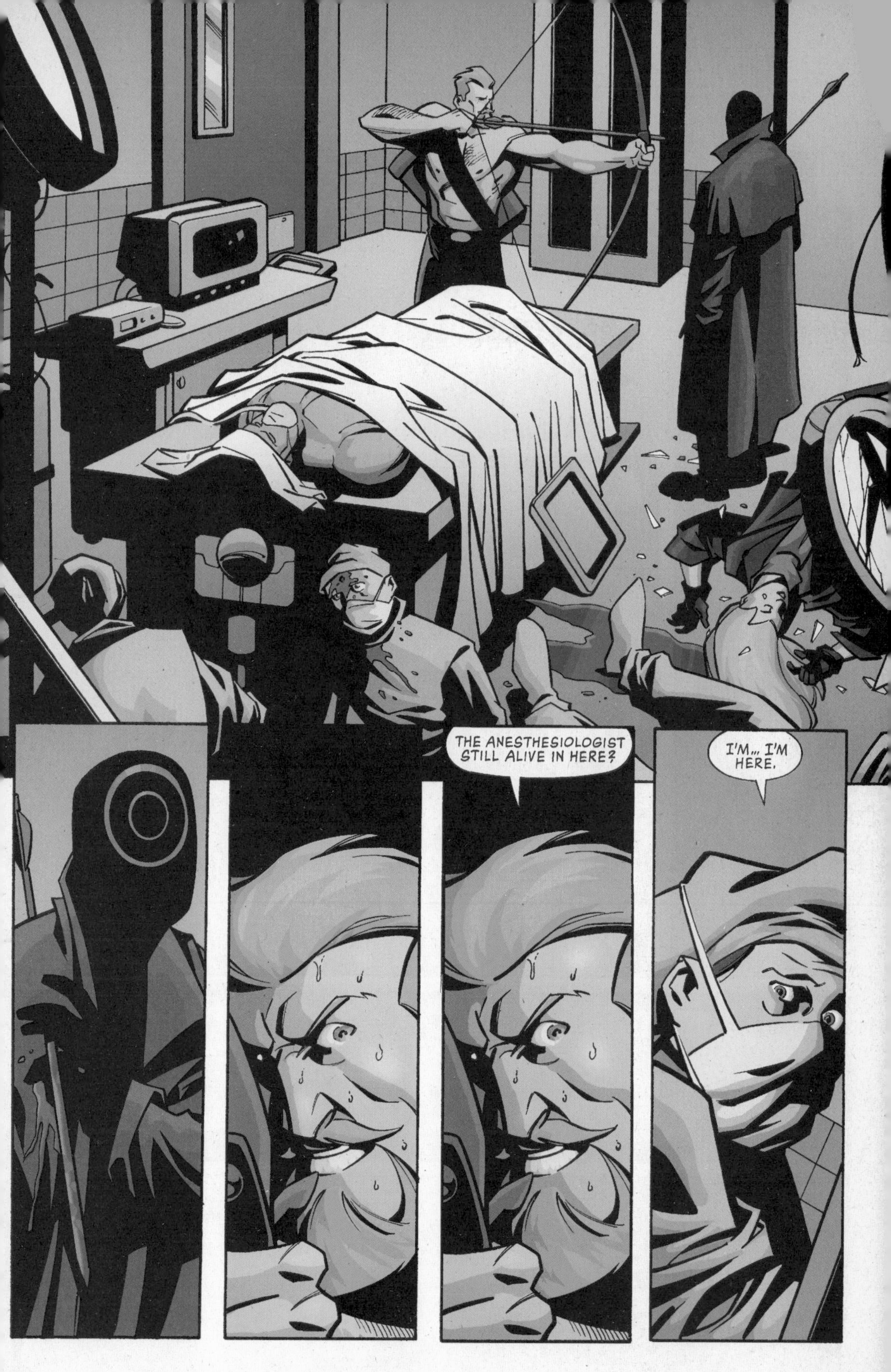
THE ANESTHESIOLOGIST STILL ALIVE IN HERE?
I'M... I'M HERE.

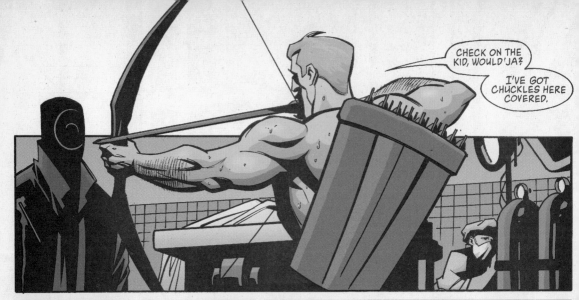

CHECK ON THE KID, WOULD'JA?

I'VE GOT CHUCKLES HERE COVERED.

NOW!

ANY NEURO-SURGEONS STILL AROUND?

HOW'S HE DOING?

Y-YES...

THE KID.

WE WERE, uh... WE WERE TRYING TO EXTRACT THE BULLET WHEN, uh...

WHEN ALL OF... ALL OF THIS HAPPENED.

SO, HE'S NOT OUT OF THE WOODS?

NO, HE'S NOT.

PLEASE... GO BACK TO WORK ON HIM.

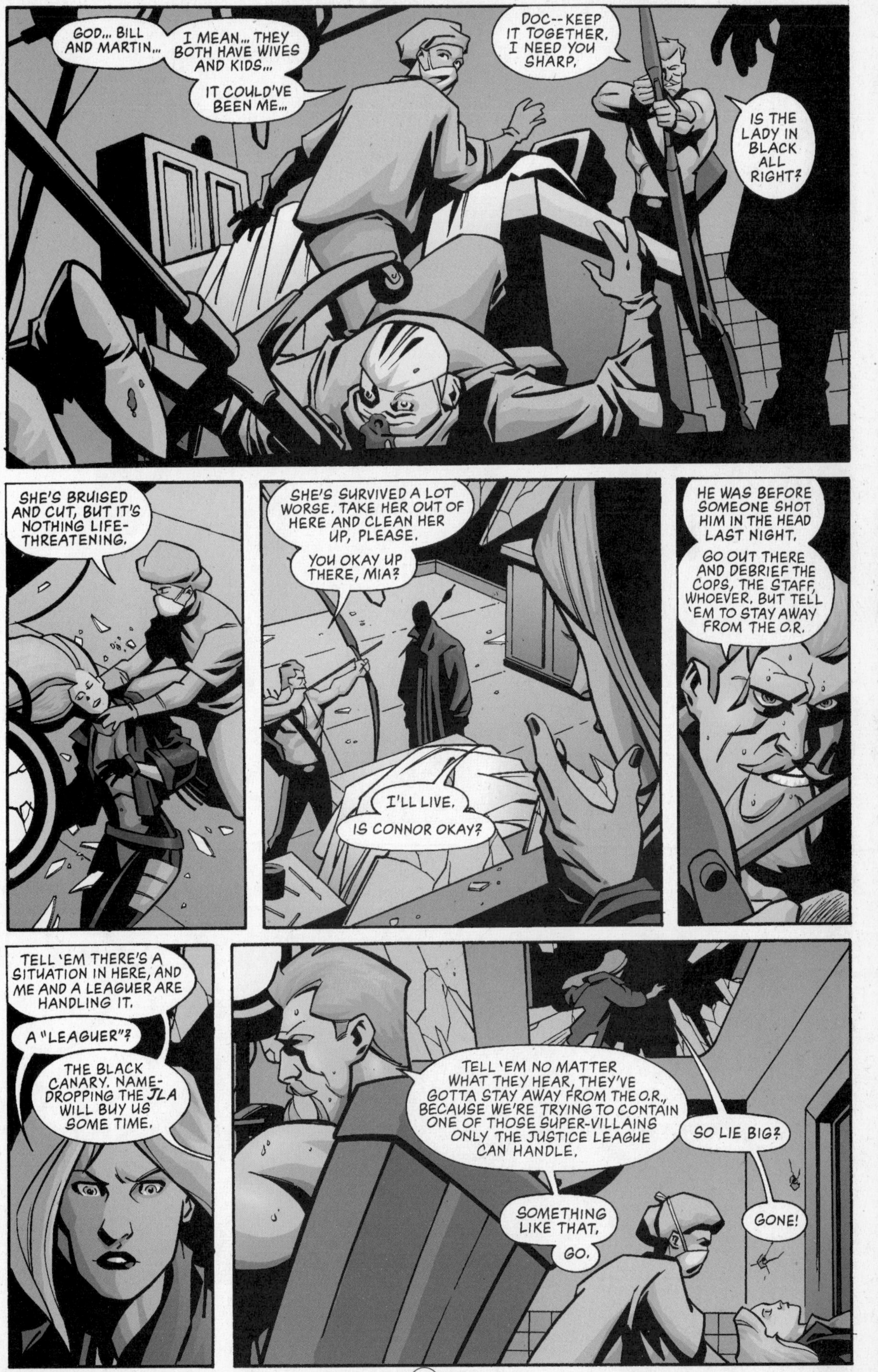
GOD... BILL AND MARTIN...
I MEAN... THEY BOTH HAVE WIVES AND KIDS...
IT COULD'VE BEEN ME...
DOC--KEEP IT TOGETHER. I NEED YOU SHARP.
IS THE LADY IN BLACK ALL RIGHT?
SHE'S BRUISED AND CUT, BUT IT'S NOTHING LIFE-THREATENING.
SHE'S SURVIVED A LOT WORSE. TAKE HER OUT OF HERE AND CLEAN HER UP, PLEASE.
YOU OKAY UP THERE, MIA?
I'LL LIVE.
IS CONNOR OKAY?
HE WAS BEFORE SOMEONE SHOT HIM IN THE HEAD LAST NIGHT.
GO OUT THERE AND DEBRIEF THE COPS, THE STAFF, WHOEVER. BUT TELL 'EM TO STAY AWAY FROM THE O.R.
TELL 'EM THERE'S A SITUATION IN HERE, AND ME AND A LEAGUER ARE HANDLING IT.
A "LEAGUER"?
THE BLACK CANARY. NAME-DROPPING THE JLA WILL BUY US SOME TIME.
TELL 'EM NO MATTER WHAT THEY HEAR, THEY'VE GOTTA STAY AWAY FROM THE O.R., BECAUSE WE'RE TRYING TO CONTAIN ONE OF THOSE SUPER-VILLAINS ONLY THE JUSTICE LEAGUE CAN HANDLE.
SO LIE BIG?
SOMETHING LIKE THAT.
GO.
GONE!

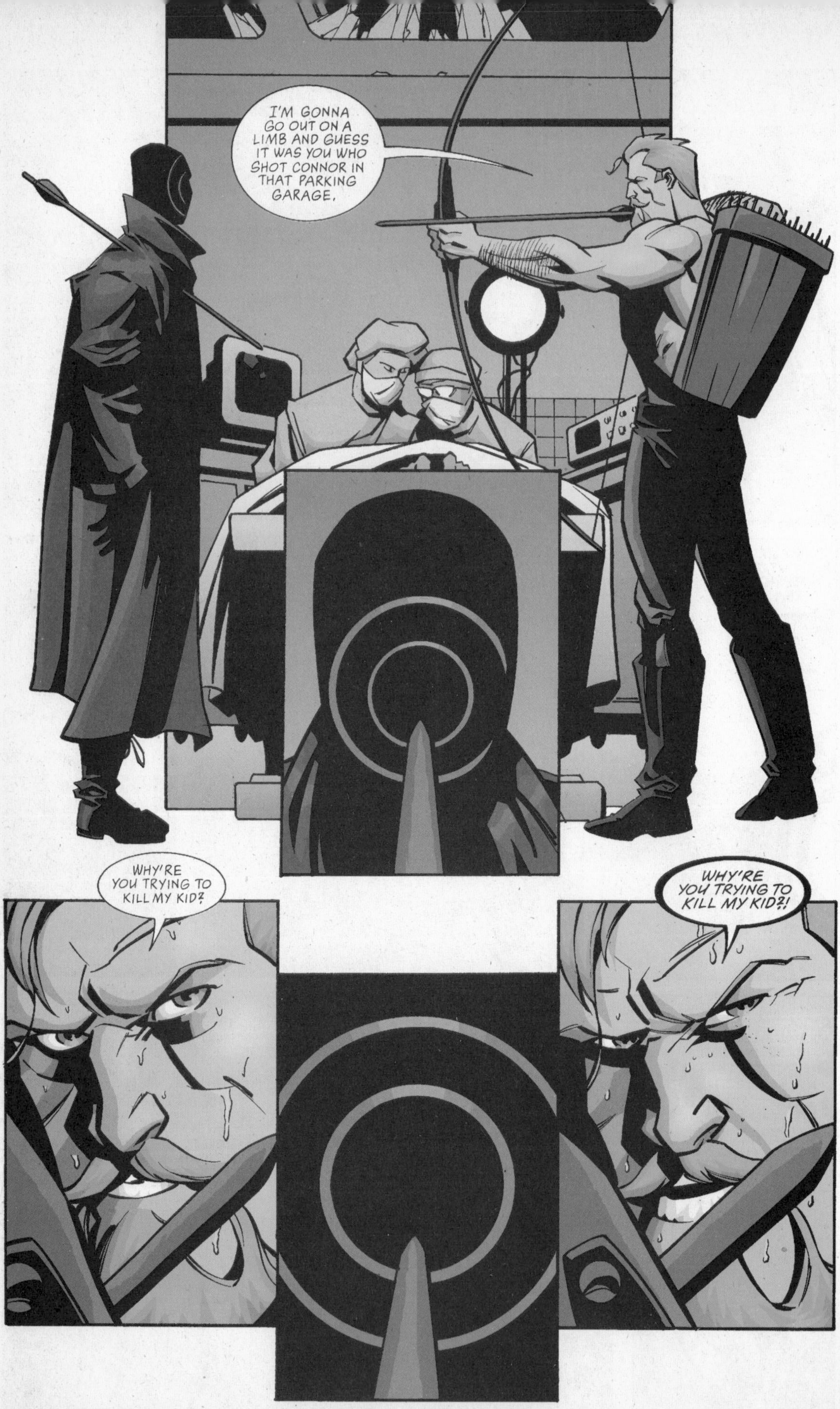
I'M GONNA GO OUT ON A LIMB AND GUESS IT WAS YOU WHO SHOT CONNOR IN THAT PARKING GARAGE.
WHY'RE YOU TRYING TO KILL MY KID?
WHY'RE YOU TRYING TO KILL MY KID?!

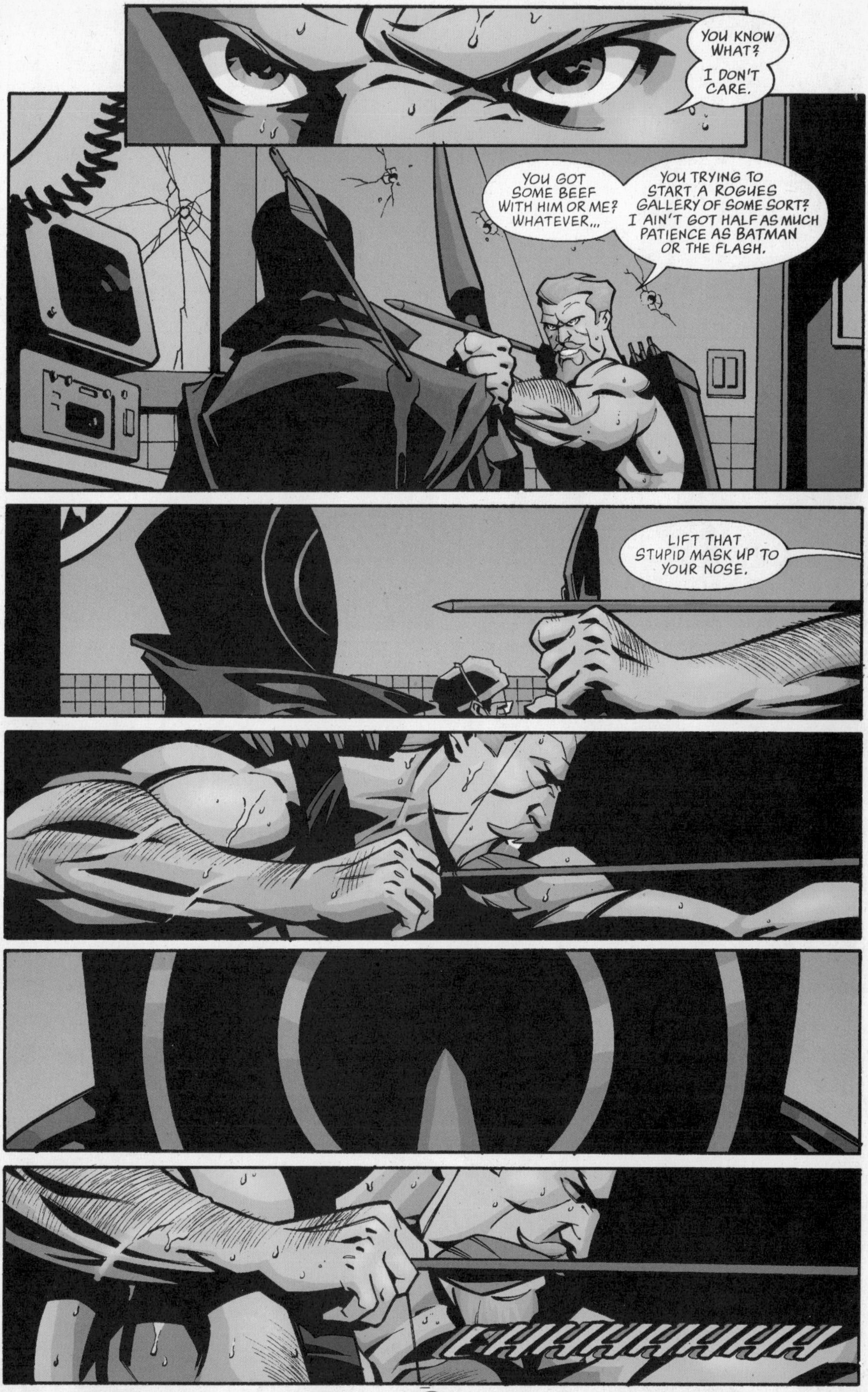
YOU KNOW WHAT? I DON'T CARE.
YOU GOT SOME BEEF WITH HIM OR ME? WHATEVER...
YOU TRYING TO START A ROGUES GALLERY OF SOME SORT? I AIN'T GOT HALF AS MUCH PATIENCE AS BATMAN OR THE FLASH.
LIFT THAT STUPID MASK UP TO YOUR NOSE.
EHHHHHHHHH

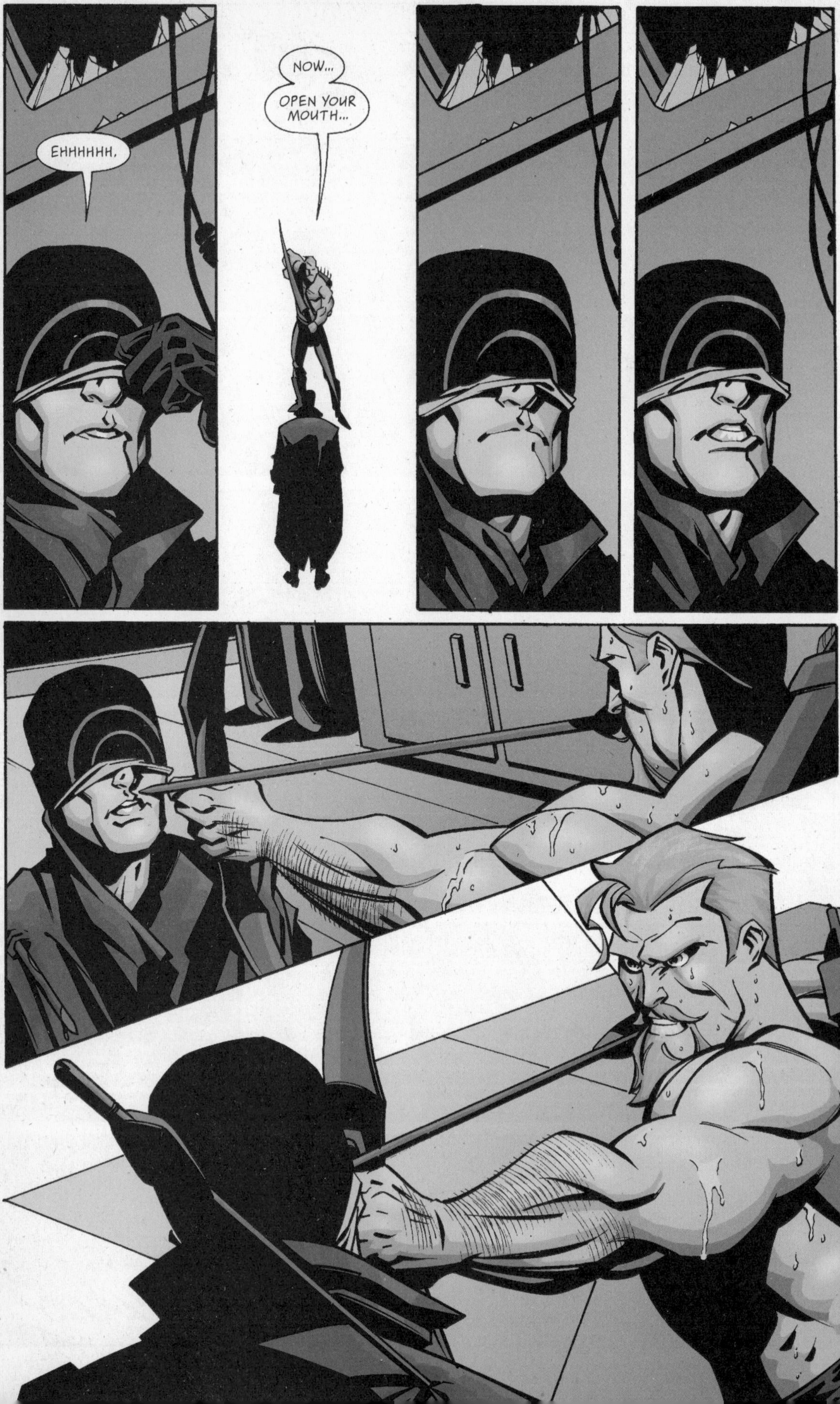
EHHHHHH.
NOW...
OPEN YOUR MOUTH...

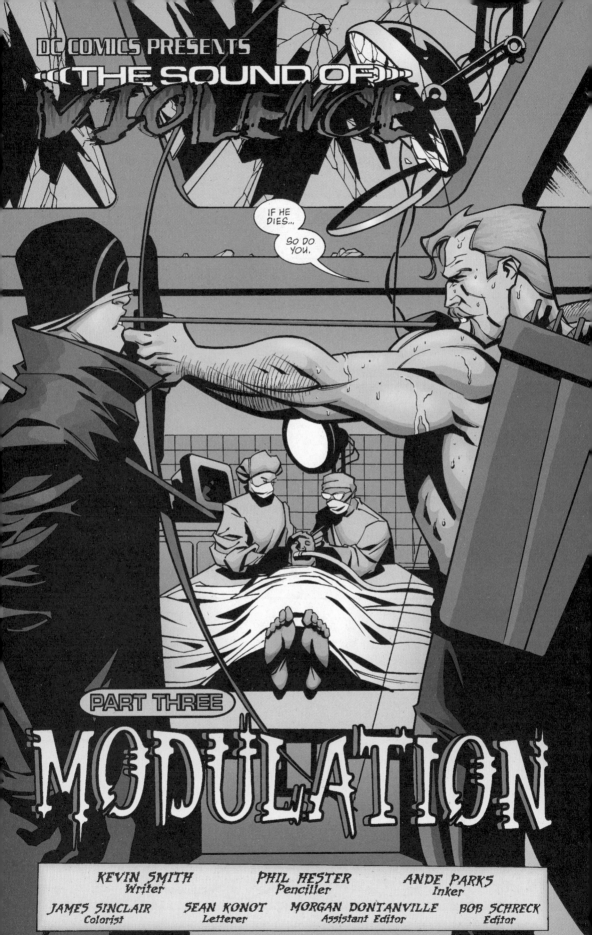

DC COMICS PRESENTS

THE SOUND OF VIOLENCE

IF HE DIES... SO DO YOU.

PART THREE

MODULATION

KEVIN SMITH
Writer

PHIL HESTER
Penciller

ANDE PARKS
Inker

JAMES SINCLAIR
Colorist

SEAN KONOT
Letterer

MORGAN DONTANVILLE
Assistant Editor

BOB SCHRECK
Editor

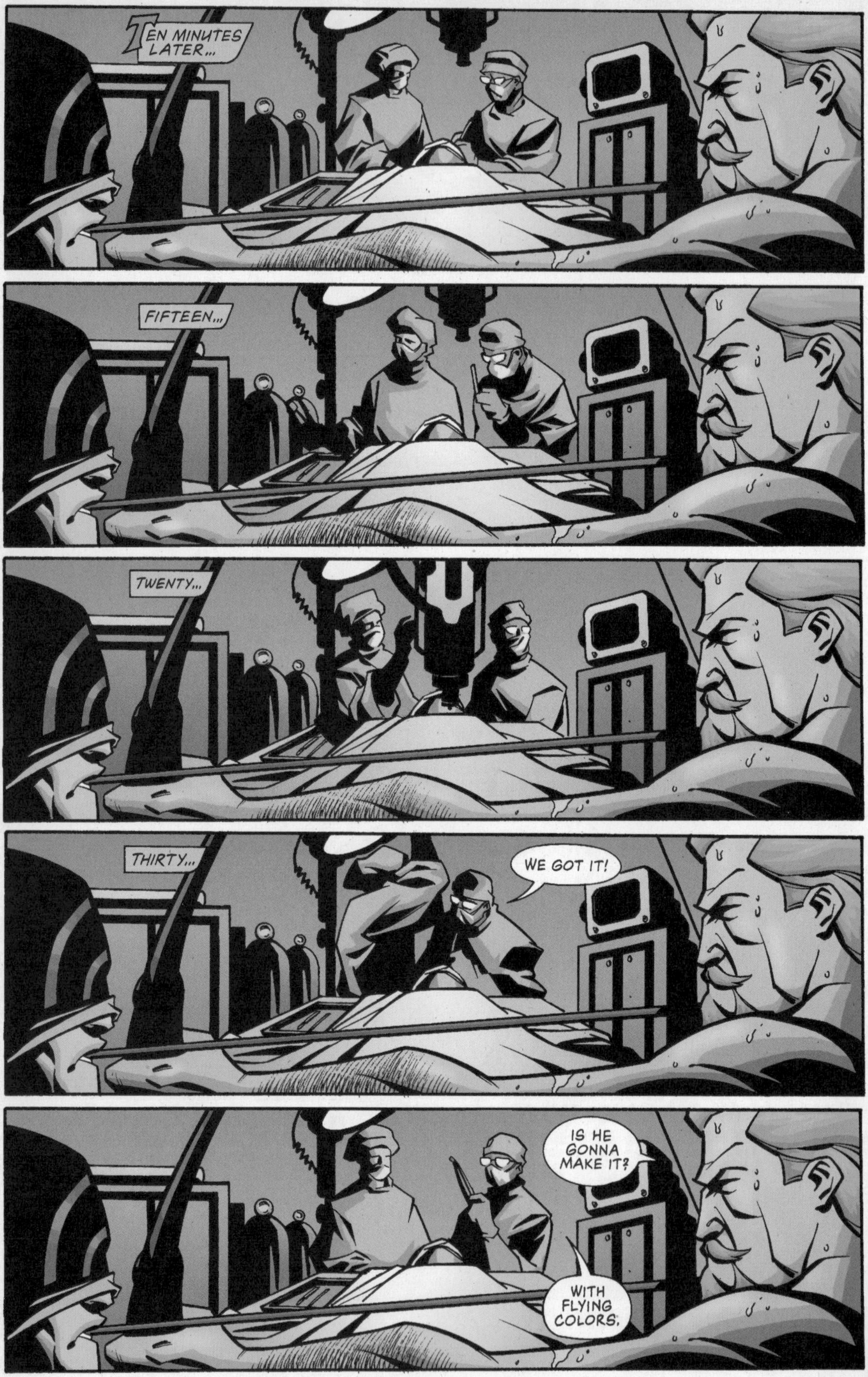
TEN MINUTES LATER...
FIFTEEN...
TWENTY...
THIRTY...
WE GOT IT!
IS HE GONNA MAKE IT?
WITH FLYING COLORS.

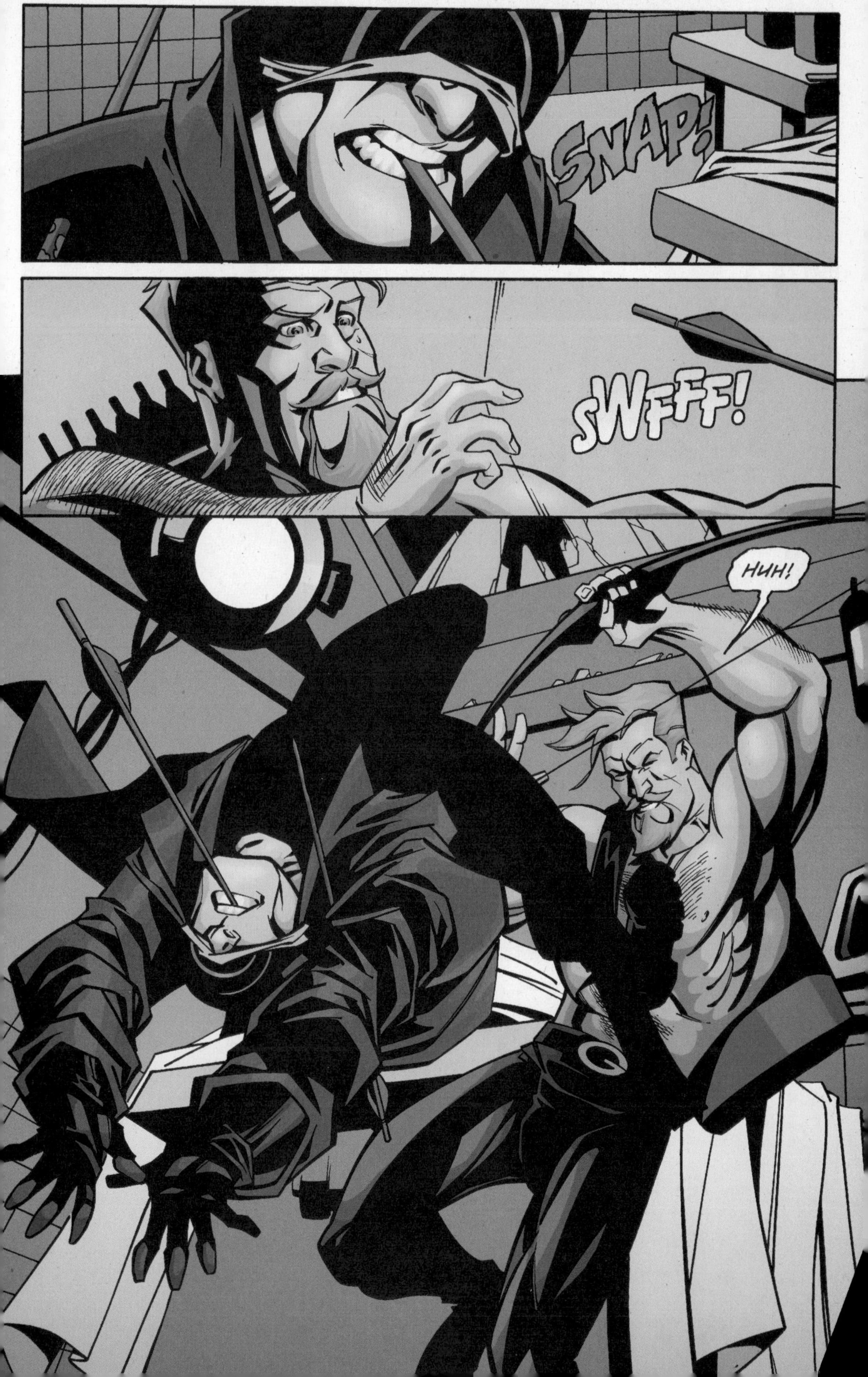
SNAP!
SWFFF!
HUH!

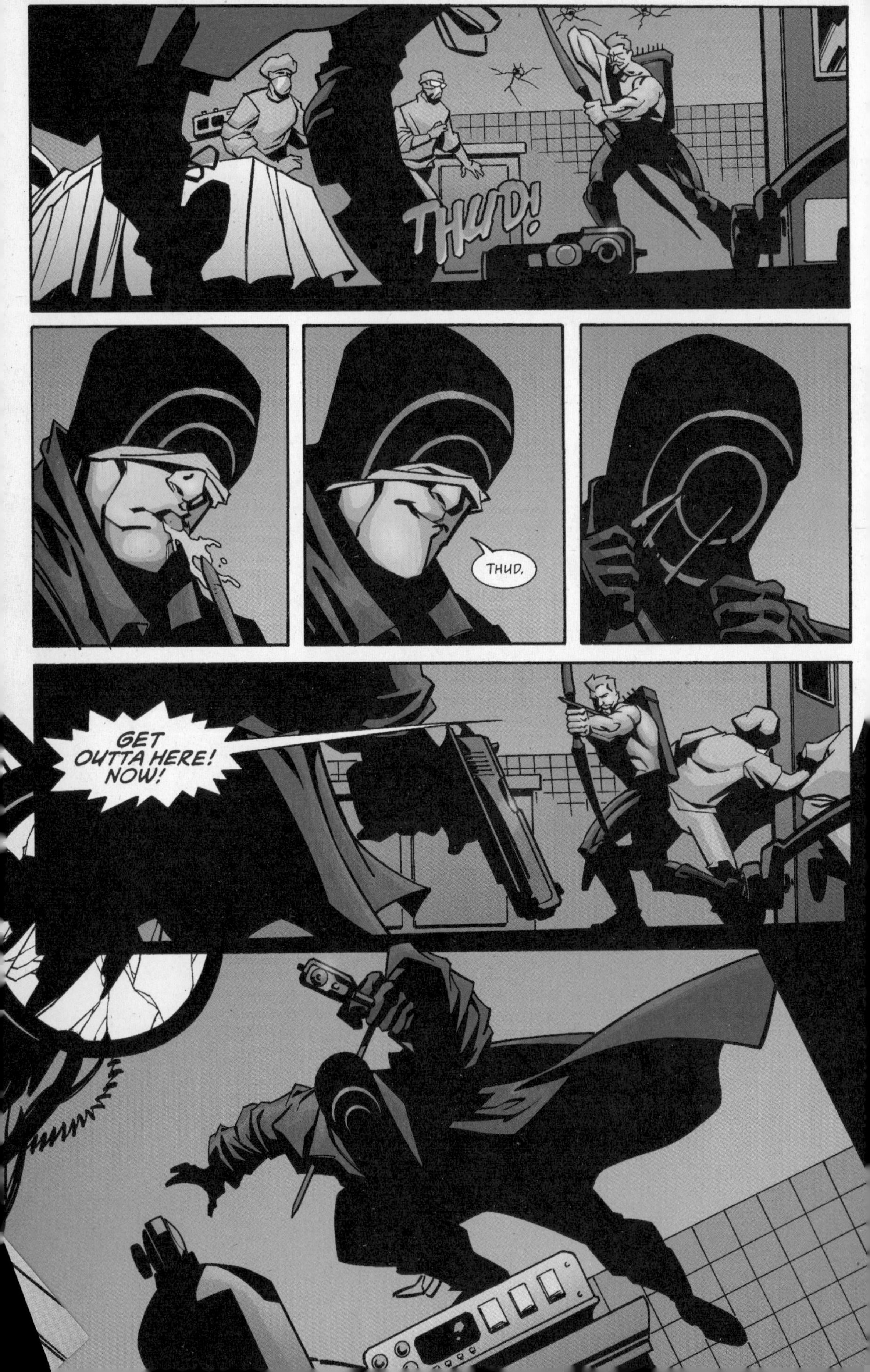
THUD!
THUD.
GET OUTTA HERE! NOW!

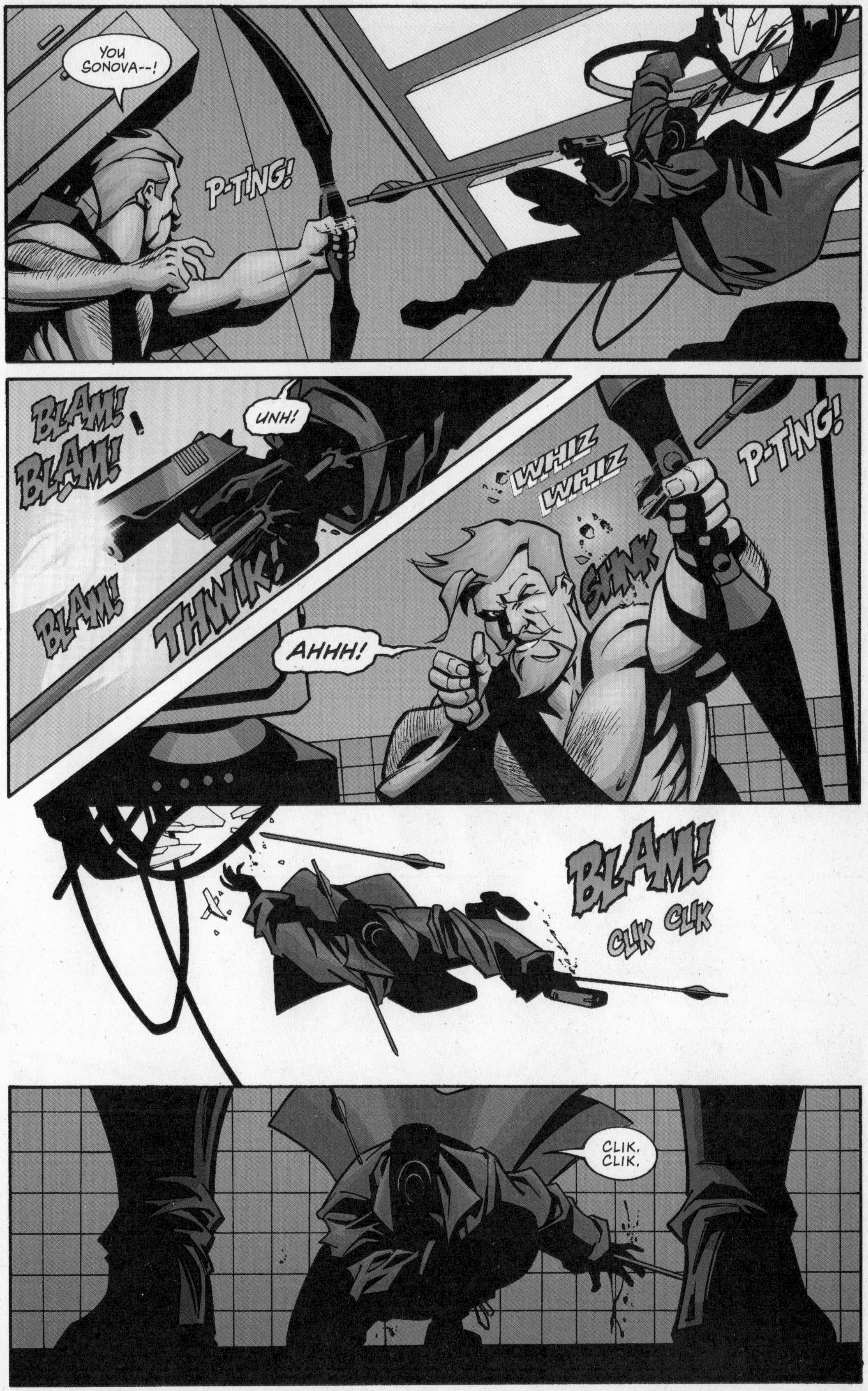
YOU SONOVA--!
P-TING!
BLAM!
BLAM!
UNH!
BLAM!
THWIK!
WHIZ
WHIZ
P-TING!
SHNK
AHHH!
BLAM!
CLIK CLIK
CLIK. CLIK.

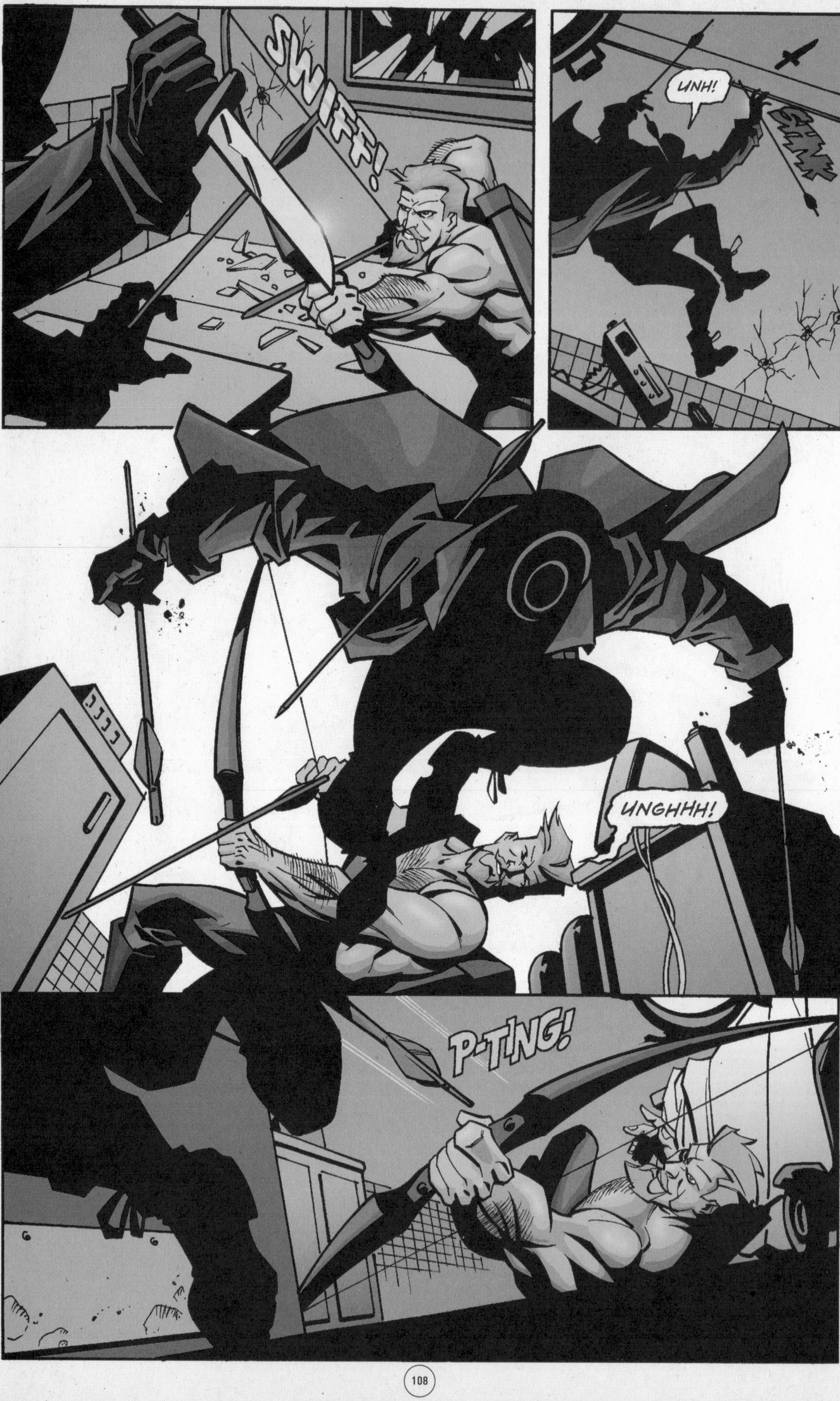
SWIFF!
UNH!
UNGHHH!
P-TING!

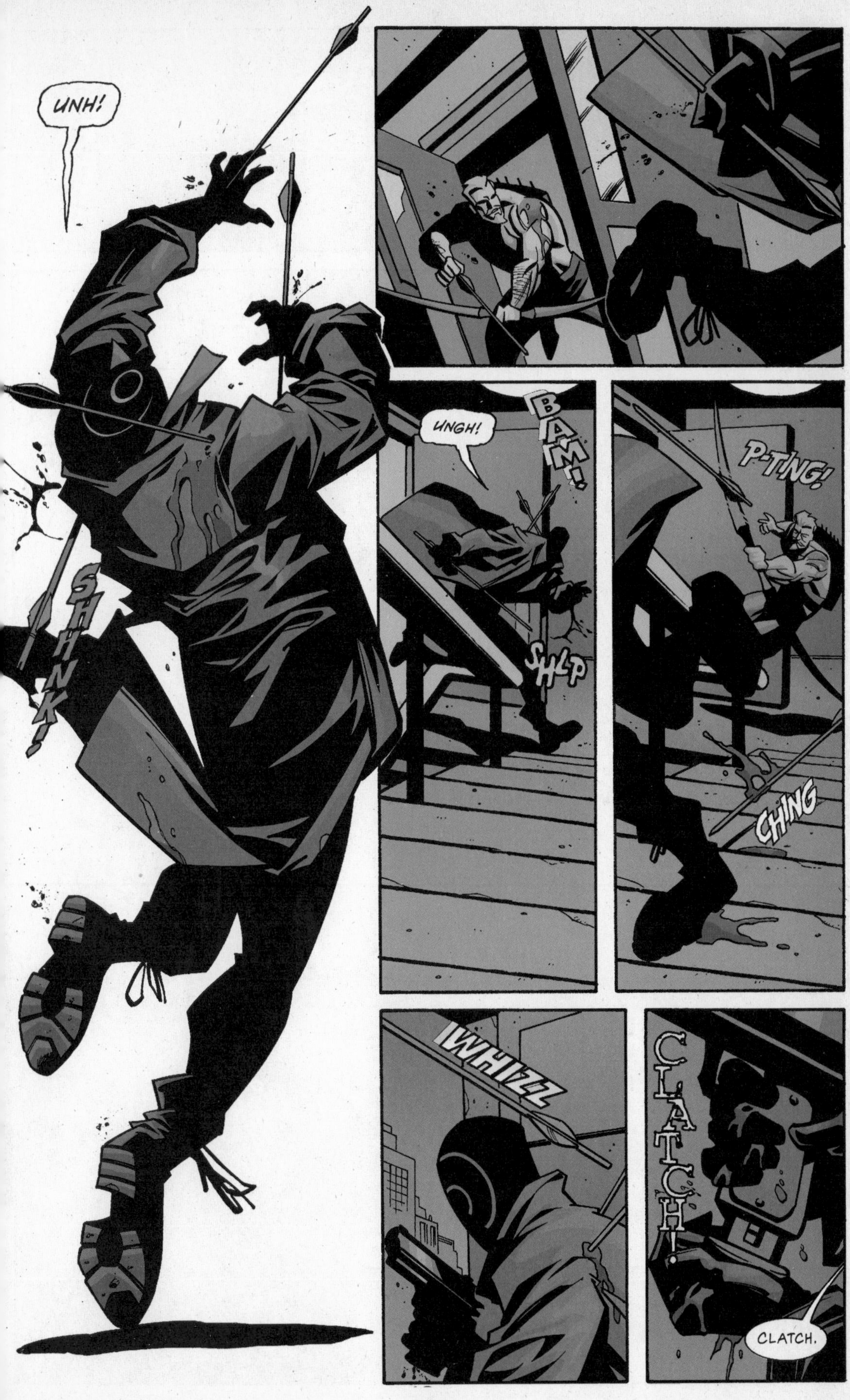
UNH!
SHHNK!
UNGH!
BAM!
SHLP
P-TING!
CHING
WHIZZ
CLATCH!
CLATCH.

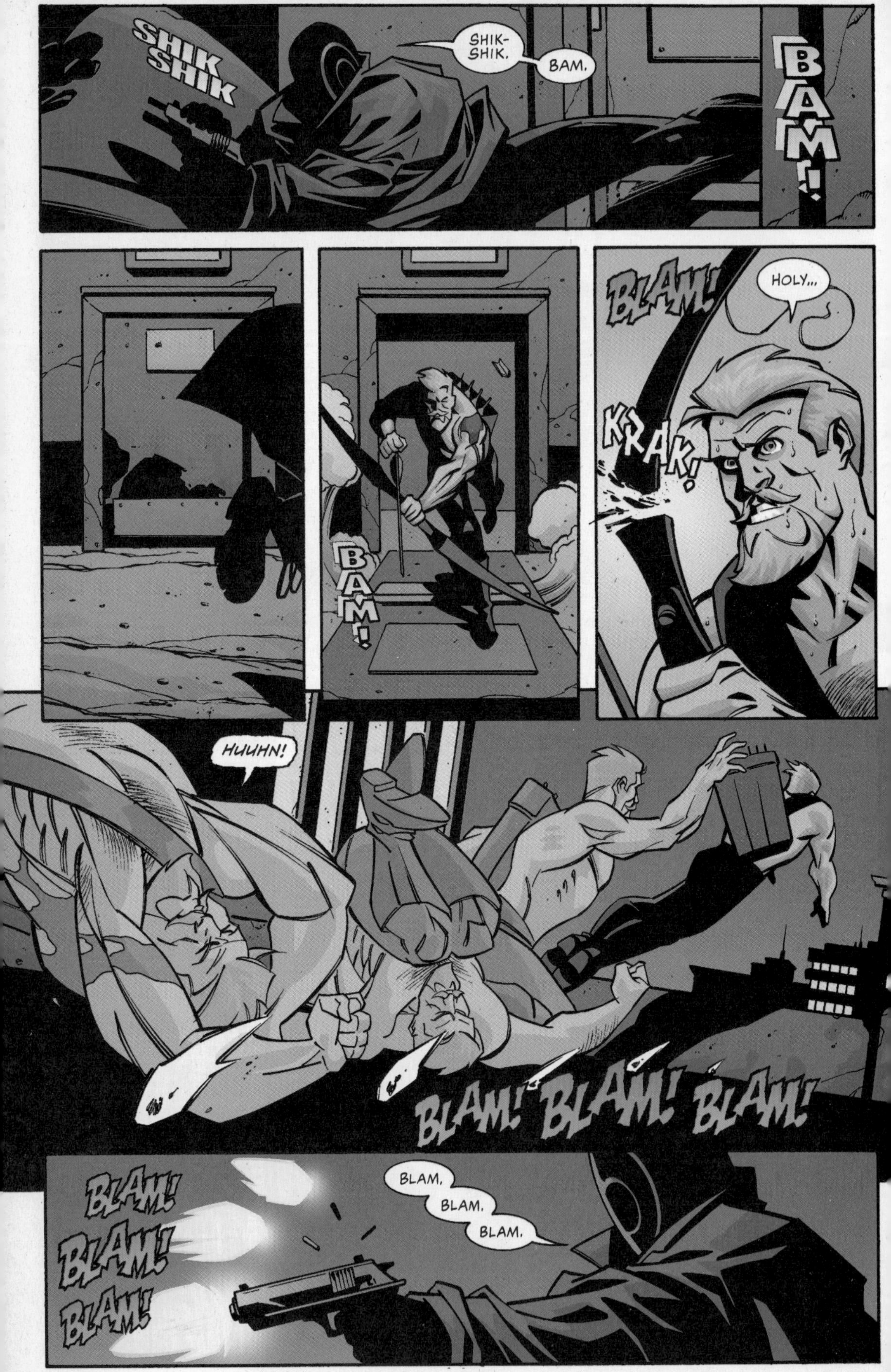
SHIK SHIK
SHIK-SHIK.
BAM.
BAM!
BAM!
BLAM!
HOLY...
KRAK!
HUUHN!
BLAM! BLAM! BLAM!
BLAM! BLAM! BLAM!
BLAM,
BLAM,
BLAM,

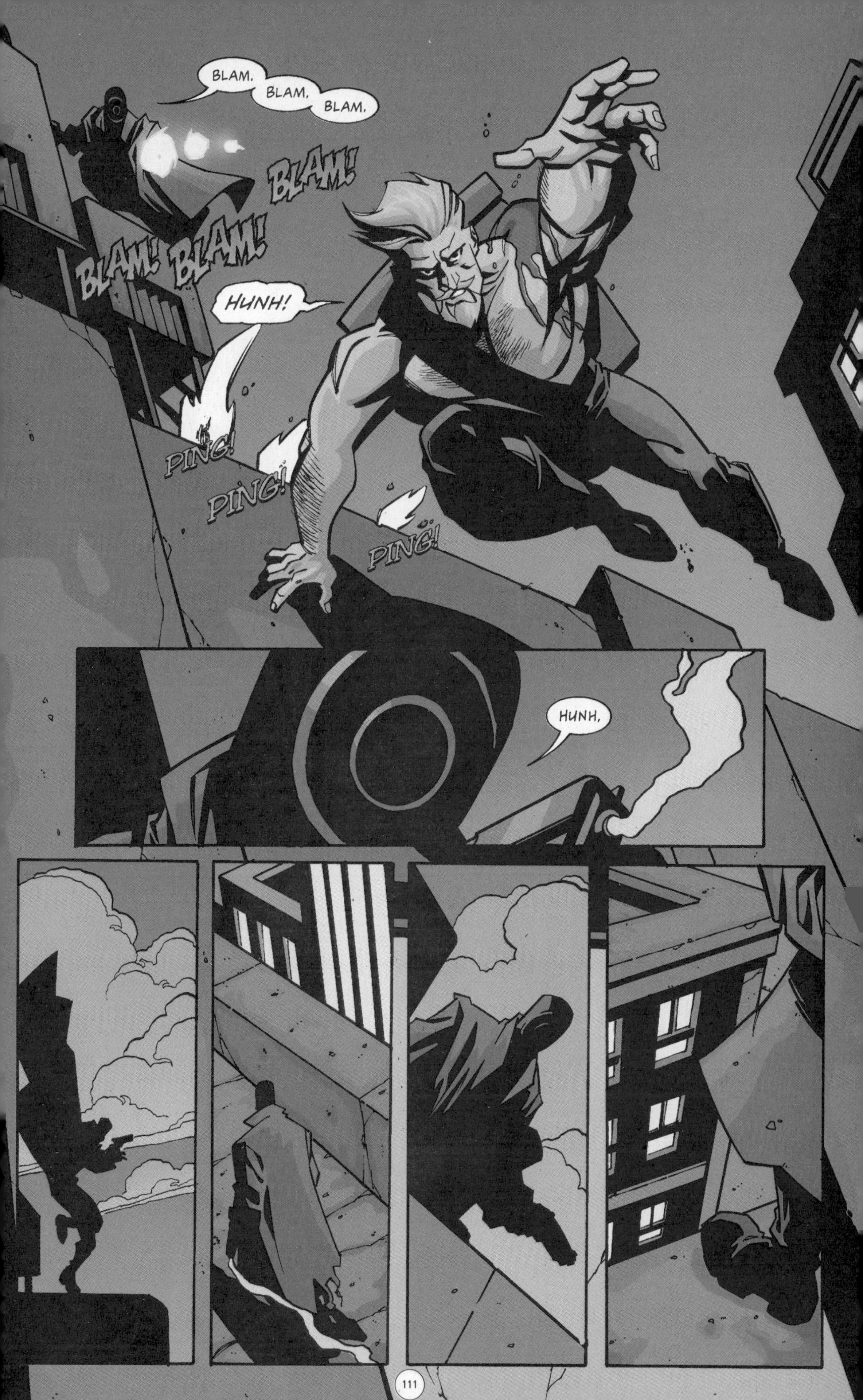

BLAM. BLAM. BLAM.
BLAM! BLAM! BLAM!
HUNH!
PING! PING! PING!
HUNH.

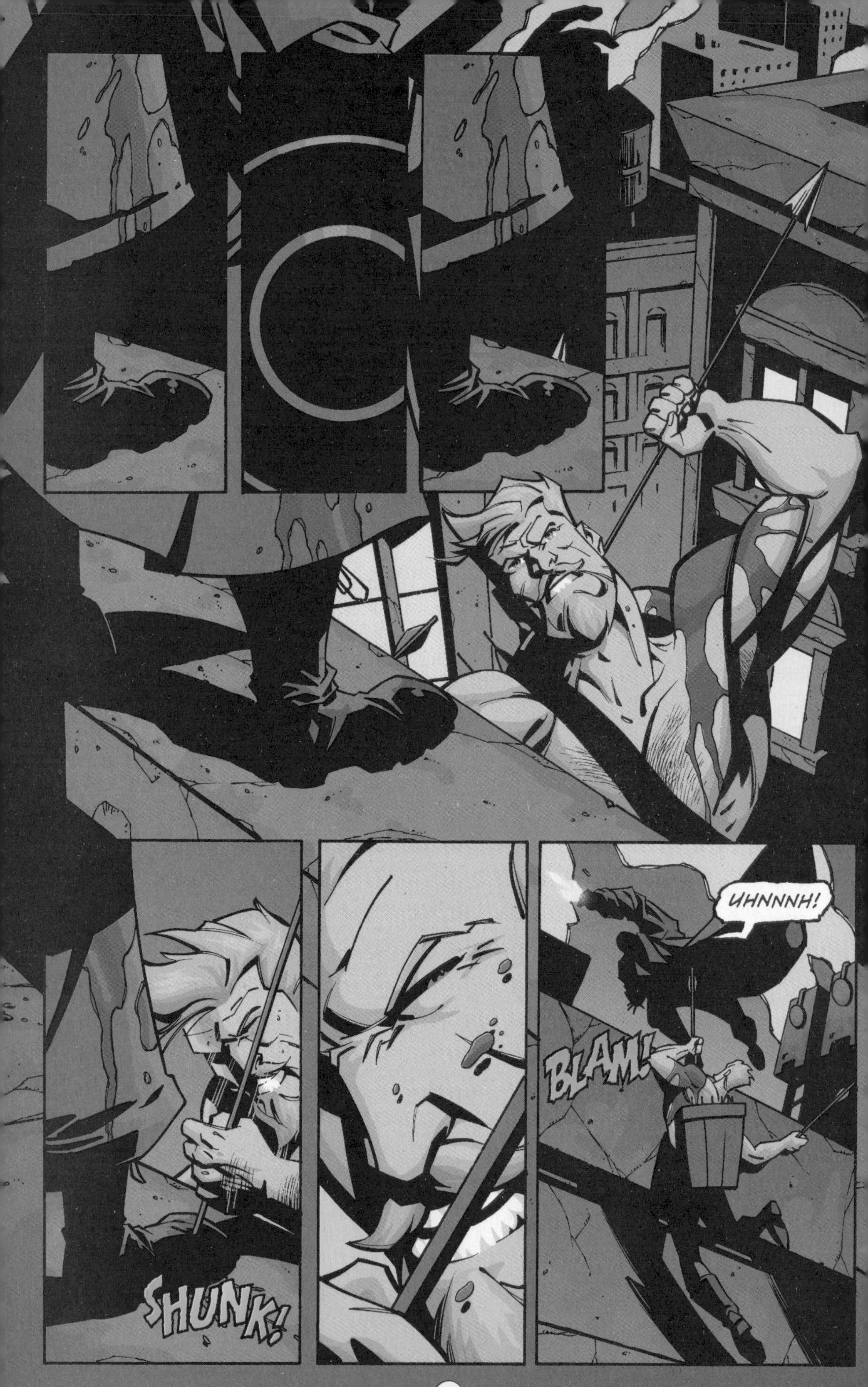
SHUNK!
UHNNNH!
BLAM!

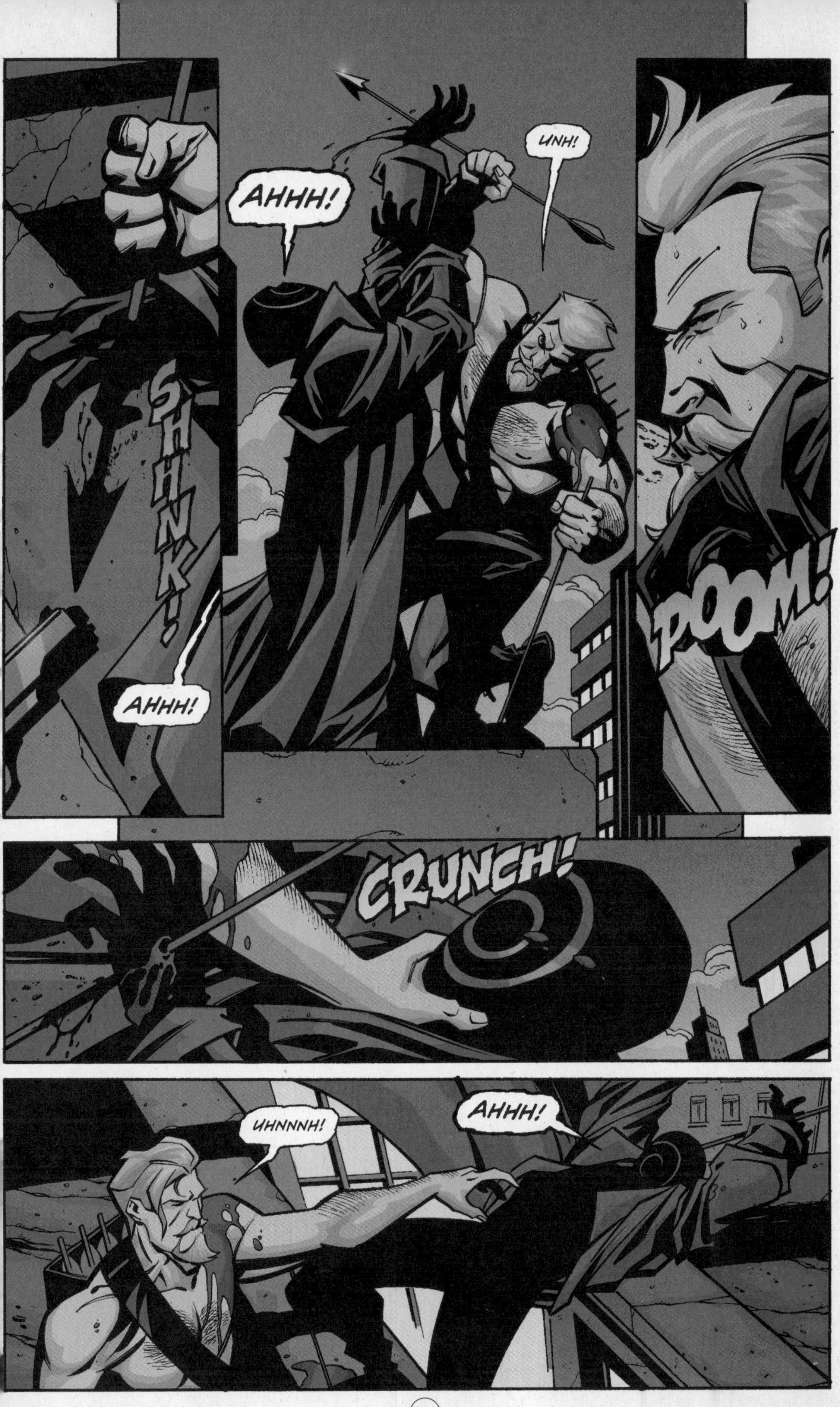
AHHH!
UNH!
SHHNK!
AHHH!
POOM!
CRUNCH!
UHNNNH!
AHHH!

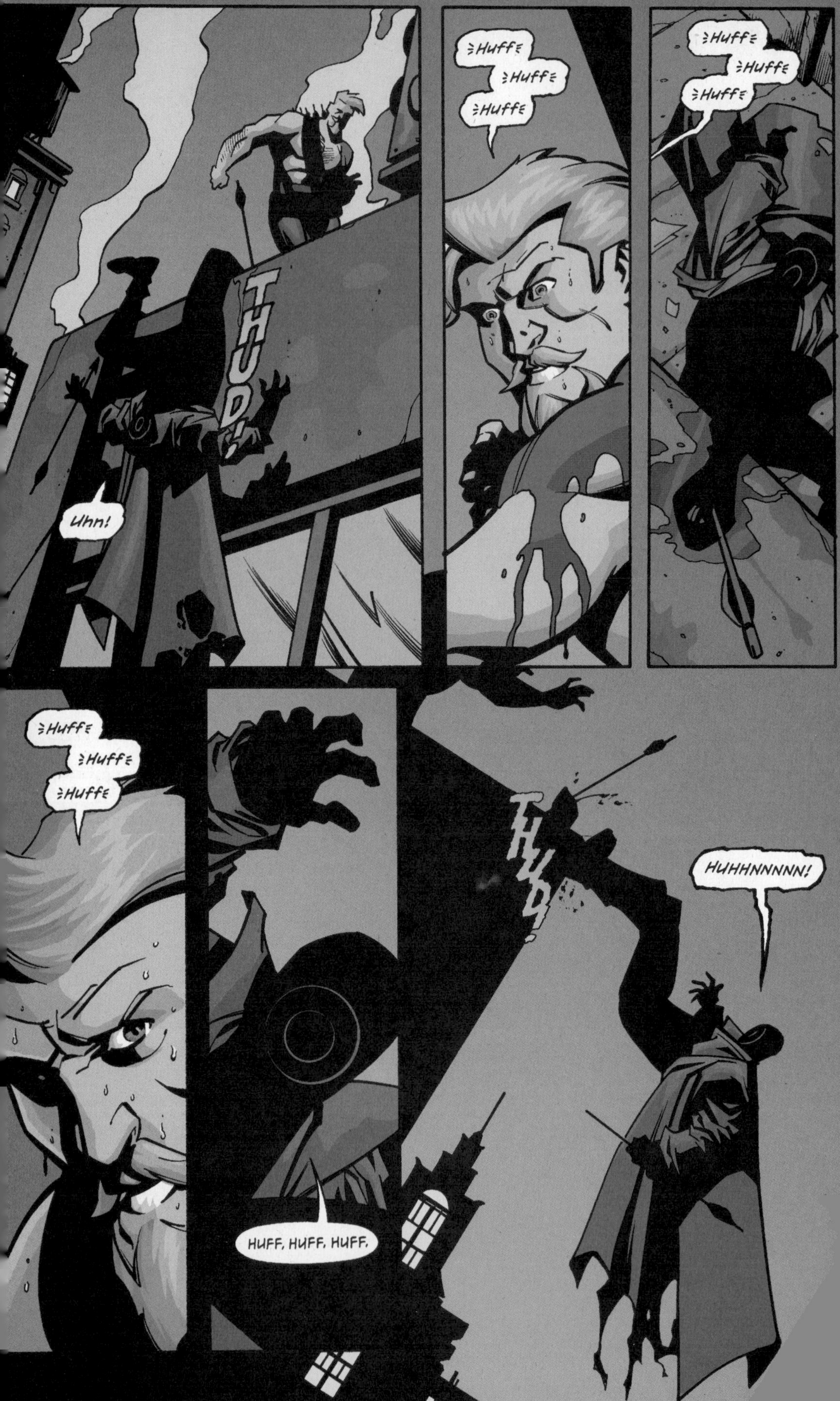
THUD!
Uhn!
Huff
Huff
Huff
Huff
Huff
Huff
Huff
Huff
Huff
HUFF, HUFF, HUFF.
THUD
HUHHNNNNN!

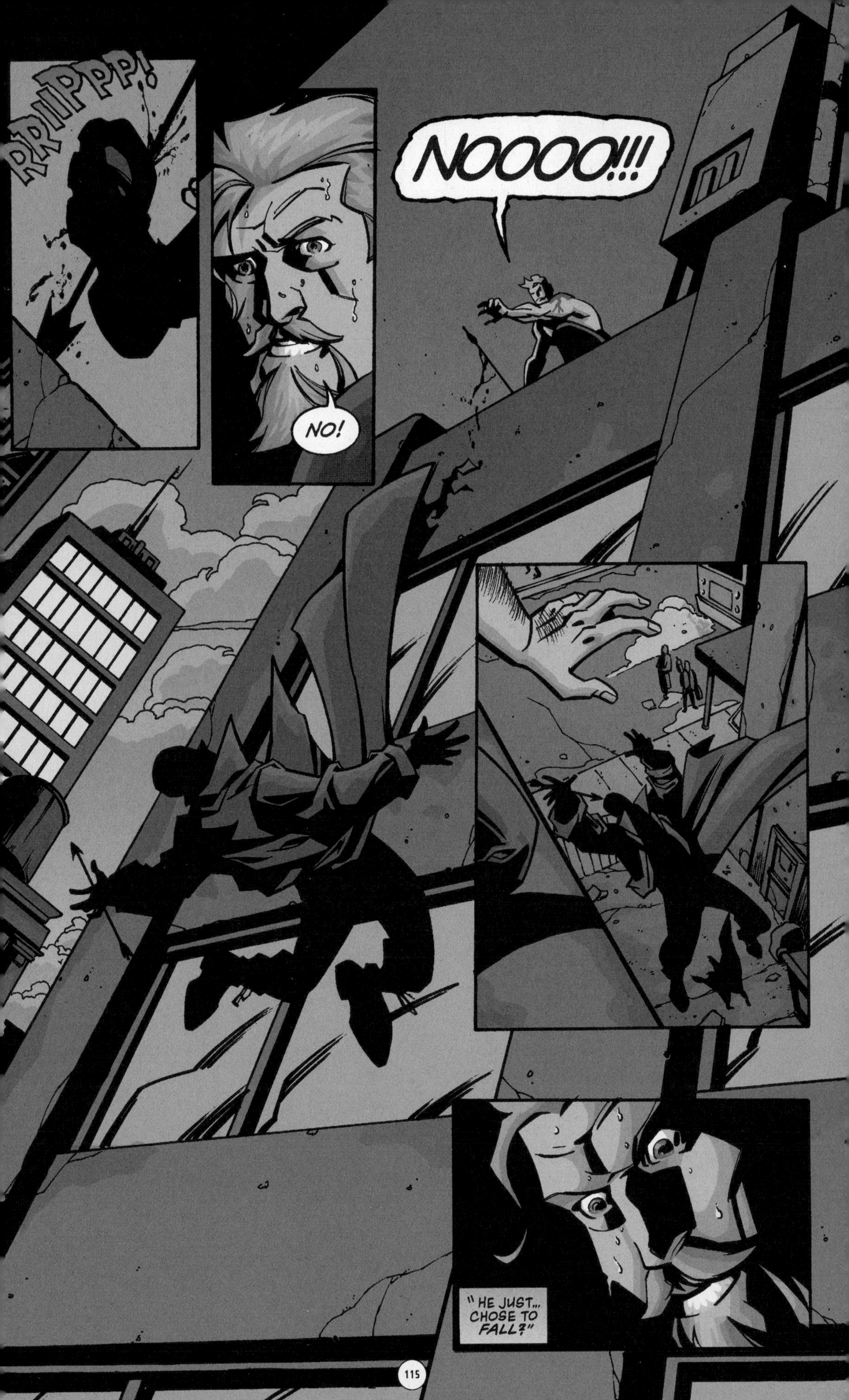
RRIIPPP!
NO!
NOOOO!!!
"HE JUST... CHOSE TO FALL?"

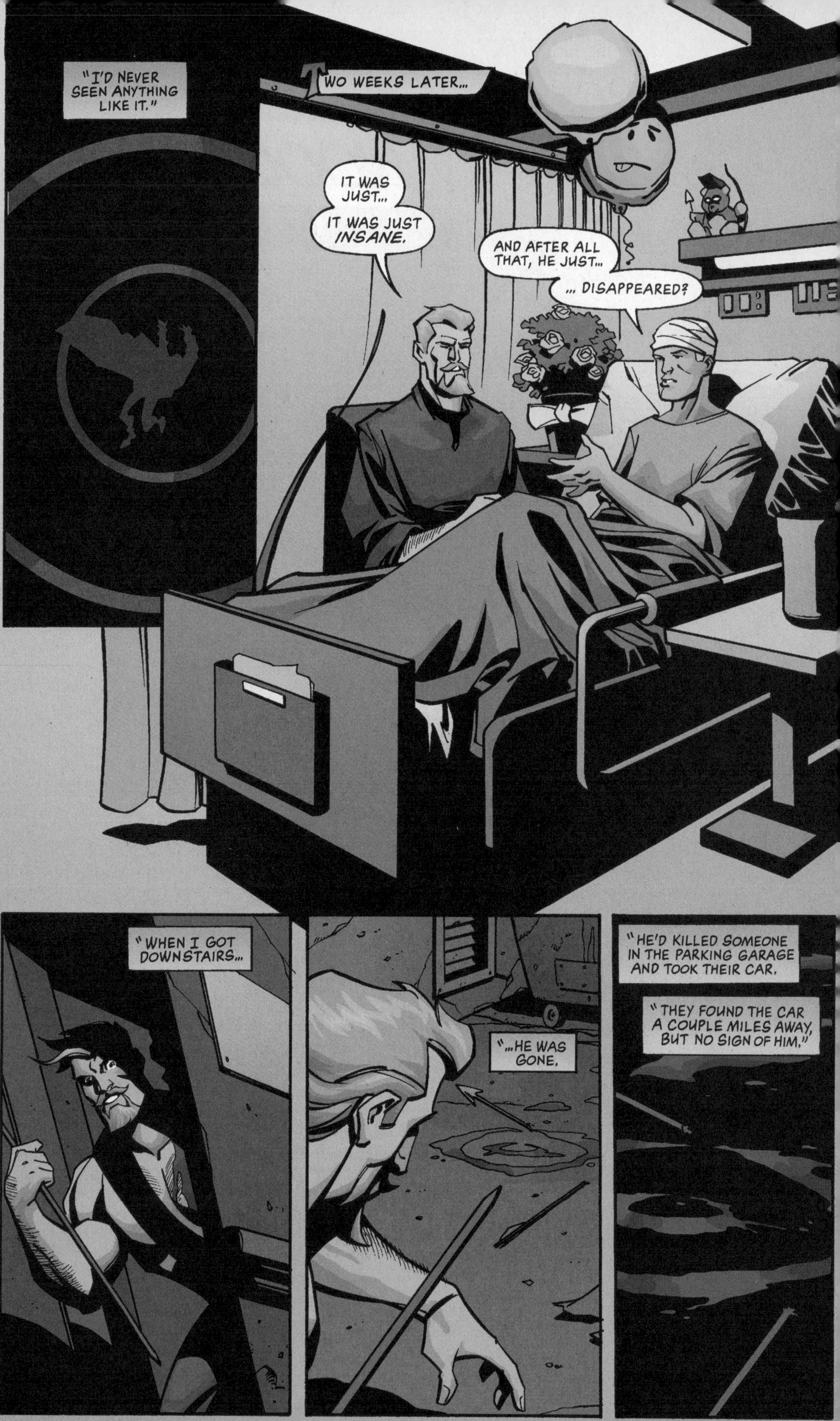
"I'D NEVER SEEN ANYTHING LIKE IT."
TWO WEEKS LATER...
IT WAS JUST... IT WAS JUST *INSANE*.
AND AFTER ALL THAT, HE JUST...
... DISAPPEARED?
"WHEN I GOT DOWNSTAIRS...
"...HE WAS GONE.
"HE'D KILLED SOMEONE IN THE PARKING GARAGE AND TOOK THEIR CAR.
"THEY FOUND THE CAR A COUPLE MILES AWAY, BUT NO SIGN OF HIM."

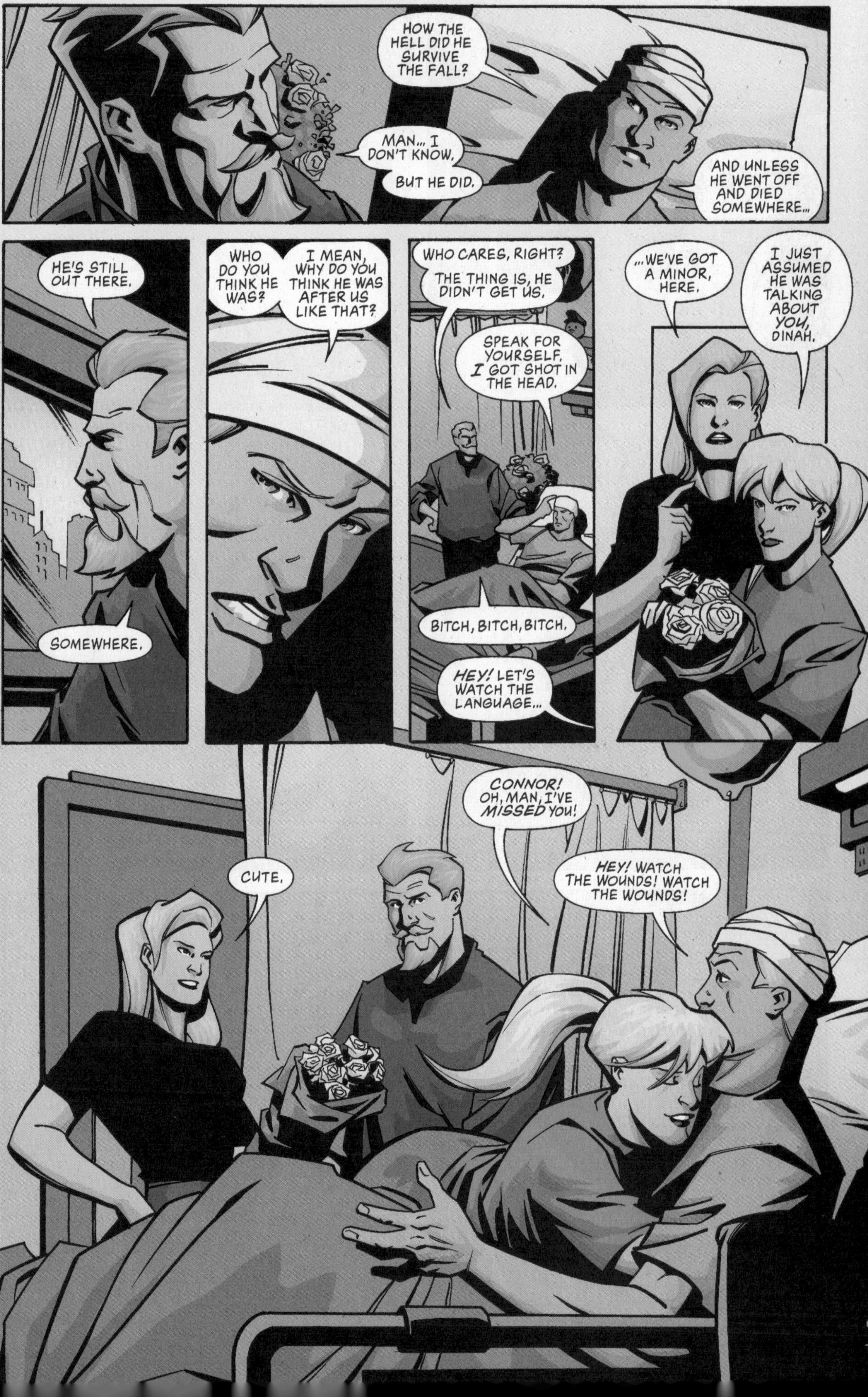
HOW THE HELL DID HE SURVIVE THE FALL?
MAN... I DON'T KNOW,
BUT HE DID.
AND UNLESS HE WENT OFF AND DIED SOMEWHERE...
HE'S STILL OUT THERE.
SOMEWHERE.
WHO DO YOU THINK HE WAS?
I MEAN, WHY DO YOU THINK HE WAS AFTER US LIKE THAT?
WHO CARES, RIGHT?
THE THING IS, HE DIDN'T GET US.
SPEAK FOR YOURSELF. I GOT SHOT IN THE HEAD.
BITCH, BITCH, BITCH.
HEY! LET'S WATCH THE LANGUAGE...
...WE'VE GOT A MINOR, HERE.
I JUST ASSUMED HE WAS TALKING ABOUT YOU, DINAH.
CUTE.
CONNOR! OH, MAN, I'VE MISSED YOU!
HEY! WATCH THE WOUNDS! WATCH THE WOUNDS!

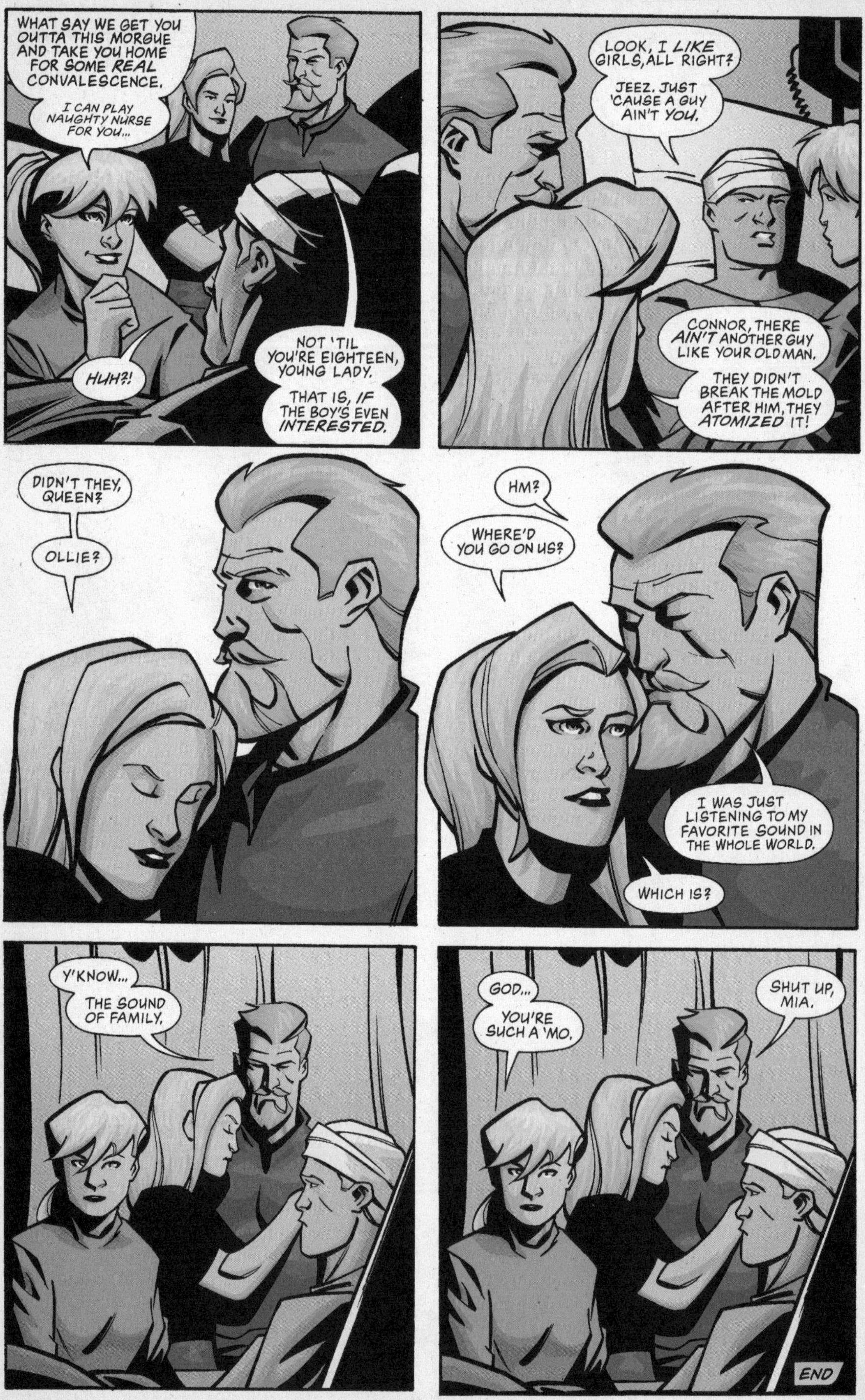
WHAT SAY WE GET YOU OUTTA THIS MORGUE AND TAKE YOU HOME FOR SOME REAL CONVALESCENCE.
I CAN PLAY NAUGHTY NURSE FOR YOU...
HUH?!
NOT 'TIL YOU'RE EIGHTEEN, YOUNG LADY.
THAT IS, IF THE BOY'S EVEN INTERESTED.
LOOK, I LIKE GIRLS, ALL RIGHT?
JEEZ. JUST 'CAUSE A GUY AIN'T YOU.
CONNOR, THERE AIN'T ANOTHER GUY LIKE YOUR OLD MAN.
THEY DIDN'T BREAK THE MOLD AFTER HIM, THEY ATOMIZED IT!
DIDN'T THEY, QUEEN?
OLLIE?
HM?
WHERE'D YOU GO ON US?
I WAS JUST LISTENING TO MY FAVORITE SOUND IN THE WHOLE WORLD.
WHICH IS?
Y'KNOW...
THE SOUND OF FAMILY.
GOD...
YOU'RE SUCH A 'MO.
SHUT UP, MIA.
END

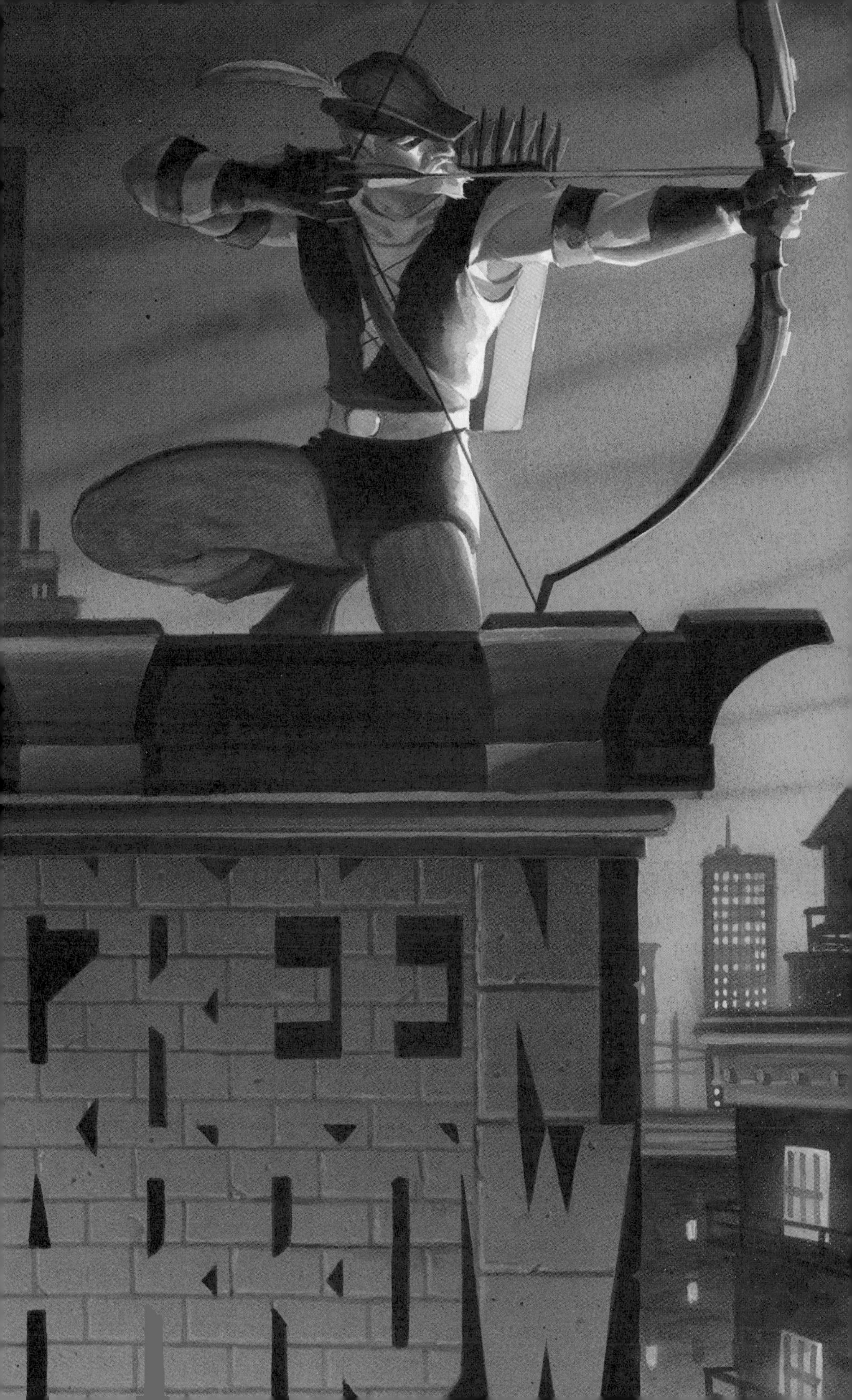

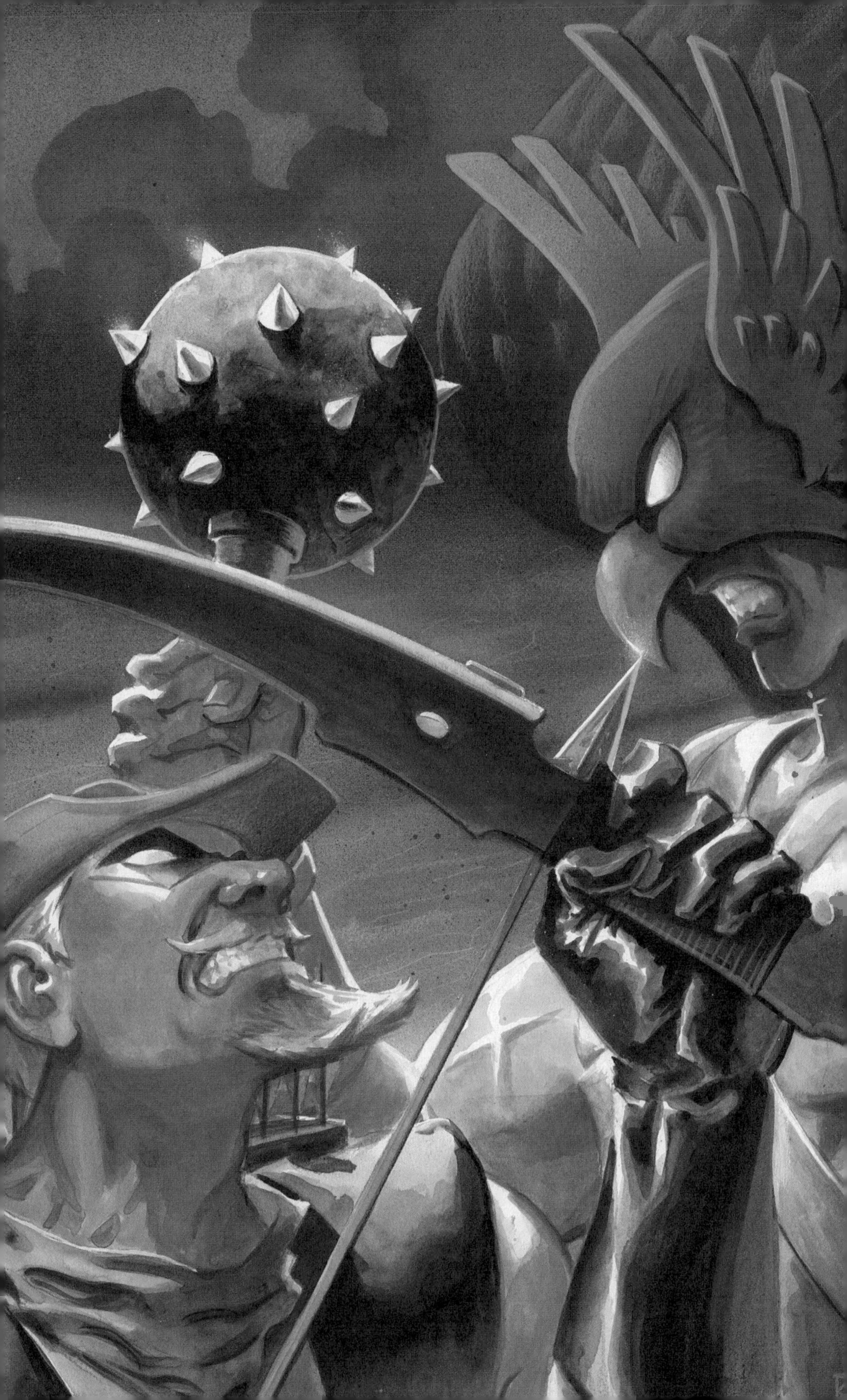

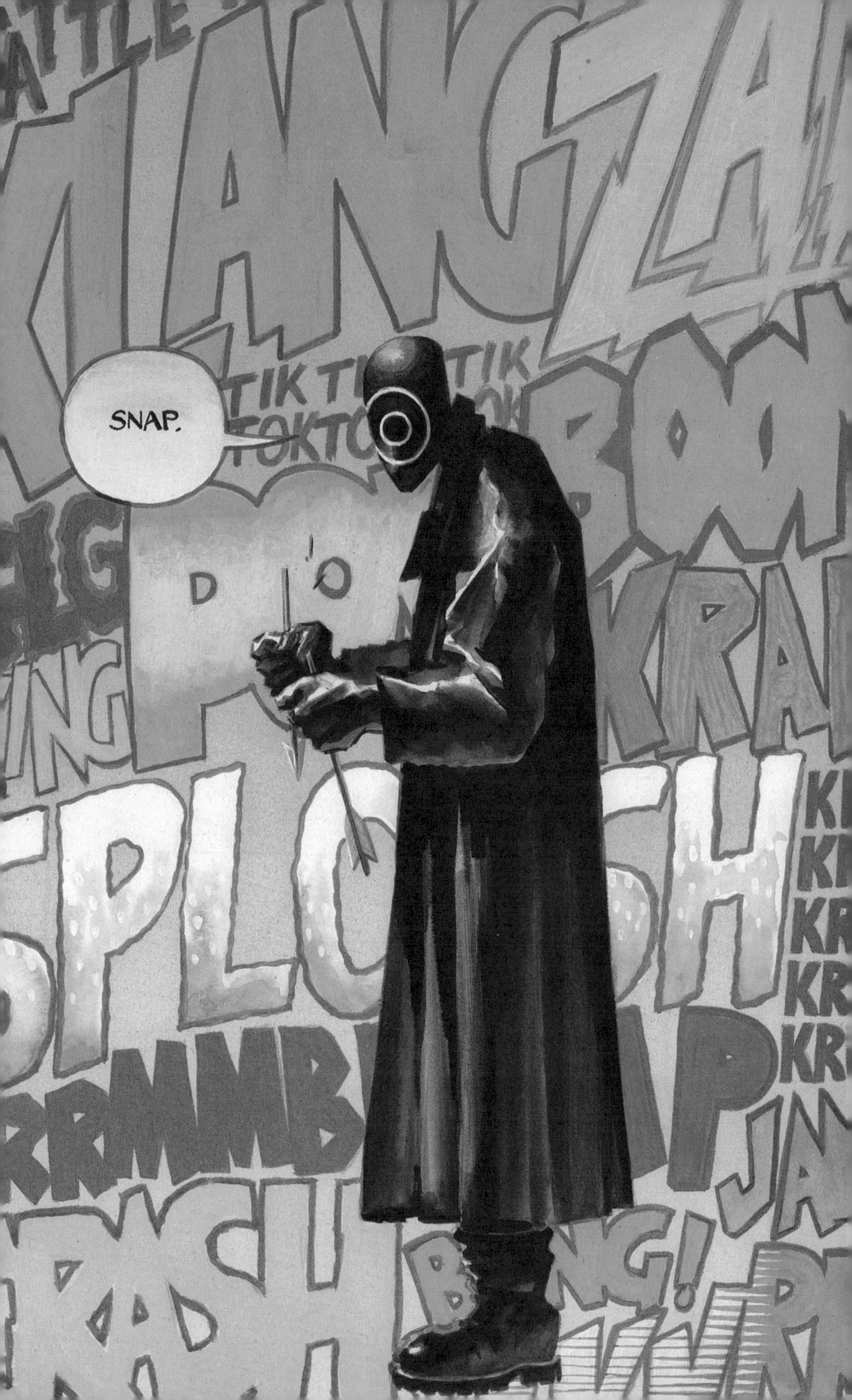
SNAP.

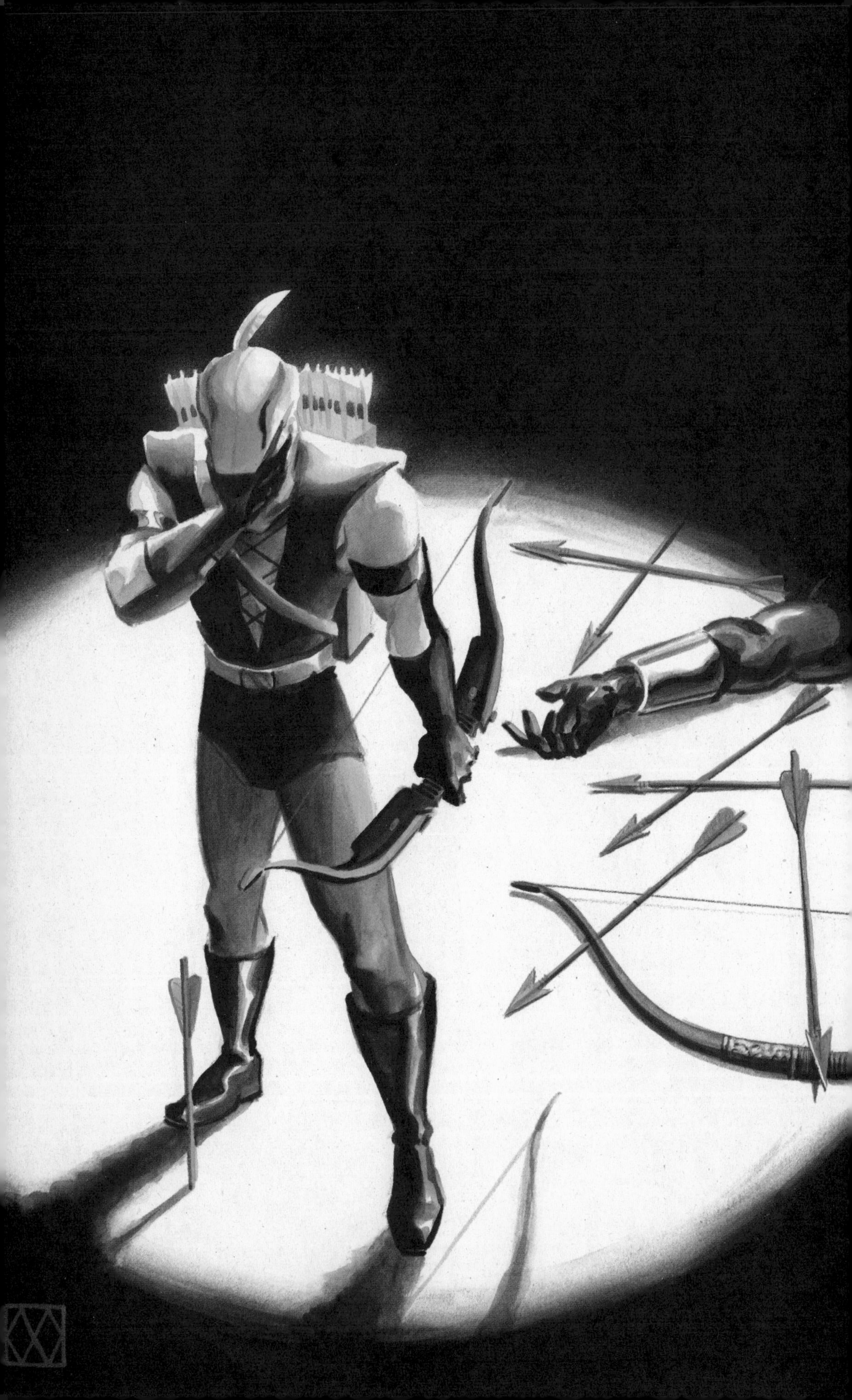

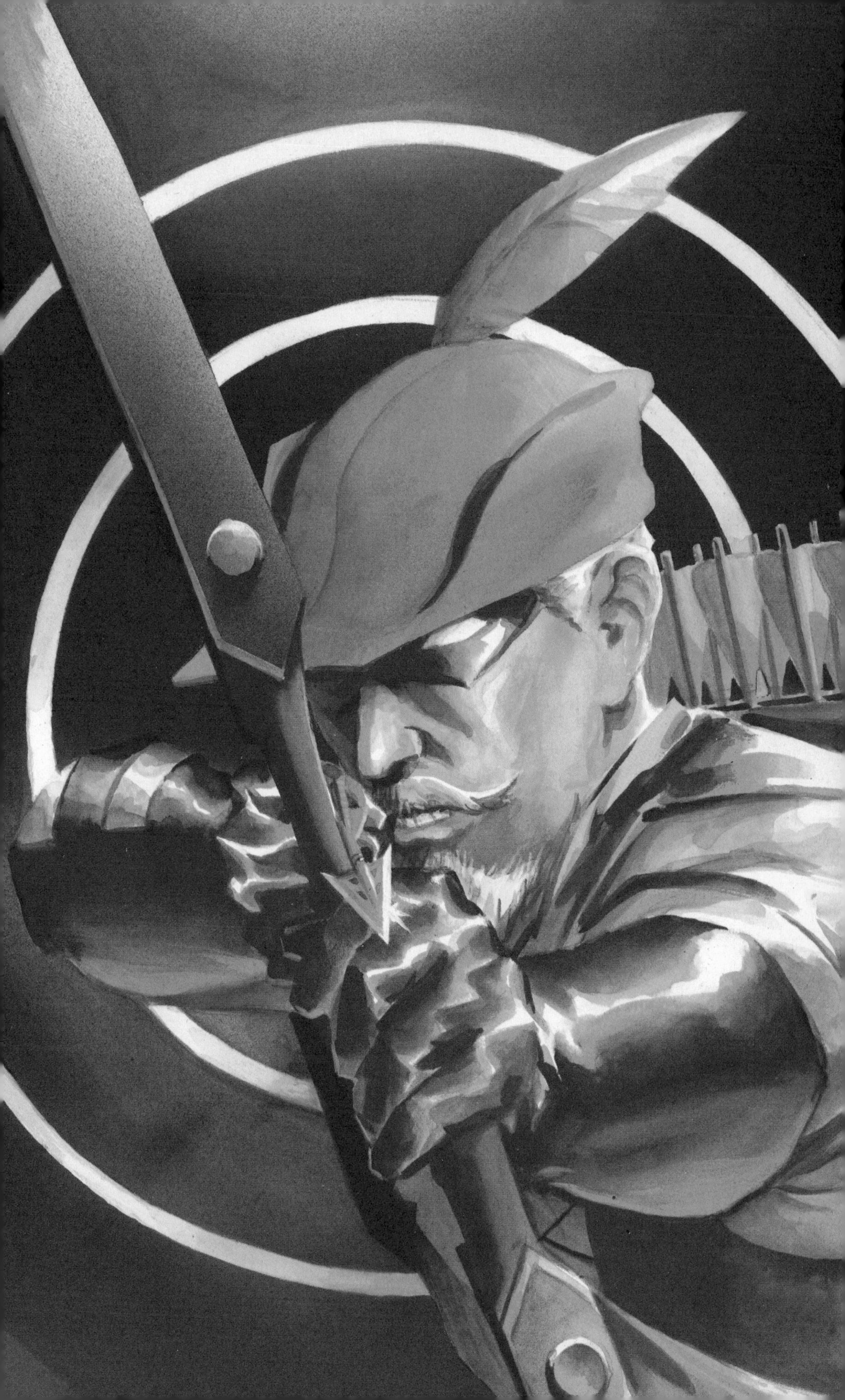

Phil Hester and Ande Parks have collaborated together for years and enjoy the process of creating new characters. On this and the following pages, we present a sampling of their page designs and character concepts.

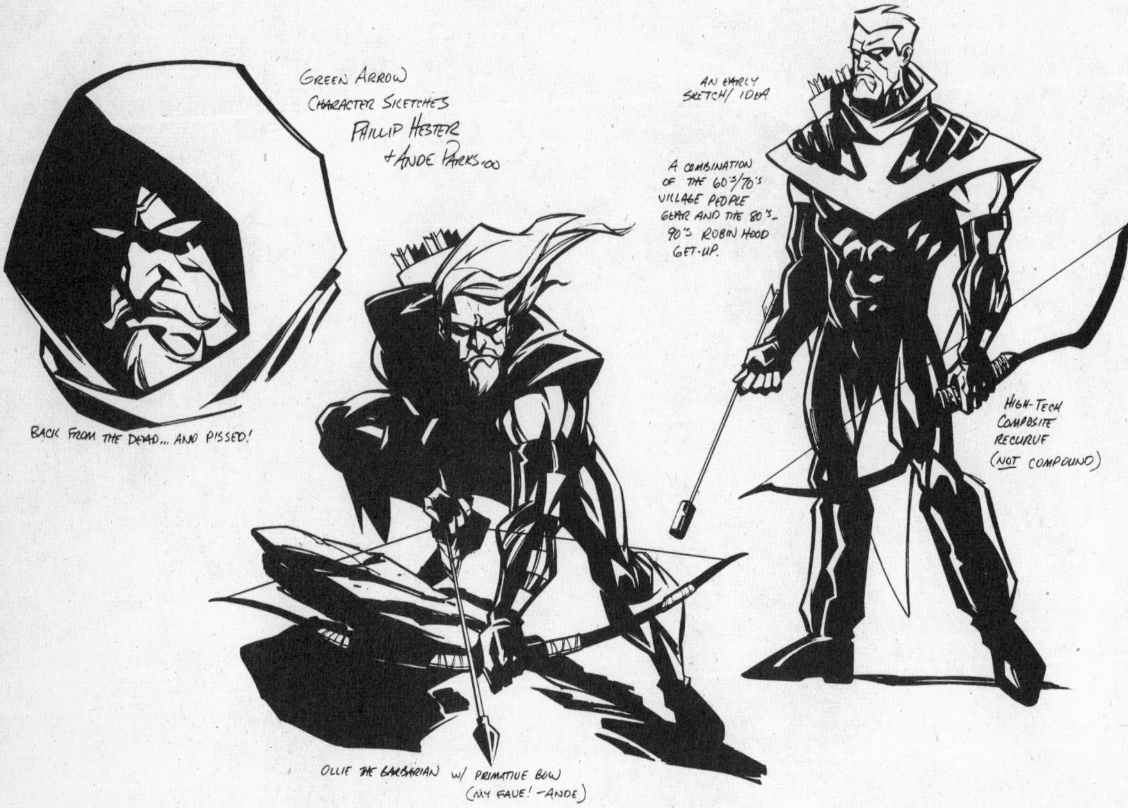
GREEN ARROW
CHARACTER SKETCHES
PHILLIP HESTER
+ANDE PARKS '00
AN EARLY SKETCH/ IDEA
A COMBINATION OF THE 60'S/70'S VILLAGE PEOPLE GEAR AND THE 80'S-90'S ROBIN HOOD GET-UP.
BACK FROM THE DEAD... AND PISSED!
HIGH-TECH COMPOSITE RECURVE (NOT COMPOUND)
OLLIE THE BARBARIAN W/ PRIMATIVE BOW
(MY FAVE! -ANDE)

The Green Arrow model sheet first appeared in *Wizard Magazine*.

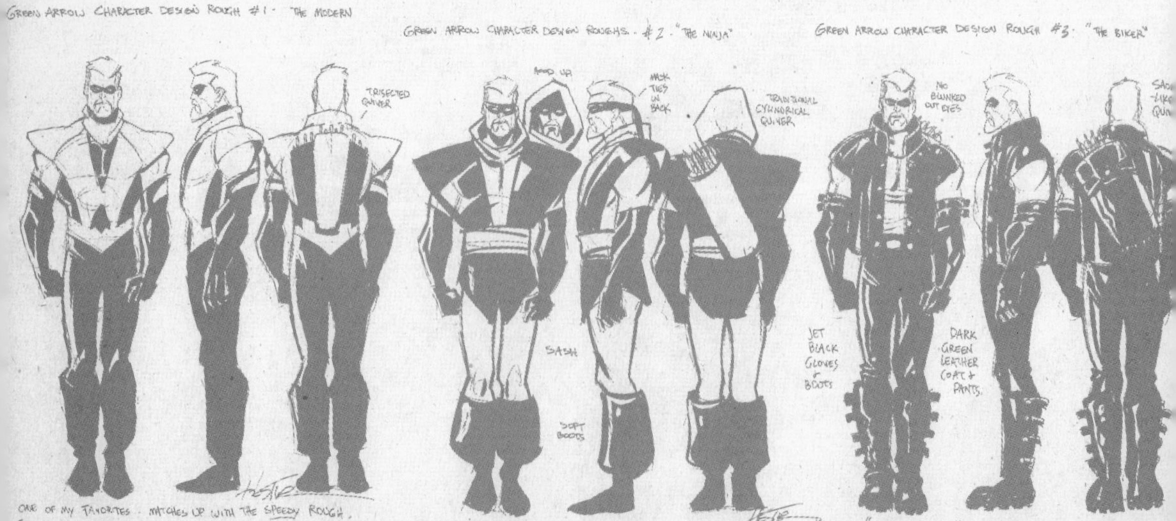
GREEN ARROW CHARACTER DESIGN ROUGH #1 - THE MODERN
GREEN ARROW CHARACTER DESIGN ROUGHS - #2 - "THE NINJA"
GREEN ARROW CHARACTER DESIGN ROUGH #3: "THE BIKER"
TRISECTED QUIVER
HOOD UP
MASK TIES IN BACK
TRADITIONAL CYLINDRICAL QUIVER
NO BLINKED OUT EYES
SASH
SOFT BOOTS
JET BLACK GLOVES & BOOTS
DARK GREEN LEATHER COAT & PANTS.
ONE OF MY FAVORITES - MATCHES UP WITH THE SPEEDY ROUGH. SLEEK, BUT ECHOES OF OLD TOGS REMAIN.
ALL CLOTH - STEALTHY - CLASSY - NICE SHAPES - ONE OF MY FAVORITES!
KIND OF "TOM OF FINLAND"... BUT AREN'T THEY ALL?

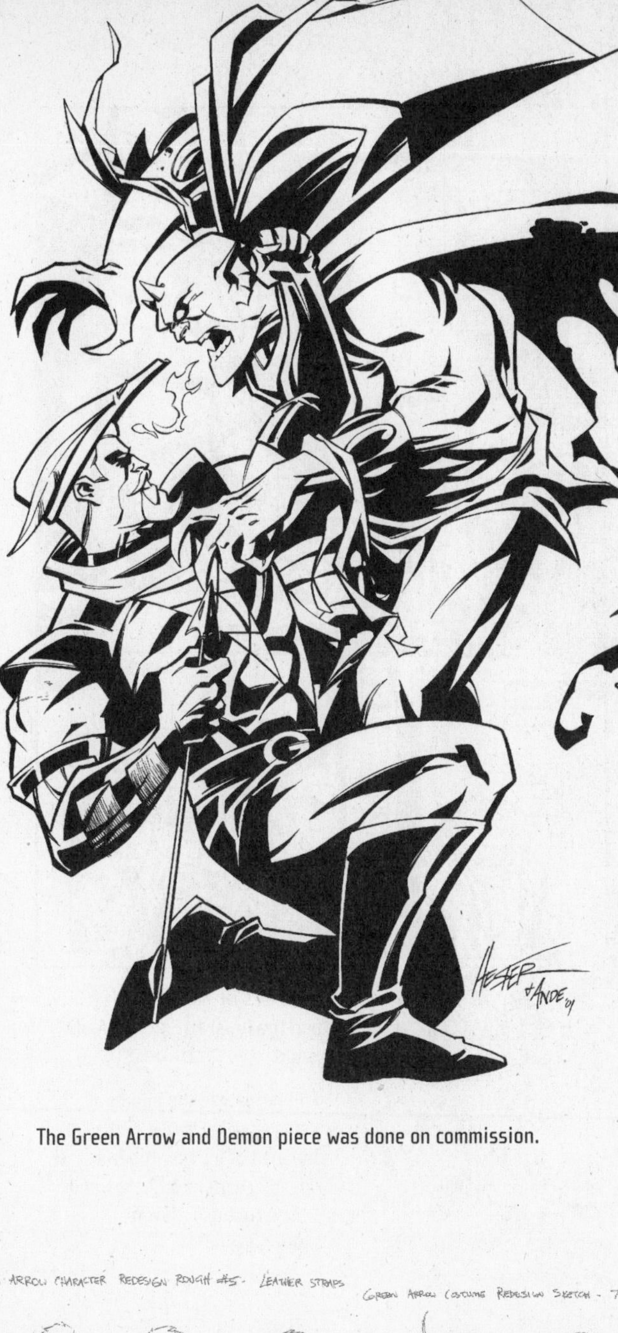

Kevin Smith as Green Arrow was done for a magazine.

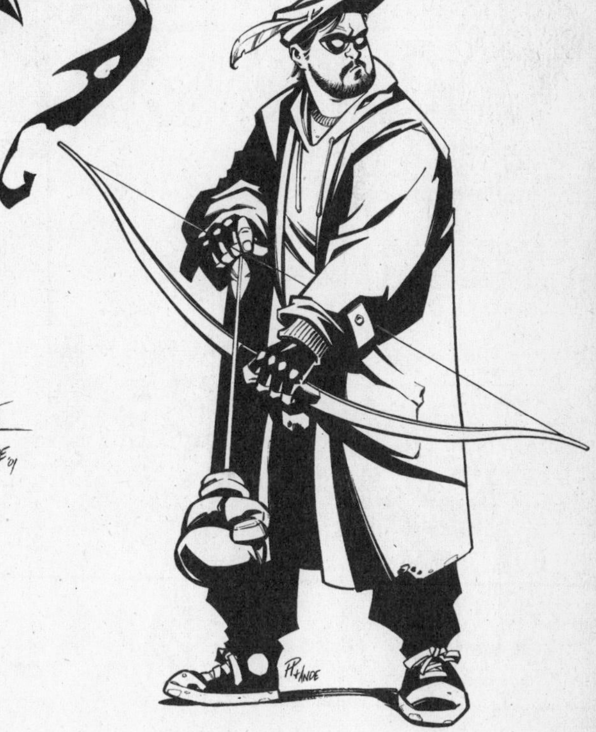

The Green Arrow and Demon piece was done on commission.

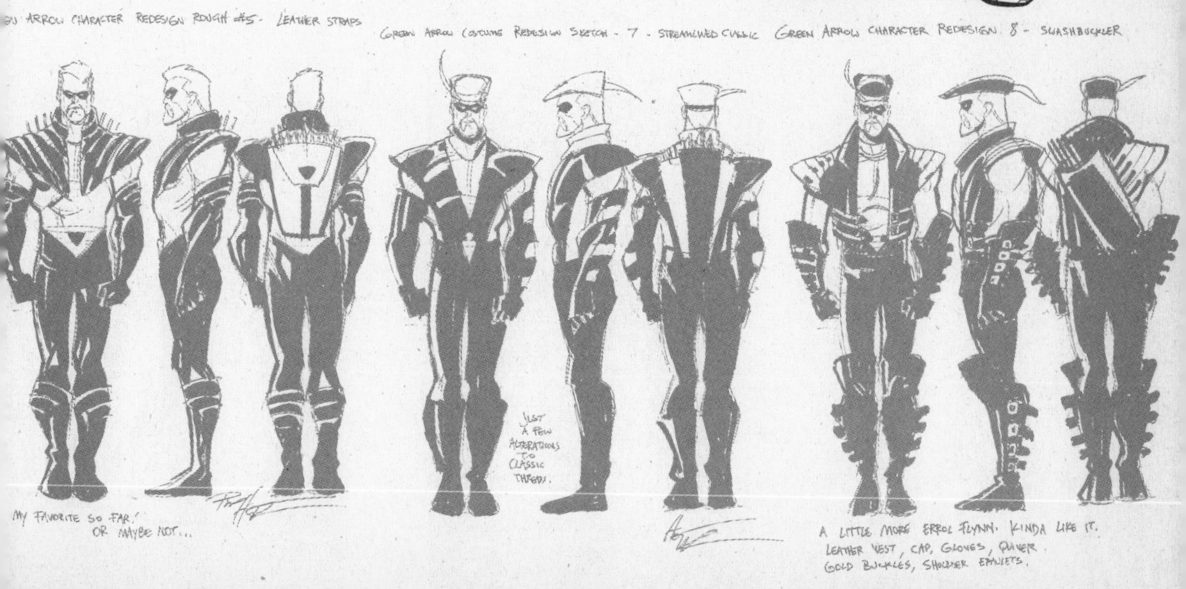

ARROW CHARACTER REDESIGN ROUGH #5 - LEATHER STRAPS
GREEN ARROW COSTUME REDESIGN SKETCH - 7 - STREAMLINED CLASSIC
GREEN ARROW CHARACTER REDESIGN 8 - SWASHBUCKLER
JUST A FEW ALTERATIONS TO CLASSIC THREADS.
MY FAVORITE SO FAR! OR MAYBE NOT...
A LITTLE MORE ERROL FLYNN. KINDA LIKE IT.
LEATHER VEST, CAP, GLOVES, QUIVER
GOLD BUCKLES, SHOULDER EPAULETS.

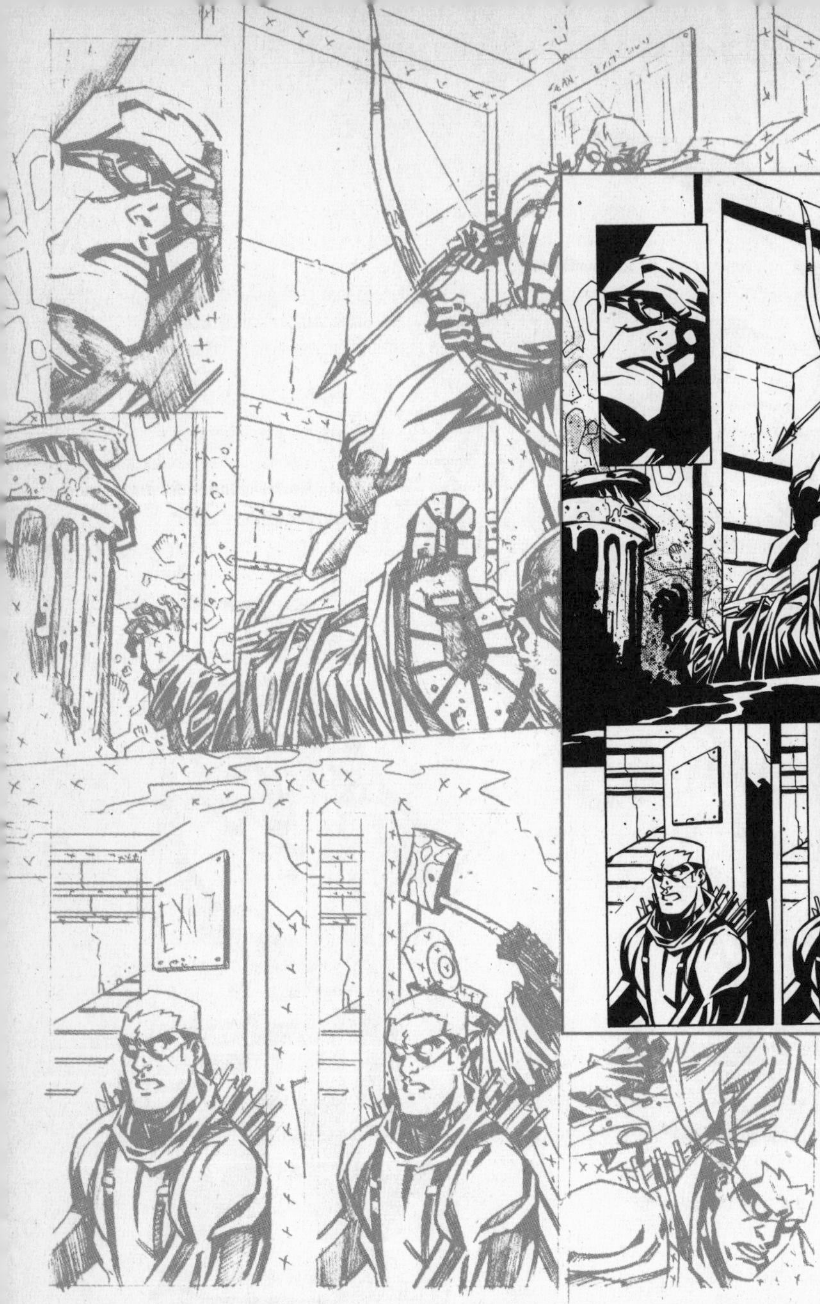

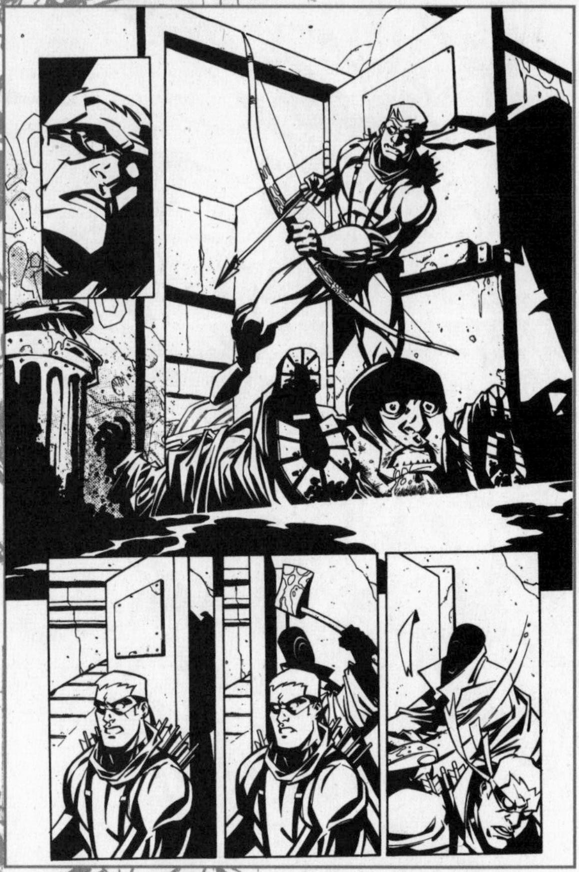

A SAMPLE OF Phil's pencils and the finished Phil and Andy page.

Phil notes, "In the middle of Kevin's run we toyed with the idea of putting Mia in a Speedy costume and changing Ollie's costume. Neither came to pass."

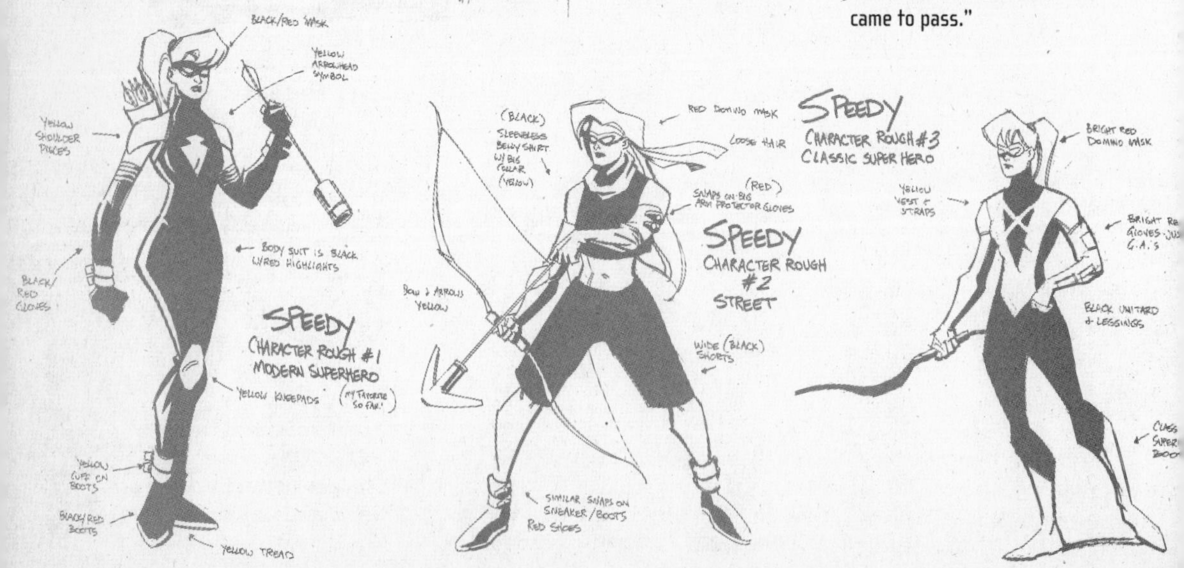
BLACK/RED MASK
YELLOW ARROWHEAD SYMBOL
YELLOW SHOULDER PIECES
BODY SUIT IS BLACK W/RED HIGHLIGHTS
BLACK/RED GLOVES
SPEEDY
CHARACTER ROUGH #1
MODERN SUPERHERO
YELLOW KNEEPADS
(MY FAVORITE SO FAR!)
YELLOW CUFF ON BOOTS
BLACK/RED BOOTS
YELLOW TREAD
(BLACK) SLEEVELESS BELLY SHIRT W/ BIG COLLAR (YELLOW)
RED DOMINO MASK
LOOSE HAIR
(RED) SNAPS ON BIG ARM PROTECTOR GLOVES
SPEEDY
CHARACTER ROUGH #2
STREET
BOW & ARROWS YELLOW
WIDE (BLACK) SHORTS
SIMILAR SNAPS ON SNEAKER/BOOTS
RED SHOES
SPEEDY
CHARACTER ROUGH #3
CLASSIC SUPER HERO
BRIGHT RED DOMINO MASK
YELLOW VEST & STRAPS
BLACK UNITARD & LEGGINGS

KEVIN SMITH

In the few years since his entry into the indie film community, Kevin Smith has seen it all — from the surprise critical and commercial success he received for his debut film *Clerks* to the disappointing critical and commercial drubbing he took on his second outing, *Mallrats*. He caught a break on his third film, the critically hailed *Chasing Amy*, and managed not to get killed by the religious zealots over his fourth film, the comedic meditation *Dogma*. Thus not deterred, Smith advanced and has written and directed the fifth and final installment in his New Jersey Chronicles, *Jay and Silent Bob Strike Back*, released by Dimension Films in August 2001. His next film, *Jersey Girl*, will be released in the summer of 2003.

Along the way, Smith has also found time to make himself a nuisance by smearing his name all over the pop culture landscape. He collaborated with indie film guru John Pierson on his best-selling book *Spike, Mike, Slackers, and Dykes*. He's published the screenplays for all four of his films. He's written comic books featuring not only his own characters (*Clerks* and *Jay and Silent Bob*), but other characters as well (the award-winning *Daredevil* at Marvel Comics, and the award-winning GREEN ARROW at DC comics). With his View Askew partner, Scott Mosier, he's also produced four low-budget, first-film efforts, including Bryan Johnson's Lion Gate release, *Vulgar*. Smith and Mosier also co-executive produced the Academy Award-winning *Good Will Hunting*, starring View Askew stalwarts (and then unknowns) Matt Damon and Ben Affleck.

Besides *Mallrats*, Smith has survived other humbling "creative" experiences which he inexplicably has failed to suppress — such as his ill-fated *Superman Lives* screenplay for Warner Bros., and his animated series version of *Clerks* for ABC primetime, which the network unceremoniously cancelled after airing only two episodes.

But, but, but, Smith was one of the first filmmakers to venture into cyberspace, establishing the insanely popular View Askewniverse website (www.viewaskew.com) in the mid-nineties. And if the film thing doesn't pan out, he does own his own comic-book store — Jay and Silent Bob's Secret Stash, in beautiful downtown Red Bank, New Jersey.

As for the hood ornaments he's collected, there's plenty of tin to go around: the Filmmaker's Trophy at Sundance for *Clerks*; the Prix de la Jeunesse and the International Critic's Week Award at the Cannes Film Festival, also for *Clerks*; The Independent Spirit Award for Best Screenplay for *Chasing Amy*; and a Humanitas Award for *Good Will Hunting*. For his writing in the comics field, Smith has received a Harvey Award, a Wizard Fan Award, and an Eagle Award.

Yet at the end of the day, the two titles Smith touts most proudly are "husband" and "father." He married his wife Jennifer in April of 1999, and celebrated the birth of their daughter, Harley Quinn, in June of that same year (you do the math).

PHIL HESTER

Phil lives in rural Iowa with his wife and two children. He began working in comics while attending The University of Iowa, from which he graduated with a BFA in drawing with minors in sculpture and painting. He has worked for nearly every comic-book publisher in the last 15 years and has been featured in over 300 issues.

Phil's past work includes SWAMP THING, DETECTIVE COMICS, *The Crow: Waking Nightmares*, *The Coffin* (writer), *The Wretch* ('96 Eisner Award nominee), THE CREEPER, *Ultimate Marvel Team-Up*, BRAVE OLD WORLD, *Fringe*, *Rust*, *Taboo*, *The Picture Taker* (writer), *Attitude Lad*, *Deadline USA*, *Negative Burn*, *Clerks: The Lost Scene* and lots, lots more.

His current and upcoming work includes: GREEN ARROW, Deep Sleeper, Firebreather, and The Operation.

He is nice and likes nice people.

ANDE PARKS

Born and raised in Kansas, Ande Parks has been employed in the glamorous world of comic-book inking for over a decade, lending his talents to such titles as SUPERMAN, WONDER WOMAN, and CATWOMAN. Often teamed with his longtime friend Phil Hester, he has won acclaim for his bold, graphic style. Parks has also created his own characters, Uncle Slam and Fire Dog. He is currently continuing his work on GREEN ARROW and is writing a gangster graphic novel. He lives in Kansas with his lovely wife and daughter.

THE STARS OF THE
DC UNIVERSE
CAN ALSO BE FOUND IN THESE BOOKS:

The Amalgam Age of Comics: The DC Comics Collection
Various

Aquaman: Time & Tide
David/Jarvinen/Vancata

Bizarro Comics
Various

Cosmic Odyssey
Starlin//Mignola/Garzon

Crisis on Infinite Earths
Wolfman/Perez/Giordano/Ordway

Crisis on Multiple Earths
Fox/Sekowsky/Sachs

DC/Marvel Crossover Classics II
Various

A DC Universe Christmas
Various

DC vs. Marvel/Marvel vs. DC
Various

The Final Night
Kesel/Marz/Immonen/McKone

Flash & Green Lantern: The Brave and the Bold
Waid & Peyer/Kitson/Grindberg

The Flash: Blood Will Run
Johns/Kolins/Hazlewood

The Flash: Born to Run
Waid/Larocque/Apara/Mhan/various

The Flash: Dead Heat
Waid/O. Jimenez/Ramos/Faucher

The Flash: Race Against Time
Waid/Augustyn/various

The Flash: The Return of Barry Allen
Waid/Larocque/Richardson

The Flash: Rogues
Johns/Kolins/Hazlewood

The Green Arrow by Jack Kirby
Various/Kirby

Green Arrow: The Longbow Hunters
Grell

Green Arrow: Quiver
Smith/Hester/Parks

Green Lantern: Baptism of Fire
Marz/Banks/Pelletier/Tanghal

Green Lantern: Circle of Fire
Vaughan/various

Green Lantern: Emerald Allies
Dixon/Marz/Damaggia/Braithwaite/Banks/various

Green Lantern: Emerald Dawn
Owsley/Giffen/Jones/Bright/Tanghal

Green Lantern: Emerald Dawn II
Giffen/Jones/Bright/Tanghal

Green Lantern: Emerald Knights
Marz/Dixon/Banks/various

Green Lantern: Legacy— The Last Will & Testament of Hal Jordan
Kelly/B. Anderson/Sienkiewicz

Green Lantern: New Journey, Old Path
Winick/Banks/Bright/Eaglesham/various

Green Lantern: Power of Ion
Winick/Eaglesham/various

Green Lantern: Traitor
S. Grant/Zeck/Kane/Kolins/Janson

Green Lantern: Willword
DeMatteis/Fisher

History of the DC Universe
Wolfman/Perez/K. Kesel

Just Imagine...Stan Lee Creating the DC Universe Vol. 1
Lee/Uslan/Buscema/J. Lee/Kubert/Gibbons

The Kingdom
Waid/various

Kingdom Come
Waid/Ross

Legends: The Collected Edition
Ostrander/Wein/Byrne/K. Kesel

Return to the Amalgam Age of Comics: The DC Comics Collection
Various

Super Friends!
Various

Super Friends! Truth, Justice & Peace!
Various

Underworld Unleashed
Waid/Peterson/Porter/P. Jimenez/various

Wonder Woman: The Contest
Messner-Loebs/Deodato Jr.

Wonder Woman: Gods of Gotham
Jimenez/DeMatteis/Lanning

Wonder Woman: The Hiketeia
Rucka/J.G. Jones/Von Grawbadger

Wonder Woman: Lifelines
Byrne

Wonder Woman: Paradise Found
Jimenez/various

Wonder Woman: Paradise Lost
Jimenez/various

Wonder Woman: Second Genesis
Byrne